The adventure

Manchester University Press

NEW ETHNOGRAPHIES

Series editor

Alexander Thomas T. Smith

To buy or to find out more about the books currently available in this series, please go to: https://manchesteruniversitypress.co.uk/series/new-ethnographies/

The adventure

Violent borders, illegal migration, and the uncertain quest for life in Morocco

Sébastien Bachelet

MANCHESTER UNIVERSITY PRESS

Copyright © Sébastien Bachelet 2025

The right of Sébastien Bachelet to be identified as the author of this work has been asserted in accordance with the Copyright, Designs and Patents Act 1988.

An electronic version of this book has been made freely available under a Creative Commons (CC BY-NC-ND) licence, thanks to the support of the University of Manchester Library, which permits non-commercial use, distribution and reproduction provided the author(s) and Manchester University Press are fully cited and no modifications or adaptations are made. Details of the licence can be viewed at https://creativecommons.org/licenses/by-nc-nd/4.0/

Published by Manchester University Press
Oxford Road, Manchester, M13 9PL

www.manchesteruniversitypress.co.uk

British Library Cataloguing-in-Publication Data

A catalogue record for this book is available from the British Library

ISBN 978 1 5261 7768 1 hardback

First published 2025

The publisher has no responsibility for the persistence or accuracy of URLs for any external or third-party internet websites referred to in this book, and does not guarantee that any content on such websites is, or will remain, accurate or appropriate.

EU authorised representative for GPSR:
Easy Access System Europe, Mustam.e tee 50,
10621 Tallinn, Estonia
gpsr.requests@easproject.com

Typeset by Newgen Publishing UK

'Au bout de l'effort, y'a la récompense, oh.
Seulement il faut savoir se battre.
Tant qu'il y a la vie,
On dit toujours y'a espoir, oh.'
[After going all the way, there is the reward, oh.
But one must know how to fight.
As long as there is life,
We always say there is hope, oh.]

        Magic System – Aventurier (Petit Pompier album, 2003)

Contents

List of figures	*page* viii
Series editor's foreword	ix
Acknowledgements	x
Prologue: Golden Sands	xii
Introduction	1
1 The making of a sub-Saharan issue	27
2 Reaching the objective	48
3 Taking a chance	67
4 Life in the ghettoes	85
Adventurers in Douar Hajja and Maâdid: a photo essay	103
5 Adventurous entrepreneurs	108
6 *Chacun sa route*	127
7 Between violence and shared dreams	146
8 Fighting illegal migration	165
Adventure: a radical movement towards life	185
References	195
Index	215

List of figures

1	Buildings in Douar Hajja and Maâdid	*page* 103
2	Two men playing games in a Malian ghetto	104
3	Ivoirian migrants cooking a communal meal on the ground floor of *le consulat*	104
4	An inscription in the Cameroonian ghetto *l'ambassade*: 'suffering is a school of'	105
5	Bedroom of Ivoirian men in *le consulat*	105
6	A Cameroonian barber in Douar Hajja	106
7	Bags and an inflatable boat in a Malian ghetto	106
8	A Cameroonian woman in her informal restaurant	107
9	Makeshift gym on a rooftop in Douar Hajja	107

All photographs © Sébastien Bachelet

Series editor's foreword

When the *New Ethnographies* series was launched in 2011, its aim was to publish the best new ethnographic monographs that promoted interdisciplinary debate and methodological innovation in the qualitative social sciences. Manchester University Press was the logical home for such a series, given the historical role it played in securing the ethnographic legacy of the famous 'Manchester School' of anthropological and interdisciplinary ethnographic research, pioneered by Max Gluckman in the years following the Second World War.

New Ethnographies has now established an enviable critical and commercial reputation. We have published titles on a wide variety of ethnographic subjects, including English football fans, Scottish Conservatives, Chagos islanders, international seafarers, African migrants in Ireland, post-civil war Sri Lanka, Iraqi women in Denmark, and the British in rural France, among others. Our list of forthcoming titles, which continues to grow, reflects some of the best scholarship based on fresh ethnographic research carried out all around the world. Our authors are both established and emerging scholars, including some of the most exciting and innovative up-and-coming ethnographers of the next generation. *New Ethnographies* continues to provide a platform for social scientists and others engaging with ethnographic methods in new and imaginative ways. We also publish the work of those grappling with the 'new' ethnographic objects to which globalisation, geopolitical instability, transnational migration, and the growth of neoliberal markets have given rise in the twenty-first century. We will continue to promote interdisciplinary debate about ethnographic methods as the series grows. Most importantly, we will continue to champion ethnography as a valuable tool for apprehending a world in flux.

Alexander Thomas T. Smith
Department of Sociology, University of Warwick

Acknowledgements

I am deeply indebted to the many adventurers who have entrusted me with their stories, dreams, and reflections. I am not able to list their names here, but I hope they find this account of their quest for a better life is true to the spirit of the adventure. This book would not have been possible without the insights, patience, and generosity of the people I met in Douar Hajja, Maâdid, and beyond. I am also thankful to the many Moroccans I met in these same neighbourhoods who also shared tales about their lives and aspirations. They too have been anonymised.

During fieldwork trips to Morocco, I have benefited from the support and guidance of many. I would especially like to thank Aadel Essadani, Aminata Pagni, Amine Oulmakki, Anaïs Dedeyan, Camille Denis, Camille Fidelin, Dounia Benslimane, Eric William Bamela, Hicham Rachidi, Khadija Souary, Lamine Tall, Mehdi Alioua, Mehdi Lahlou, Nadia Khrouz, Nabil Ben Ali, Ndlend Fils Vermont, Patrick Kit, Pierre Delagrange Kesseng a Beyeck, Said Tbel, Sara Soujar, Soufiane El Hamdi, Stéphane Julinet, Yemoh Odoi, and Youssef Atlas. In Fez, I was lucky to study at the Arabic Language Institute with the wonderful teachers Abdennebi El Haloui and Nouzha El Yamani. I also wish to thank Ross Holtan, Philip Murphy, and Stéphane Julinet for their companionship. For her encouragement and advice on the series of photographs included here, I express gratitude to Leila Alaoui. Her generosity, kindness, and dedication to portraying social outcasts as more than simply victims remain an inspiration for all those who had the chance to meet her before her tragic death. She is sadly missed.

The research for this book started at the University of Edinburgh. I am intellectually indebted to Anthony Good and Tobias Kelly for their generous criticism. I am grateful for the encouragements of Henrik Vigh to turn the thesis into a book. Special thanks to Laura Jeffery for her continuous guidance, mentorship, and support in further developing this work. I wish to thank my friends and peers within the Social Anthropology department in Edinburgh for their encouragement and stimulating discussions, their hospitality, and for sharing anxieties and excitements throughout the PhD programme. Special thanks to Agathe Mora, Andreas Hackl, Diego Maria Malara, Don Duprez, Jenny Lawy, Jon Schubert, Koreen Reece, Leila Sinclair-Bright, and Luke Heslop.

At the University of Manchester, I am grateful to my colleagues Michelle Obeid and Katherine Smith for reading several drafts and providing detailed and constructive feedback. I am thankful for the trust and support from Anthony Simpson in helping me to settle in the Department of Social Anthropology. At the University of Keele, I would like to thank Donna Bailey and Harry Mace for generously hosting me during the last stages of the writing process. I would like to thank colleagues for their insights and comments on various parts of the work developed in this book during conferences, workshops, writing groups, and other research settings, especially Alexandra D'Onofrio, Annika Lems, Constance Smith, Dorte Thorsen, Elena Borisova, Jamie Coates, Jelena Tošić, Lauren Woodard, Heath Cabot, Leslie Gross-Wyrtzen, Lorena Gazzotti, Madeleine Reeves, Malika Bahovadinova, Maria Hagan, Mériam Cheikh, and Nauja Kleist. Warm thanks to Amandine Coquaz for her help with proofreading and editing the writing.

Thanks to Shannon Kneis from Manchester University Press for her guidance throughout the process of developing this book. I am grateful to the anonymous reviewers who have offered encouraging and productive feedback on the book proposal and manuscript. I acknowledge the support of the Economic and Social Research Council for generous funding which enabled this research project, especially funding for my PhD (ES/I012567/1) and a New Investigator Grant (ES/T016485/1).

Finally, I am very grateful to Alice Bachelet and Mariangela Palladino for their enduring love, patience, and counsel along this journey and towards new adventures.

Prologue: Golden Sands

On a Sunday morning in spring 2013, I hopped into one of the city's blue *petits taxis* near the flat I was renting in L'Océan. I was crossing Rabat, the Moroccan capital, to meet some of the young men from Western and Central Africa I had been conducting research with in Douar Hajja, a peripheral neighbourhood that felt far away from the city of light's centres of power and historical sites. After speeding by the old medina and the parliament, amidst little traffic, the taxi drove past the eighteenth-century Assouna Mosque, continued between the Quartier des Ministères and the royal palace, to emerge out of Bab Zaers on to the large Avenue Mohamed VI. Explaining yet again why a Frenchman wanted to visit Douar Hajja, I listened to the usual words of advice from the middle-aged taxi driver. The same I had heard almost every day for the past year. These '*clandestins*' (clandestine people) were '*msākn*' (poor, indigent), but I should be careful. Many were '*khṭīrīn*' (dangerous).[1] 'Why are so many people bothering about these Black people when Moroccans have so many problems?' he asked.

Leaving behind the Almohad outer city wall and tourists' buses heading towards the medieval ruins of the Chellah, the driver followed the road which cuts across central and affluent residential neighbourhoods (Agdal and Souissi) west of the avenue, and more modest neighbourhoods (e.g. Youssoufia, Takaddoum, and Hay Nahda) on the east side, by the humid Bou Regreg river. Turning left and crossing through Youssoufia, the driver stopped on Avenue Al Haouz, on the edge of Douar Hajja, a densely populated working-class neighbourhood hosting a growing number of migrants from Western and Central Africa. I got out at a place known as *château* amongst Moroccans and migrants alike because of the water tower (*château d'eau* in French) standing nearby.

On weekdays, this area was bustling. Moroccan inhabitants emerged early out of a maze of narrow and tortuous alleyways to catch a crowded bus or squeeze into a collective *grand taxi*, on their way to work across the city. Many women could be seen travelling to more affluent neighbourhoods to resume their day job as cleaners. In a place where unemployment was high, men of all ages also emerged from their houses on the narrow and humid streets of Douar Hajja, to sit on the sunny terraces of cafés dotted along Avenue Al Haouz, chatting over slowly sipped glasses of coffee. A large group of migrants usually lined up at the beginning of the main avenue from dawn till noon. They awaited contractors who selected them, often according to physical characteristics, for jobs on construction sites in more affluent areas of Rabat, or for casual work in the agricultural sector in the countryside.

Police vans regularly turned up. Sometimes to target the Moroccan informal street vendors, trading food and second-hand clothes. But larger displays of police forces were deployed for raids targeting Black migrants, assumed to be 'sub-Saharan' and therefore identified as 'clandestine migrants'. *Château* was the locus of dangerous morning games of cat and mouse, which had increased in frequency since I first started visiting in spring 2012. Migrants frantically dispersed at the sight of police vans emblazoned with '*sûreté nationale*' (national security), chased into the maze of narrow alleyways in Douar Hajja by agents of the Moroccan state tasked with upholding law and public order. Presenting a valid visa, or paperwork confirming their status as asylum seekers, was often not enough to prevent the authorities from pushing migrants into police vans. Arbitrary detention, marked by violence and the theft of belongings, was the first stage of an expeditive process migrants were recurrently subjected to, culminating in deportation to the desert by the Algerian border. Migrants then needed to painstakingly make their way back to Douar Hajja to tend their wounds, figure out what to do next, and find new resources to pay rent and fund their next border-crossing attempts.

On Sunday mornings, fewer migrants stood on the pavement. A couple of men sat chatting on a concrete slab next to a stand selling tea and fried doughnuts, in case an odd job requiring some manual labour, like a removal, turned up. Work opportunities were scant on Sundays. Migrants often stayed in their accommodations to avoid trouble and to rest. I walked away from *château* and made my way into the heart of Douar Hajja, to one of the derelict and overcrowded buildings, which migrants called 'ghettoes'. I entered the ground floor of a building its Ivoirian and Cameroonian inhabitants had nicknamed *le consulat* (the consulate), to pick up my Ivoirian friend Moussa for a long-planned trip to the beach. 'Today, the beach will be Black,' Moussa repeated ecstatically. Some of his roommates decided to join too. They asked me about my recent trip to visit family in Italy. A trip that was also necessary to renew the three-month period I could be in Morocco without requiring a residency permit. My own free movement contrasted with the '*attaques*' (attacks) migrants from Douar Hajja organised when seeking to cross the fences around the Spanish enclaves of

Ceuta and Melilla in the north. The mood lightened when I produced some colourful thread bracelets – the kind of cheap lucky charms sold on Italian beaches. They laughed at my '*gris-gris*', teasing me that by wearing such talismans, I showed I also believed in 'chance'. They joked about whether these bracelets were enough to help them '*boza*' – to successfully cross into Europe irregularly. Moussa was already sporting one, a gift from a previous trip to Europe. It had brought him no luck so far.

Our little party walked to *château*, where we met up with a few other Cameroonian and Ivoirian young men. My flatmate Stéphane, a French jurist working in a Moroccan organisation supporting migrants, arrived too. The men were in a jovial mood and cracked jokes about my flatmate and I being two wealthy Europeans 'picking up Blacks' to work in our lavish villa. By then accustomed to such humorous taunts and their disturbing implications, I joked about the kinds of jobs awaiting them in our imaginary villa, though we lived in a flat in L'Océan, an area known as the '*petits blancs*' (little white people) neighbourhood in the colonial period.

Fifteen of us boarded a local bus for the first leg of the journey towards the Golden Sands (*les Sables d'Or*), a sandy beach fifteen kilometres south of Rabat. It was not the first time I had travelled to this beach with some of my informants. These occasional trips allowed me to carve out time, away from overcrowded ghettoes, to interview close informants, but mostly they were about having fun with people who, like me, were in their early twenties and had become friends. As the white, French researcher who enjoyed greater mobility, status, and disposable income, it was tacitly assumed I would pay for transport, cigarettes, and other essentials. The young migrants wore their best clothes for the beach, but many still looked dishevelled, following their recent return from informal forest 'camps' in the borderlands near the Spanish enclave of Melilla. One Cameroonian man walked with crutches. He had been beaten by Spanish and Moroccan border guards after trying to scale up the fences separating Europe and Morocco. Some of the other passengers on the bus stared at us. The young men brushed off my concerns about being too noticeable and we continued our journey, rythmed by more jokes and laughter.

We reached the Golden Sands by mid-morning, bought snacks from street vendors, and dropped down on the sand. The young men took deep breaths as they admired the view, sharing that they had come along to forget, momentarily at least, their worries about money, border violence, and their slim chances of reaching Europe. One of Moussa's roommates talked about how the adventure – the name these young men gave to their dangerous and hopeful migratory journeys – requires constant self-control. Being at the beach, he said he could finally let go. Moussa mocked me for applying sun cream, teasing me about white skin and its weakness. While we laughed about many things, their lives in Morocco – where they experience daily forms of violence, abuse, and racism – and their imagined futures elsewhere remained, unsurprisingly, an important topic of conversation and jokes on this day trip. A few of the men spotted a small fishing boat, unattended on the shore, and made the by-then almost customary jokes about stealing it to paddle across the Atlantic Ocean, playfully arguing about which country they would reach in a straight line across the ocean, and how long it would take.

We enjoyed that peaceful time by the seaside, with two towels to share between us all, taking deep breaths from the salty ocean breeze, our toes pressed into the warm sand. This tranquillity was interrupted for a moment when a police patrol on horseback strode towards us along the beach, stopping a few metres away from Fabien, one of my main informants. He was brooding, lying on his back with the newspaper he had snatched from me to shield his face from the sun at its zenith. He did not budge when the patrol stopped next to us but everyone else tensed up. For a few seconds, the policemen stared at Roméo, a Cameroonian man who was ostentatiously crumbling a piece of hashish and staring back at the officers through his sunglasses. I discouraged Roméo from getting up to brazenly take a selfie next to the horse, even though I could not imagine a mounted patrol would arrest migrants and take them away on their horses. The patrol resumed their gentle stroll on the sand, paying no more attention to us.

After a while, Roméo walked towards the shore. He stood with water up to his knees, looking intensely at the rolling ocean waves. His roommate, Alain, later explained that Roméo had never seen the sea and that the day after, they would be travelling to Tangier to attempt crossing into Spain with an inflatable rubber dinghy (known as 'a zodiac'). The mood was joyful. Yet, the choice of location for this trip was unlikely to provide substantial respite amongst migrants whose daily lives were oriented towards finding ways to cross the sea into Europe, whose pressing concern was to leave Douar Hajja and Morocco for good.

Later, two young Moroccan women in bikinis approached Roméo and Alain as they stood in the water. This drew disapproving looks from Moroccan men walking along the beach, perhaps because of their choice of swimwear, or because of their proximity to Black men. Young men in Douar Hajja often shared their frustration at the near impossibility of forging romantic relationships with Moroccan women. It was dangerous, not least because of the everyday racism these men encountered. As the two women drew closer and addressed Roméo and Alain, most of the other men, who had been leisurely lying on the sand, jumped to their feet to join their friends and these two women in the water. 'These Moroccan [women] kill us Blacks!' exclaimed Moussa, before getting up nonchalantly and performing a series of backflips and other somersaults in an evident, but unrewarded, effort to impress the women. Only Fabien, still sulking, stayed behind, with the newspaper covering his face. My informants and the two women were busy playing and laughing in the water, splashing each other copiously. Curious about what they might be chatting about, I left Fabien and Stéphane behind. I approached the young people just as one of the women asked Alain in French whether they were all 'clandestine migrants' trying to get to Europe. Alain laughed and looked around at his companions from the Douar Hajja ghettoes. 'Europe?' he replied to the woman. 'We are from Spain. We are businessmen. We are on holiday here in Morocco.' There was a short pause, and a knowing look exchanged between the two women, before all burst out laughing. They did not seem to believe this story, but they stayed a bit longer in the water with the men before leaving.

We got ready to return but the local bus we were expecting did not turn up. Without enough cash to get taxis for the first leg of the journey back to Rabat, we had no choice but to walk a few kilometres to the nearest town. Sandy and thirsty, we walked in a line along the busy coastal road for about an hour. Armed guards in their uniforms outside some official-looking buildings gave us suspicious and puzzled looks. The mood grew sombre. Some were complaining about having to return 'to the same problems' back in Douar Hajja. One of the Cameroonian men from *le consulat* protested this was a 'forced march', comparing our walk to migrants making their way back, on foot, from the no man's land at the Algerian border following arrest and deportation by the Moroccan security forces. A few people asked what had happened to the 'transport money', complaining that they could have afforded the taxi fare themselves and avoided the walk. Aboubacar from the Ivoirian ghetto in *le consulat* reprimanded my flatmate and I, saying we could have done a better job negotiating with taxi drivers, prompting us to remind him exasperatedly that we were not his mum and dad. Aboubacar gave me an angry stare and stopped talking to me.

Moussa shrugged and told me not to worry, but the following day, I went back to *le consulat* to apologise for my snide remark, delivered in frustration after a tiring day. I did not want Aboubacar to think I had been unwilling to pay for the fares. I meant to say that Stéphane and I were not in charge of deciding all the details of the day trip for everyone. I told him I was sorry I had angered him. On the beach, I had enjoyed the company of people who had become friends. The return journey had sharply brought back into focus the deeply entrenched inequities between myself and my informants. Aboubacar replied that he was not concerned about the money at all. I had reminded him that although I had taken them out of Douar Hajja for the day to enjoy the beach, I could not solve their problems on their behalf. Moussa added, 'in the adventure, we are *les enfants de nous-mêmes* [our own children]'. Sat in the humid and windowless flat in *le consulat*, I listened as they explained that adventurers needed to demonstrate courage and strength in the face of hardship and suffering, to overcome obstacles in the hope of reaching the life they aspired to. Moussa mentioned he was again getting ready to travel north to the borderlands. We decided to go back to the beach the following Sunday before he left. Maybe, this time, for good.

Note

1. For Arabic transliterations, I follow the standards from the *International Journal of Middle East Studies*.

Introduction

This book explores the everyday lives of young, male migrants from Central and Western Africa 'stuck' in Morocco. It sheds light on migrants' own experiences and understandings of their entrapped mobility in Douar Hajja and Maâdid, two peripheral neighbourhoods of Rabat, the Moroccan capital. After long and dangerous journeys, these young men faced a precarious existence, marked by violence, and an uncertain future. They strove to carve out a better life for themselves, which they imagined away from Morocco. They usually pinned their hopes on continuing their dangerous journeys towards Europe. Their fragile anchoring in Douar Hajja and Maâdid was marked not just by the brutal infringement of their rights and a suspended existence, but by struggles towards self-making, the negotiation of unequal relationships, and creative efforts to reach a more fulfilling and dignified life. Departing from reductionist public discourses centred around the trope of crisis, this book seeks to deepen, nuance, and humanise understandings of 'sub-Saharan migration'.

The book examines the emic notion of '*l'aventure*' (the adventure) as an epic quest to carve out a better life and future. The young men referred to themselves and their companions as '*aventuriers*' (adventurers) who were looking for their 'selves' (*se chercher*) and their 'lives' (*chercher sa vie*). Idrissa, a young man from Burkina Faso, stressed that the adventure was about leaving behind '*la galère*' (adversity, hardship) and preparing himself for his 'future'. The notion of the adventure evoked courage and strength amongst young men from Western and Central Africa, the prospect of a future better life for themselves and their loved ones, but also danger, violence, suffering, and the possibility of failure and death. A focus on the notion of the adventure foregrounds migrants' own imaginaries, hopes, and understandings of their uncertain journeys and future-making attempts. Their efforts were met with hostile politics of migration, which fostered precarious living conditions and denied them the future they aspired to. For Moussa, Fabien, and others living in Douar Hajja and Maâdid, no matter how many times they failed, there was always 'a chance' they would make it.

In this book, I theorise the emic notion of the adventure as an existential yearning for a better life and future, an individual quest for emancipation and opportunities amidst a collective endeavour that defies transnational efforts to govern (and often curb) people's ability to settle and circulate. The adventure entails a mode of being in (and moving through) the world for migrants facing violent, racialised migration regimes marked by abjection and inequities amidst ambiguous collaborations between nation-states. I argue that the adventure provides analytic tools to apprehend with nuance both the mechanisms that drove migrants' forced immobility in Morocco, and their struggle to unfetter themselves and reach the lives and futures they aspired to (usually projected towards Europe). To explore migrants' fraught but hopeful journeys, I maintain that a focus on the adventure is crucial to foreground how migrants cultivate fragile but necessary dispositions, skills, and relationships to navigate deadly bordering measures stretching across and beyond the Mediterranean region. Those who made it to Morocco after long and arduous journeys faced further seemingly insurmountable obstacles prescribed by European but also African nation-states. Exploring what it means to be an adventurer sheds light not only on the tensions and ambiguities between staying and leaving for migrants in a hostile country such as Morocco where they have become (often unwillingly) anchored, but how migrants struggle to hold steadfast through repeated cycles of failed border-crossing attempts that threaten to leave them dead or mad. The adventure holds heroic promises for those intrepid and lucky enough to 'take the road' and seize victory, but it requires a difficult balancing act ('keeping the right mentality') in the face of precarious living conditions and an uncertain future.

In Morocco, irregular migrants from Western and Central Africa navigated hostile politics of containment marked by abuse, suffering, and violence. Through an ethnographic emphasis on how these young men articulated and enacted the adventure as an existential yearning, the book sheds light on the moral, gendered, affective, social, and political aspects of their lives and the cultivation of their selves as adventurers. Steering away from ubiquitous aesthetics of despair, victimhood, and criminality, which have been a privileged emphasis in migration studies and strands of (dark) anthropology, the book focuses on young men's efforts to face up to and overcome bordering practices to retain control over their lives and mobility. In doing so, the book brings into focus everyday activities such as finding money in the informal economies located along the adventure, setting up temporary accommodations to live in between border 'attacks' (i.e. mass border-crossing attempts), forging fragile but necessary relationships with one another, and collectively organising themselves in migrants' associations to articulate claims in a fraught political context. However, it is crucial for such analysis not to sensationalise the violence and suffering migrants were subjected to, nor romanticise their own capacity to act.

The emic notion of the adventure is embedded in migratory processes from Western and Central Africa, but its analytical purview echoes other struggles against violent border regimes across the Maghreb and beyond (e.g. USA–Mexico). The book's theorisation of the adventure (as an existential yearning requiring the cultivation of dispositions, skills, and relationships) provides insights that are crucial to analyse the workings and consequences of violent migration regimes fostering a global apartheid system in which many struggle to make a life and carve out a path for themselves. Indeed, accounting for how adventurers made sense of their dangerous journeys, forced immobility, illegalisation by transnational bordering regimes, and uncertain future stuck in Douar Hajja and Maâdid raises questions about the inequities of transnational efforts to manage (and stop) migration. It highlights how such practices are entangled with enduring dynamics of race, and narratives about whose mobility is deemed desirable, deserving, or dangerous. Processes of illegalisation enacted by state and non-state actors targeting the young men at the heart of this ethnography are deeply entangled with their racialisation as Black migrants in (post)colonial imaginaries that underpin migration policies and practices in Europe as well as in southern Mediterranean countries. Calls for decentring (or provincialising) Europe in the analysis of migratory phenomena must also account for the workings of racialised constructions in the governance of South–South migration. The book's focus on the adventure in Morocco contributes to the unstitching of the Eurocentric focus in the analysis of migration across the Maghreb, unpacking how the global apartheid is maintained through various border and migration regimes. In Morocco, the mobility of African citizens is hampered by another (North) African nation-state colluding (if uneasily) with European states while pursuing its own geostrategic interests.

A focus on migrants' own articulation of their entrapped mobility as an adventure offers important insights to critically engage with prominent concepts and categories (e.g. illegality, immobility, uncertainty, suffering, transit) within policy debates and interdisciplinary scholarship. The adventure is a quest for *'une vie plus supportable'* (a life more bearable), a hopeful and risky journey to become the person one aspires to be, to reach a place where one's dignity and rights would be respected. Examining the fragile and ambiguous anchoring of migrants in Morocco is especially relevant at a time of uncertain transition in Morocco's politics of migration, a transition marked by continued abuse and violence. As migration continues to be a key political issue within Maghrebi nation-states and in their relationships with European and other African countries, the book sheds light on the brutal consequences of transnational efforts to curb and manage migration in the wider region. Relevant well beyond the Moroccan context, this ethnography examines hostile practices and discourses targeting illegalised and racialised migrants. In foregrounding the emic notion of the adventure as an existential yearning, the book transcends established modes of representing, analysing, and legislating over (illegal) migration to provide analytical insights relevant to other border zones where those constructed as undesirable (and irregular) must cultivate the necessary skills, dispositions, and relationships to continue living (and moving).

Crisis narratives

Migration is one of the most contentious and ubiquitous issues on the global stage, and one that is often narrated and analysed using the same discursive frames. Since the 1990s (see Chapter 1), Morocco has been at the centre of the global governance of mobility, and increasingly, it has become a focal point within migration studies, especially scholarship focused on forced immobility, violence, and illegality (e.g. Pian, 2009; Khrouz and Lanza, 2015; Stock, 2019; Tyszler, 2019; Alexander-Nathani, 2021; Gross-Wyrtzen, 2021; Bachelet and Palladino, 2024). The movement of migrants from sub-Saharan Africa into, through, and out of Morocco has become a privileged target of bordering efforts. '*La question subsaharienne*' (the sub-Saharan issue) has mobilised a growing array of policymakers, non-governmental organisation (NGO) practitioners, activists, journalists, and researchers in Morocco and beyond. It has been the topic of complex and fraught negotiations seeking to tighten transnational collaboration (Andersson, 2014; El Qadim, 2015; Norman, 2016; Gross-Wyrtzen and Gazzotti, 2021; Natter, 2022).

On the southern shores of the Mediterranean Sea and beyond, migrants are the target of hostile transnational migration politics, articulated through a broad range of policies and measures to selectively stop, manage, contain, deter, and deport them. Violent and abusive policies and practices involving state and non-state actors coalesce into a 'militarized global apartheid' (Besteman, 2019: S26) – with deadly consequences for those denied safe and legal routes, who then risk their lives crossing deserts, seas, and barbed wire. Hostile migration politics vividly illustrate how, in parallel to the increased circulation of information, goods, and capital, the movements of some men and women continue to be subjected to 'heavier and heavier limitations' (Balibar, 2004: 113). While this dynamic is not restricted to the Mediterranean region, Europe's southern external border has been a laboratory for the deployment of administrative, legislative, technological, and militaristic means in the war waged against 'illegal migration' (Bigo,

2022; Boswell, 2003; Feldman, 2012; Jones, 2016; Panebianco, 2022). The rising number of deaths amongst migrants – in recurrent tragedies at sea, in detention centres, or along the fences of Ceuta and Melilla – are not signs of failure, nor are they mere collateral damage. Such violence is inherent to the cynical logics of border and migration regimes. The political and moral justifications of deadly policies and practices stress the uncanny entanglement of compassion and repression in the global governance of migration, and the uneasy cohabitation of humanitarian and securitarian imperatives (Fassin, 2005; Ticktin, 2006; Pallister-Wilkins, 2022).

What is at stake across the Mediterranean region is the fostering of what anthropologist Ghassan Hage calls 'colonial spatial politics' (2016: 38) to uphold the division between spaces of exploitation and spaces harbouring the good life, to control who can circulate and how. To remain 'a space of morality and goodness' (Dzenovska, 2014: 281), the European Union (EU) entails the construction of 'a gated community' (Van Houtum and Pijpers, 2007), rather than an impenetrable fortress, to sustain and protect (unequally distributed) levels of comfort. The movement of people and its policing must be situated in the shared (post)colonial history of 'uneven exchanges' (Gaibazzi *et al.*, 2017: 4) between the two continents (Tošić and Lems, 2019). The selective and unequal distribution of the ability to stay, move, and settle elsewhere is inscribed in enduring hierarchies and inequities, in which race and colonial legacies figure prominently (Jones *et al.*, 2017; De Genova, 2018; El-Enany, 2020; Mayblin and Turner, 2020). In Morocco and across the Maghreb, the targeting of racialised Black migrants entails the reproduction of local racialised dynamics that have long shaped patterns of voluntary and forced mobility between Morocco and Central and Western Africa (Hannoum, 2020; Menin, 2020; Gazzotti, 2021; Gross-Wyrtzen, 2023).

Public debate continues to peddle the trope of crisis. Especially when figures lead the discussion in news reports about migrants scaling the land border between Morocco and Spain, around the enclaves of Ceuta and Melilla. Or when news emerges of yet another mass drowning of men, women, and children, seeking to reach Southern Europe on rickety boats. These narratives partake in the reproduction of a myth that Europe (as well as Morocco) is under attack, which is fuelled by arguments about migration statistics and what they really mean (De Haas, 2023). This myth sustains fallacious arguments about a Europe that cannot afford to welcome all the misery of the world and must protect itself against profiteering and menacing hordes. Such narratives overlook not only historical and contemporary ties between Europe and the Global South, including many former colonies of European countries, but also how Europe contributes to creating and reproducing a 'problem' of (at least partially) its own making by repeatedly rolling out 'more of the same response' (Andersson, 2016: 1055).

Crises are portrayed as turning points requiring decisive and urgent decisions to resolve an unstable situation (Redfield, 2005). But it is more productive analytically to apprehend them as a 'condition' (Vigh, 2008: 9): not just a chaotic period that will pass (pending the right decision), but a chronic socio-political state. As with financial crises (Roitman, 2013), designating a series of events (but also spaces and people) as a crisis allows only certain narratives to be audible. It fosters the erasure of 'history and context' (Cabot, 2019: 264): held beyond polymorphous and diffuse borders, migrants are also discursively contained within the confines of a dehumanising world floating 'either beyond or above politics' (Malkki, 1995: 518). The putative crisis unravelling across the Mediterranean region is manufactured by migration politics, but it is also intimately linked to wider political and economic processes and struggles, not least the accumulation of capital (De Genova and Tazzioli, 2016).

Painting the movement and displacement of people as exceptional denies the coevalness of policymakers, migrants, and researchers (Ramsay, 2020). Crisis narratives conveniently shift the issue of responsibility from socio-political and economic processes and the myriads of decision-makers towards others, including migrants who come to embody the crisis. Beyond regimes of power which select and restrict transnational human mobility, the discourse of crisis also points to fears and imaginaries about Europe and its future (Holmes and Castañeda, 2018). The depiction of mostly non-white mobility at the borders of Europe as a crisis and anxieties over what European identity constitutes and how to protect it are 'mutually constitutive' (De Genova, 2018: 1768).

These critics have provided crucial insights into the analytical shortcomings of a notion of crisis that is politically productive in sustaining the status quo over how migration is conceived, narrated, and managed. Cabot warns us that as a 'temporal, spatial, aesthetic, and affective frame' (2019: 266), crisis has insidiously found its way within scholarship, influencing the design of research projects, the choice of field sites, the availability of funding, and the representative strategies in scholarly writing. In response, it has become even more pressing to de-exceptionalise displacement by 'disrupting epistemological and political boundaries, and examining erosions in the capacity for flourishing lives and livelihoods unfolding across diverse categories of membership' (Cabot and Ramsey, 2021: 292).

Unpacking the logics of bordering regimes requires more than deconstructing powerful concepts and the labels generated by transnational migration politics, that categorise people to enforce their selective control. It requires the serious consideration, within the analysis itself, of the ways people embarking on increasingly uncertain journeys understand and relate to their entrapped mobility and the regimes of power they face. Being privy to stories of clandestine journeys, anthropologists can make them and the suffering they entail more 'imaginable' (Coutin and Vogel, 2016). This is best achieved by centring migrants' own idioms in these stories – rather than forging new ones and adding to the ever-expanding plethora of labels, concepts, and categories in migration studies, which are not always ethnographically grounded nor relevant (Hage, 2005). Critically engaging with migrants' understanding of their entanglements with mighty regimes of power restraining their mobility, without confining them to experiences of violence and suffering, is needed to depart from the kind of stories which we 'already know' (Kleinman, 2019: 5). Amongst young men stuck in Morocco, tales of their journeys were articulated around the notion of the adventure, pointing to both the consequences of violent, racialised migration regimes as well as their continuous struggle and existential yearning for a better life and future.

Adventure

Young men from Western and Central Africa in Douar Hajja eschewed the labels commonly deployed in policymaking, the media, and scholarship to categorise them (e.g. 'irregular', 'clandestine', 'illegal').[1] They used the trope of the adventure to make sense of, articulate, and act on their entrapped mobility in Morocco and beyond. They were 'adventurers' (*aventuriers*) courageously facing up to the violence and uncertainty of hostile migration politics seeking to contain them. As argued by Agier in his study of refugee camps, scholars of migration ought not to confuse 'the object of research with that of the intervener who creates this space and this category' (2011: 68). In migration and refugee studies, scholars exploring the subjectivities and experiences of migrants have deconstructed categories and labels (Zetter, 2007; De Coninck, 2020; Hamlin, 2021), notably by approaching illegality, with its 'products and excesses' (Andersson, 2014: 8), as a theoretical and ethnographic object (Willen, 2005). Illegality is neither self-generating nor random (De Genova, 2002). As a set of juridical and sociopolitical statuses, reflected in everyday, embodied processes, illegality entails the incomplete exclusion of migrants and their consignment to what Coutin calls 'the space of non-existence' (2000: 29).

To examine migrants' entanglement with these processes of exclusion and abjection, this book contributes to the growing corpus of studies that have explored in earnest migrants' narrative framework of the adventure (Timera, 2009; Bredeloup 2013, 2014; Olwig, 2018; Kleinman, 2019) and related emic notions in other languages spoken across Western and Central Africa (Alpes, 2014; Gaibazzi, 2015b). The adventure has become a prominent lens through which to examine mobility issues in the wider region. Such journeys for emancipation unsettle assumptions about migrants as criminal or miserable subjects. Adventurous journeys from (and within) Western and Central Africa are quests for self-fulfilment, success, and escape from circumstances that fail to deliver the life people aspire to. They predate European colonisation (e.g. pilgrimages) and have taken many forms in recent history, such as the young 'jaguars' in Ghana and the Ivory Coast, the '*sapeurs*' on both sides of the Congo River, and the diamond traders of the Senegal River Valley (Rouch, 1956; Gandoulou, 1989; MacGaffey and Bazenguissa-Ganga, 2000). 'Venturing off' is a form of escape for migrants seeking to 'construct [themselves] in an enduring fashion' (Bredeloup, 2013: 180). Yet, the adventure does not necessarily mean the reversal of established hierarchies. Going on the adventure, as a rite of passage, provides a socially sanctioned alternative way to find one's social place (Bredeloup, 2016). Explorations of the emic notion of the adventure across diverse contexts show it is not a 'deterministic cultural pattern but rather a malleable resource' (Kleinman, 2019: 12).

The book contributes to interdisciplinary scholarship on these issues by developing the notion of the adventure as an existential yearning for a better life and future. Exploring the lives of adventurers stuck in Morocco sheds light on the violence of bordering through a closer focus on migrants' (limited) ability to act, as well as their own imaginaries of (im)mobility, illegality, and uncertainty. Adventurers in Douar Hajja and Maâdid described their journeys in epic terms ('a quest'): the search for 'one's life' (*chercher sa vie*) (looking for one's life) and the search for 'one's self' (*se chercher*) (looking for one's self). I theorise the adventure as a way of being in (and moving through) the world that requires the cultivation of necessary but fragile dispositions, skills, and relationships for migrants to be able to continue their journey. Rather than centring nation-states' concerns with spatial and/or legal transgressions, the book deploys the notion of the adventure as an existential yearning to account for and examine these young men's efforts to maintain their 'capacity to *live*' (Jackson 2005: xi; original emphasis) amidst circumstances over which they had limited control. This is crucial to examine migrants' dangerous journeys and efforts to face up to transnational bordering efforts to contain them, as well as their fragile and ambivalent anchoring in Morocco.

The book examines how adventurers in Douar Hajja and Maâdid strove to reach what they called 'the objective', seizing the life they aspired to by successfully crossing borders and overcoming danger and obstacles to achieve victory ('*boza*'). Everyday life in marginal spaces and 'attacks' on the border required the honing of important skills like '*débrouillardise*' (resourcefulness) and learning to understand and act within 'the environment' where hostile actors (e.g. Moroccan and Spanish border security forces) impeded their lives and mobility. Failure, and the shame associated with it, was a tangible prospect for migrants who continued to seek out creative ways to confront risk and obstacles but remained stuck in Douar Hajja and Maâdid, following repeated border-crossing attempts. Failure often entailed losing everything, could incur injuries (or death), and required resources and time to heal and recover. Adventurers needed to cultivate and display 'the right mentality': balancing efforts to exhibit 'strength and courage' with a recognition that success was a matter of 'chance' which lay beyond their immediate control and would only be granted by greater forces (e.g. destiny, God). 'Controlling one's heart' and cultivating the right mentality were primordial for adventurers. 'Going in circles' (from one failed attempt to the other) and on the brink of 'becoming mad', they found comfort and support amongst each other in the marginal spaces they inhabited collectively (e.g. ghettoes). The relationships adventurers cultivated with one another were necessary for facing the hardship of everyday life in Morocco as well as organising collective border-crossing attempts. Yet, such relationships, like the ties that anchored them into Morocco, were precarious.

Adventurers did not form a neat and close-bound community. Researchers have stressed how young men from across Western and Central Africa draw on a shared vocabulary of the adventure (Bajalia, 2021). Yet, the book explores how the adventure is an individual journey amidst collective endeavours – amongst other people attempting to cross borders and those in 'home' countries who anxiously await the outcome of these journeys. As adventurers, these young men stressed they needed to fend for themselves and carry the burden of their loved ones' expectations. Staying close to travelling companions had moral and practical significance, but it was sometimes necessary to leave people behind. I trace how being an adventure required mutual help but could also entail the conditions for betrayals, especially when the small window of success for one's journey required breaking off from companions. Adventurers needed to negotiate multiple relationships amongst themselves, with their distant families, as well as with a range of state and non-state actors in Morocco (e.g. NGOs, neighbours, Moroccan authorities, etc.).

Focusing on the narrative of the adventure amongst these young men brings new insights to the study of the logics and experiences of bordering. Everyday practices of enforcing and confronting the regulation of mobility entail diverse 'operations of morality, ethics and rights' (El Qadim *et al.*, 2021) which are not limited to the workings of compassion and repression within the humanitarian governance of migrants. Taking the road was the only option for these young men to assert themselves as 'actors within the global arena' (Olwig, 2018: 156). Denied visas and other means to travel regularly, they were forcefully attempting to gain a seat within 'the circle of full humanity' (Ferguson, 1999: 236). Their uncertain journeys were about reclaiming their place in an unequal world, where not everyone has the same opportunities to travel or the same control over their lives. This emphasis on migrants' aspirations and search for, or rather carving of, opportunities to realise themselves is at odds with the two dominant portrayals of migrants in public discourse: scroungers and criminals threatening (European) nation-states and their culture, economy, and health, or voiceless victims embodying suffering and misery (Szörényi, 2006; Crawley et al., 2016; Wilmott, 2017; Brambilla and Pötzcsh, 2017). Adventurous journeys point to the clash of different 'imaginaries' about mobility and belonging amongst conflicting forces navigating, transgressing, and enforcing regimes of mobility (Vigh, 2006; Alioua, 2009; Salazar, 2011; Alpes, 2014; Bal and Willems, 2014; Schielke, 2020; Ménard and Bedert, 2021). Considering migration as necessary to their quest for 'a worthy existence' (Vigh, 2009b: 103), adventurers were trying to reimagine their lives and themselves, breaking away from the monotony of their living conditions to become the 'authors of their own destinies' (Bredeloup, 2013: 174).

The adventure is then akin to a 'moral experience' (Bredeloup, 2016: 134): migrants are driven by a deep desire to live more intense and dignified lives. In the book, I examine how the adventure's moral experience also translates into political subjectivity and the articulation of complex (and sometimes seemingly contradictory) political claims. The notion of the adventure not only points out global injustices, but also provides insights into migrants' political subjectivities as they face up to the borders impeding their quest. Such struggles were not confined to the borders of Morocco. Adventurers readily drew connections between their arduous predicament as migrants in Morocco, the harshness and inequities that beleaguered their lives in the 'home' countries and which they needed to escape, as well as future challenges they anticipated facing if they ever made it into Europe. A focus on the adventure is then crucial to steer away from the kind of research which produces 'a "migrantology" that is capable of little more than repeatedly illustrating and reproducing itself' (Römild, 2017: 70). It sheds light on migrants' experiences of wider social forces that impede on their lives across multiple nation-states, and their refusal of the obstacles obstructing their quest for a life more bearable.

In the context of rising numbers of women undertaking these journeys and facing additional forms of vulnerabilities (Schmoll, 2020; Friedman et al., 2022), studies of the adventure have increasingly stressed how such epic journeys of self-becoming are undertaken by women too (Escoffier, 2008; Stock, 2012; Bredeloup, 2013; Tyszler, 2018). Researchers have also explored the mobilisation of the notion of the adventure amongst queers (e.g. Gouyon, 2022). Mobility is a crucial lens through which to examine how 'specific kinds of gendered people' (Elliot, 2021: 142) are (re)defined. Mobility and gender are relational, they are mutually constitutive, and they entail the (re)production and transformation of gender roles and expectations (Osella and Osella, 2000; Melly, 2011; Mortensen, 2021). In the book, while I draw on interviews with a few female interlocutors (especially Chistine, introduced in Chapter 5) and a few older migrants, I focus more particularly on the journeys and lives of young men (i.e. in their early twenties and younger), who were by far more numerous in the neighbourhoods of Douar Hajja and Maâdid. I trace how these migrants negotiated the affective challenges (e.g. shame) of struggling to reach the goals of their initiatory journeys while cultivating their adventurous selves. Adventurers were stuck in a place where their masculinity was curtailed, notably by the near impossibility to forge amorous relationships with Moroccan women. They could not sustain the expectations of families left at home, who often were unable or unwilling to continue providing support to adventurers stuck in Morocco.

The book's focus on the idiom of adventure resonates with Michael Jackson and Albert Piette's call for 'direct engagements with the lived experiences of *particular* human beings' (2015: 3; original emphasis). In examining complex, often non-linear journeys, I take inspiration from studies which have applied an existential anthropology lens to the exploration of mobility. The adventure was a fraught quest not just towards success and (material) wealth, but also towards crafting more meaningful and dignified lives (Willen, 2019). As explored by Hans Lucht in his ethnographic work with Ghanaian fishermen travelling to Italy, such dangerous migratory journeys amount to 'an attempt to revitalize life by *re-establishing connections between* individual and social desires and the many promises and constraints of outside reality' (2011: xii; original emphasis).

By engaging with the idiom of adventure amongst young men stuck in Douar Hajja, the book looks more closely at the complex aspirations of migrants involved in the 'unremitting task' (Jackson, 2005: xx) of struggling to be in a moving world where forces shaping one's life are beyond one's full control. At the heart of the impetus to live for these young men lies what Hage, in his work on transnational Lebanese migration, calls 'existential mobility': 'a form of imaginary mobility, a sense that one is "going somewhere"' (2009: 97). Highlighting how dynamics of immobility and containment entail physical and existential states is necessary to refine the analysis of multiple forms of dispossession and ruptures that lead to experiences of 'existential displacement' (Obeid, 2023; see also Hage, 2009; Jackson, 2013; Jansen, 2014; Tošić and Lems, 2019). Such a focus challenges common dichotomies between forced and voluntary migration, as there is often no clear demarcation between choice and constraint (Salazar and Smart, 2011). Alongside diverse experiences of poverty and repression, this feeling of not going anywhere and of unrealised talent led my young male informants to take to the road. In Morocco, they found themselves 'going in circles'. They needed to keep going, to display the necessary qualities and dispositions of young men on the adventure (courage and strength), while acknowledging that the success of their next border crossing did not depend entirely on them but on 'chance'. Maintaining this balance was hard and could lead to '*devenir fou*' (becoming mad).

The everyday lives for adventurers in Douar Hajja highlighted how their hopeful orientations towards their existence and future entailed both uncertainty and potentiality (Di Nunzio, 2015; Kleist and Jansen, 2016; Kleist and Thorsen, 2016). The narratives and journeys of these young men illustrate how the distribution of hope is a political phenomenon (Hage, 2003). People are not equally recognised as worthy humans nor endowed with the capacity to give meaning to life and the world around them. Adventurers refused to 'wait out' (Hage, 2009: 97) the crisis and projected themselves towards a better future by scaling fences and crossing the sea on rubber dinghies. They embarked on difficult and arduous journeys that showcase how hope entails something that 'drives us to continue to want to live, no matter what we are facing' (Zournazi and Hage, 2002: 151). Yet, in Morocco, the epic narratives about their adventurous journeys contrasted with an enduring reality, marked by abjection, violence, and the continuous infringement of their rights. They hoped that tomorrow would bring them opportunities but could not be sure. They were ready to seize them or carve them out. The adventure entailed elements of faith (Bredeloup, 2013) that one's efforts in enduring suffering would be rewarded. Hence, the examination of migrants' efforts to cultivate their adventurous selves calls for a focus on the violence and suffering they experienced. Suffering especially was often described by migrants as intrinsic to the adventure. It was a 'school of life'. They did not seek out painful and violent experiences purposefully, but for adventurers there could be no reward, or successful crossing, without some form of suffering. Scholars have warned against the pitfalls of a certain type of 'dark anthropology' (Ortner, 2016) marked by the emphasis on depression in the face of the harshness of social life. While it is important to depart from uncritical accounts of trauma within scholarship as well as the wider miserabilist aesthetics that has become ubiquitous in representations of migration (along with other dehumanising tropes), taking migrants' understanding of the adventure seriously shows how hope, suffering, and violence were deeply entangled for young men who depicted themselves in epic terms. In the analysis of migrants' fraught journeys and efforts to seize a better life for themselves, an anthropological account oriented towards the good (see

Robbins, 2013) cannot leave out suffering. Nevertheless, it is important not to romanticise adventurers' capacity (or willingness) to endure the harshness of border regimes (see Chapter 6).

In striving to realise themselves and keep hopeful about the possibility of reaching this better existence in the future, migrants in Douar Hajja and Maâdid also sought to improve their precarious existence, becoming increasingly emplaced in Rabat. I return to such contradictions in the book to examine the fragile and ambivalent anchoring in time and space of these young migrants. Dwelling in the peripheral urban neighbourhoods of Rabat entailed transformative instances of 'real life' (Agier, 2011: 86). Douar Hajja was referred to as the 'African neighbourhood' with the growing but precarious presence of migrants, visible in the narrow streets, businesses, and houses.[2] Most of them were relentlessly seeking to leave yet were spending increasingly long periods in Douar Hajja and Maâdid, forging relationships with Moroccans characterised by solidarity but also racism, opening businesses they were ready to abandon if the opportunity to cross arose, setting up political organisations to better the rights of migrants while planning their next trip.

In exploring issues around the forced immobility of migrants in Morocco, the book engages with forms of emplacement that point to the entanglement of future and home-making processes with mobility, including in situations marked by violence and uncertainty (Jansen and Löving, 2008; Kleinman, 2019; Boccagni et al., 2020; Boccagni and Miranda Nieto, 2022). Scholars have called for closer attention to be paid to the dynamics of placement within displacement, through a focus on the 'particularity and everydayness of being-in-place' (Lems, 2016: 315; Lems, 2018). The exploration of the adventure in a peripheral Moroccan neighbourhood sheds light on the fostering of ambiguous forms of belonging and emplacement in conditions of 'transience' (Kleinman, 2019: 18). Young adventurers were keen to escape Morocco, to use Douar Hajja as a temporary stage post along their initiatory journeys for self-fulfilment and realisation, but they kept coming back and found it difficult to gather the necessary resources to try leaving again.

Thus, the notion of the adventure points to both analytical categories and emic descriptions. It transcends common understandings of and stories about migration, to provide crucial insights into how migrants denied safe routes conceive of their lives and journeys, in a world marked by inequities, power differentials, and discriminations that affect more than one's capacity to cross borders. I take inspiration from researchers who have highlighted the adventure's heuristic potential to spell out how migrants 'make sense of and act in a world of enduring risk' (Kleinman, 2019: 8). In a word of warning, Bredeloup warns against efforts to essentialise it and stresses that it is foremost 'a social construction offering insights into societies and their imagined utopias' (2016: 134). The adventure provides 'a template' (Kleinman, 2019: 12) for individuals who have left their families, to embark on long and dangerous initiatory journeys to search and realise themselves. However, in examining the cultivation of an adventurous way of being and moving amongst people who have become stuck and are forcibly immobilised in Morocco, this book foregrounds the contradictions and ambiguities embedded in this emic notion of the adventure – as a template, it is fraught with paradoxes.

Doing research with adventurers

The book draws on enduring ethnographic research on migration from Western and Central Africa in Morocco. It focuses particularly on fieldwork carried out in the peripheral neighbourhoods of Douar Hajja and Maâdid in Rabat, between May 2012 and August 2013, a period marked by the escalation of institutional violence against migrants across the country, but also intense mobilisation amongst civil society (see Chapter 1). The book sheds light on the tumultuous period that preceded the announcement of a shift in Moroccan politics of migration in September 2013, a few weeks after I completed fieldwork. The book is also informed by continuous engagement with this topic through regular research trips to Morocco, between 2014 and 2024, for projects on migration, illegalisation, repression, and activism. Ten years after the start of the 'new' politics of migration, the analysis of my informants' adventurous stranded mobility in Douar Hajja and Maâdid highlights continuities in the contemporary brutal treatment of migrants seeking to carve out a better life for themselves, in Morocco or elsewhere. Their fragile anchoring in Morocco is evidence of the shortcomings of Moroccan politics of migration and of a failure to substantially improve migrants' living conditions. Disillusioned by the prospect of staying in Morocco, adventurers from Western and Central Africa must decide whether to continue enduring difficult conditions in Morocco, return to their country of origin, or carry on with their journey, often towards Europe.

Ethnographic work entailed having informal discussions and semi-structured interviews in dilapidated migrant ghettoes, walking with migrants along Douar Hajja's and Maâdid's tortuous alleyways (and other neighbourhoods in Rabat), as well as setting up interviews with humanitarian workers and human rights activists actively engaged with migration matters in Morocco. In the 2012–2013 period, I spent most of my time 'hanging out' with a core group of around twenty young men, spread across the two neighbourhoods, and I interacted with numerous others (e.g. roommates, friends, and neighbours). I also spent significant periods of time with the Moroccan youth in this densely populated area of Rabat, especially since my adventurous informants tended to disappear with little notice, if any. An analysis of the adventure must also include parallels between migrants' struggles and the lives and aspirations of my informants' Moroccan neighbours. This is crucial to foreground how processes of dispossession, entrapped mobility, and abjection affect not just migrants but citizens too, thereby also calling into question such dichotomies (Çağlar and Schiller, 2016).

As the neighbourhoods were the locus of regular police raids and my interactions with migrants were visibly the focus of attention from curious neighbours, exasperated landlords, and suspicious authorities, I decided not to live in the same neighbourhood for security reasons (mostly to protect my informants). The places I inhabited in other parts of Rabat (Hassan, L'Océan) were also useful meeting points to spend time with friends and informants away from crowded migrant houses. But they were also uncomfortable reminders throughout fieldwork of the different positions we occupied in the racialised hierarchies of mobility. Initially, I settled in a more central neighbourhood of Rabat in the hope of conducting fieldwork across multiple sites within the Moroccan capital city, and beyond. Though I made short trips to significant sites related to migration across Moroccan cities (e.g. Tangier, Fez, Oujda, Nador, etc.), the focus in this book is on Douar Hajja and Maâdid, two marginal neighbourhoods in Rabat (see below).

The informants with whom I developed the strongest bonds, and who have generously shared the most insights into their adventurous journeys, were named – through pseudonyms – in the Prologue to this book. There were several others (especially Idrissa from Burkina Faso) who did not attend that trip to the Golden Sands, because, by then, they had successfully crossed into Europe, were temporarily staying in the borderlands, or had taken the difficult decision to return 'home'. Most of these young men were from Cameroon and the Ivory Coast and lived in large ghettoes like *le consulat* (the consulate) and *l'ambassade* (the embassy), and in smaller accommodations in Douar Hajja and Maâdid. A significant number of my informants were also from Guinea, Burkina Faso, and Mali. All had undertaken long journeys before reaching Morocco, stopping for several months, and sometimes years, along the way, in countries such as Algeria or Mauritania (see Chapter 2). Most of them entered Morocco irregularly via Oujda. Many did not have passports; they were lost, stolen, or confiscated on the way. Others had fraudulent passports, sometimes purchased from staff in sub-Saharan consulates. But some had (until they expired or were lost or stolen) valid passports and visas which offered little, if any, protection in the face of racialised regimes of migration that constructed them as undesirable, irregular migrants (see Chapter 1). A few amongst my informants had lodged asylum claims with the United Nations High Commissioner for Refugees

(UNHCR) and received paperwork attesting their claim was being considered. This made little difference to how Moroccan authorities treated them.[3] Most of them had arrived in Morocco in 2010 and 2011. A few had entered Morocco for the first time several years before. By the time I left in late summer 2013, most of these young men were still in Morocco. Some had crossed and a few had returned to their countries of origin. Several had just disappeared.

Like most migrants in this area of Rabat, almost all my informants were men.[4] Most were, like myself, in their twenties, which was instrumental in fostering friendships with some of them. Several were older, mostly in their thirties and a handful in their forties and older. There were many unaccompanied minors too. Biographical details were not always clear. People had many names, which they selectively gave, depending on the context and their interlocutors. It was widely assumed that presenting oneself as Muslim, and changing one's first name accordingly, could lead to better treatment. I knew my informants by many nicknames and was not always sure what their 'real' names were. The adventure also rhymes with secrets: keeping one's plans for departure, true nationality, and resources secret from others, including researchers. I did not seek to enforce the kind of truth demands that are regularly imposed on to migrants' stories and bodies to assess the validity and deservingness of their claims (Fassin and d'Halluin, 2005; Salter, 2006; Friedman, 2010; Bachelet and Palladino, 2024). In fostering counter-narratives of migration, I have sought to create spaces for self-expression with adventurers, which resisted normative expectations of authenticity and the revelation of one's 'true self' (Greatrick and Fiddian-Qasmiyeh, 2017: 3). I explored with them, through conversations and observations, what being an adventurer meant to them and how it informed their everyday life in Douar Hajja and Maâdid. The book's structure and the scope of the different chapters reflect what the adventurers I met highlighted as issues that deserved (critical) attention for this study. For the analysis, I have sought patterns and recurring topics in the data I collected (i.e. field-notes, interviews, etc.) but remained particularly attentive to the notion of the adventure as well as the wider range of idioms my informants used daily and stressed as crucial to understand their lives and journeys (e.g. the right mentality, etc.).

Researching migration and illegality entails numerous ethical concerns. The book does not include detailed descriptions of migrants' tactics to overcome bordering practices. There was suspicion amongst some migrants that my interest in the adventure could reveal sensitive information. We had many discussions over what it means to document and expose '*les vraies réalités*' (the true realities) of migrants. Some were concerned not just about their identities being revealed, but about their friends and families at home becoming aware of gruesome details adventurers kept secret from them – out of shame or because they did not want to worry their loved ones. As Nancy Scheper-Hughes suggests, anthropologists do not necessarily have 'a responsibility to honor *community* secrets' (2000: 126; original emphasis). While such concerns are legitimate and care has been taken to protect the identities of my informants here, many in Douar Hajja and Maâdid were keen for the consequences of migration politics to be documented and highlighted. Not describing such arduous living conditions would make any research on the subject impossible. I was often solicited to take pictures of my informants for their social media profiles. Such pictures often presented inaccurate or plainly deceiving portrayals of their everyday life in Morocco. Such deception was often a focus of debates amongst migrants. The book is illustrated with another series of photographs taken in Douar Hajja and Maâdid, used with the permission of the pictured individuals. In order to appease my informants' concerns and protect their identities, I have swapped their names and nicknames (including those of my Moroccan informants) with pseudonyms. I have selected pictures where people are not readily identifiable.

While undertaking language training in Fez between October 2011 and May 2012, I conducted preparatory visits to Rabat in the hope of finding an organisation that could facilitate access. This was met with reticence and suspicion. I had no specialised skills (e.g. medical or juridical) which could benefit overburdened organisations, at a time when they were also increasingly solicited by researchers and students. I nevertheless forged close relationships with some activists and practitioners. We have often looked back humorously at some of our early encounters. In our first meeting, I was strongly rebuffed by the coordinator of a Moroccan organisation, which became a partner for a subsequent project, when I clumsily explained I was interested in 'transit' migration – a term many organisations contested, in their effort to compel the Moroccan authorities to support and respect the rights of migrants staying for increasingly long periods.

I established relationships with adventurers in Douar Hajja and Maâdid early on, through a series of serendipitous encounters. Soon after settling in Rabat, I was introduced by a flatmate, a Moroccan man who had worked on projects about interculturality, to Pierre. From Cameroon, Pierre was then the president of *Collectif des Communautés sub-Sahariennes au Maroc* (CCSM) (The Collective of Sub-Saharan Communities in Morocco). We quickly became friends, and Pierre took me under his wing for the first few weeks. Since there was little to do, he brought me along to a theatre workshop with young Moroccans and migrants. There, I met Idrissa, a young Burkinabé man who lived in Maâdid, and his Moroccan neighbour, Youssef. It was also Pierre who introduced me to Cameroonian men in *l'ambassade*, a Cameroonian ghetto located in Douar Hajja. These men wanted to set up a new migrants' organisation ('*association de migrants*') and sought Pierre's help in getting started. Along with Pierre, I was given the title of advisor, and I became closely involved in the activities of the organisation, befriending some of its core members and, with them, forging relationships with other activists from Moroccan civil society in Rabat. I remained deeply involved with this association in Douar Hajja throughout fieldwork and beyond (see Chapter 8), and interactions with its members were crucial to discussing multiple aspects of the adventure.

In articulating her challenging notion of 'militant anthropology', Nancy Scheper-Hughes argues that as anthropologists 'we can make ourselves available … as *comrades* (with all the demands and responsibilities that this word implies) to the people who are the subjects of our writings, whose lives and miseries provide us with a livelihood' (1995: 420; original emphasis). With this exhortation in mind, I took an active part in the activities of the organisation, especially helping close informants compile reports, though I sought to limit my role within the association to helping members formulate their own ideas and act on 'objectives' they themselves set. In the politically charged field of migration, no research project can pretend to be neutral. This book was made possible thanks to ongoing political engagements with migrants' associations as well as Moroccan NGOs (e.g. GADEM) in collaborative projects. This reflects my long-standing commitment to scholarship on migration that is not only critical of the brutality of migration regimes, but can serve to analyse, amplify, and support indignant refusals of bordering policies, discourses, and other practices that violently disregard people's right to mobility.

Doing research with a highly (im)mobile population poses numerous methodological issues. Everyday life was focused on locating the necessary resources (e.g. money, information) to organise border-crossing attempts. Adventurers often failed and returned to tend their wounds and restart the process of finding the necessary resources for the next trip. They could be gone for days, weeks, or longer. I sought to forge relationships with adventurers in different ghettoes. There were times when almost all of them were around, which could be difficult to manage. There were also periods when almost nobody I knew well was around. This prompted me to spend a lot of time with the Moroccan youth in Douar Hajja and Maâdid, especially Youssef and his group of friends, but also others, like Ali, a homeless Moroccan man who had befriended some of the Ivoirian men in *le consulat*.

The initial research plan had been to spend a few months in Rabat, exploring urban neighbourhoods, then move north, to focus on informal forest camps. Rather than a deliberate decision, it was the progressive connections I established with migrants and Moroccan youths across Douar

Hajja and Maâdid that highlighted the relevance of these peripheral neighbourhoods in the study of migrants' fragile and ambivalent anchoring in Morocco. Following adventurers' sinuous and difficult journeys to the borderlands and the camps was neither practical nor advisable, because of the increase in violent interventions by the Moroccan authorities, especially in the late-2011 to mid-2013 period. Focusing on Douar Hajja and Maâdid became an obvious, if serendipitous, choice for a form of 'arbitrary location' (Candea, 2007: 167), in response to the pitfalls of multi-sited ethnography (Marcus, 1995). Studying illegalisation and other fraught migration processes entails important methodological choices that can facilitate but also preclude the collection of certain data. I have chosen to focus on the experiences of migrants themselves, but other researchers have taken up different approaches and focuses (e.g. bureaucratic encounters with the state, the materiality of border infrastructures, the negotiation and use of European funds for migration, etc.). As a heavily politicised object and a central aspect of many people's lives, migration requires and deserves to be studied from various angles. Zooming in on the adventure as an existential yearning offers much-needed insights into how adventurers articulate and make sense of their own journeys, thereby tracing the connections between lives lived and aspired, risky journeys, and migration regimes embedded in historical processes marked by racialised understandings of deservingness, dangerousness, and desirability. Instead of reducing migrants to 'metaphorical figures' (Tošić and Lems, 2019: 3), the book exposes their efforts to cultivate adventurous selves to reach a life more bearable, highlighting in the process how they unwillingly became precariously anchored into marginal Moroccan neighbourhoods. It provides fewer insights into the workings of policymaking, transnational collaborations amongst nation-states, or the ambiguities of humanitarian assistance. But the ethnographic exploration of migrants' lives and journeys with a focus on how they themselves imagine and act on their mobility is a story that is too often ignored in fearmongering accounts of migration.

Douar Hajja and Maâdid

Ali was lying in the shade of a tall eucalyptus tree opposite the Sofitel hotel. The heat was excruciating on that late-August morning. Along the busy road circling the Almohad outer city wall, Moroccan flags, motionless for the lack of wind, were hanging on allocated poles in preparation for a royal visit. Apart from the occasional roar of a sports car driving out of the upmarket hotel, it was mostly quiet for Ali and a few other homeless people taking a nap. Later, crowds of Rabatis, inhabitants of Rabat, would gather to run in the adjacent park before their *ftour*, the meal to break the daily fast during Ramadan.

Skinny and short, with large brown eyes and dark skin, Ali, whose family originated from the disputed territories in Southern Morocco (i.e. the Western Sahara), was in his forties. He was born in Douar Hajja. Since he had been disowned by his father a few years before we met, he was sleeping rough around Douar Hajja and other places. He had a peculiar sense of humour and often joked about what life was like for ordinary Moroccans, mocking the government and the King. 'I cannot stand TV; you see the King's face on it all the time. I don't have a TV. I am alright. I have no TV; I have no house,' he told me when we first met, before breaking off into his frantic laughter. Ali enjoyed practising his fluent English with me and recalling trickster stories about his life in Dublin, where he had lived without documents for eight years before being deported. Sitting in the grass, Ali was laughing: 'How are you dealing with fasting? Me, it is forty years I fast. I am fasting from work, housing, and human rights here.' A few weeks earlier, he had been arrested by the police in Douar Hajja for smoking hashish. Ali could not afford to pay to be let free. He argued and was beaten up. He had been talking for a while about reaching out to a human rights association, but he did not really expect anything would happen: '[Abroad], they say that [Morocco] is getting democratic, that there are human rights; it is not going democratic, there is nothing here.'

Ali and I shared news about Moussa. It was my Ivoirian informant from *le consulat* who had introduced us. We joked that he would return soon from the borderlands, on account of his recent spate of misfortune in the north. Ali had a lot of sympathy for migrants in Douar Hajja. He had witnessed the sharp increase in the migrant population in his neighbourhood. But he often steered the conversation towards 'Moroccan people's problems', stressing that the authorities were brutal towards migrants but could exercise even more violence against their own citizens. Ali regularly pressed me to spend time with Moroccan inhabitants whom he referred to as the 'original people' from Douar Hajja. There were often striking similarities between the conversations I had with adventurers, who talked about the need to '*sortir*' (get out) of their countries and reach '*le dehors*' (the outside) to find their lives, and those I had with Moroccan youths, who discussed the lack of opportunities in Morocco and dreamed of 'the outside' (Elliot, 2021). Ali stressed how '*l-brrā*' (the outside) was widely seen as a solution to inequality and lack of freedom. He contrasted it with '*l-ḥgra*' (oppression, injustice): 'if you stay here, you go to prison. Here, it is *ḥgra*, but if you go *l-brrā*, you can have your *droits de l'homme* [human rights]. You get respect. Here, you cannot get respect.' He would often repeat that in Europe, one could save money towards a house, but in Douar Hajja, one could work forty years and get nothing. 'Being illegal there is better than being legal here. Here, you are legal only in your pocket,' Ali often joked. 'In Morocco, we might have nice food and lovely weather, but we are like strangers in our own country. That is why we run away.' But he was often critical of young people who thought that Europe was just a paradise. He had experienced hardship first-hand as an irregular migrant. He underlined that the focus on the outside made 'people live in *l-ḥulm* [dream] not *l-ḥaqīqa* [truth, reality]. Some think you can just go to Paris and find money behind the cafés and bring it back. They say I am stupid. I was in Europe eight years, and I did not learn how to make money.' He complained that some of the Moroccan migrants, who returned every summer to Douar Hajja, perpetuated lies about what life was like for migrants in Europe.

Shortly before *ftour*, Ali and I left the park to make our way back to the market in Douar Hajja. Sat on a concrete slab, at a crossroad not far from the Cameroonian ghetto *l'ambassade*, we watched people rushing to buy food, before returning home on time to break the fast. Next to us was a stall selling *msemmen*, Moroccan pancakes, and, beyond the counter, some sniffing drugs in plastic bags. Ali pointed at people working in the market who had spent time in prison for drug charges and other offences. He joked that in Douar Hajja, prison was called *Hajj* (pilgrimage). A man selling fruits and vegetables opposite us used to go all the way to Fez to steal. 'He gave me one advice: "stay away from aggressions",' Ali laughed. As it was soon time for the prayer marking the end of the fast, we got up and walked deeper into Douar Hajja.

In Rabat and beyond, Douar Hajja was widely portrayed as a dangerous neighbourhood – a platform for drugs, prostitution, and other forms of criminal activities. A 2008 headline from Moroccan newspaper *Al Bayane* called this neighbourhood '*une plaie hideuse*' (a hideous scar) in Rabat. This was mostly directed at the insufficient response of the state to the problems of Douar Hajja and Maâdid, rather than at the inhabitants themselves. Places such as Douar Hajja and Maâdid are associated in Moroccan public discourse with ' "urban abnormality" – they are inhabited by undisciplined, wild, filthy and uneducated people' (Navez-Bouchanine, 2003: 9).

Maâdid and Douar Hajja are two densely populated, peripheral neighbourhoods of Rabat. Migrants often referred to them as Takaddoum (meaning progress in Arabic), the neighbourhood directly along Avenue Al Haouz. Takaddoum, a modest neighbourhood where none of my informants could afford to live, originates from the development of subsidised housing for families with lower revenues, which began during the French Protectorate. The adjacent neighbourhoods of Douar Hajja and Maâdid are not the result of *ex nihilo* development programmes.[5] Neither are they shanty towns, although they were often referred to as 'bidonvilles' by migrants and

Moroccans living in other parts of the city. They are 'illegal districts [with] concrete buildings which more or less resemble traditional buildings, or cheap houses, but ... built on purchased plots of land without any permits' (Navez-Bouchanine, 2003: 5). As stressed by Essahel (2011) in his analysis of illegal habitats, inhabitants have bought plots of land and secured the necessary acts from notaries, but the plots are located in areas prohibited for urbanisation or deemed non-constructible.[6]

In Douar Hajja and Maâdid, buildings of unequal heights hazardously lean against one another on an unstable terrain, rising in a jagged pattern. Over-urbanisation, high population density, over-elevations without adequate foundations, surface run-off water forming gullies, a topography marked by natural slopes, and the geological configuration increase the risk of collapse and form a structurally hazardous place (Alain-El Mansouri, 2004). Official attitudes towards such neighbourhoods have oscillated between indifference, destruction, and a posteriori attempts at regularising and updating them, turning them into 'a sort of intermediate product, between the medinas and the legal low-income housing estates' (Navez-Bouchanine, 2003: 17). The tortuous and humid alleyways, often poorly lit and bearing painted numbers rather than street names, are narrow, crooked, and slippery. Migrants called them '*couloirs*' (corridors).

After a short walk, Ali and I stopped so he could receive food, donated by people he knew. We were sat near his parents' house. He always ate there during Ramadan 'to shame them'. When the *takbir* marking the start of the prayer resonated, Ali broke his fast. Some of the youths sitting nearby lit their first joints. A few minutes later, a woman was trotting down the street, talking on the phone: 'Have you had your *ftour* yet? Yes, yes, I am having my *ftour* right now. Yes, I am home.' She smiled at Ali, who translated what she said next, while walking past us: 'It is months you are in prison and then you ask me if I am having my *ftour*!' Ali laughed, 'She is right – if he is jealous, he should just not have fucking gone to prison and stayed with his wife.' Like migrants, many of the Moroccan youths I spoke to in Douar Hajja and Maâdid called these neighbourhoods 'a prison with an open roof'. They spoke of the poverty and difficulties many people faced. As in other places marked by structural exclusion, the response could be equally self-destructive (Bourgeois, 2008). Ali talked about Douar Hajja as the 'country of the bomb', where people could explode at any moment from the abjection and stigma they suffered. Ali complained that policemen, upon checking his ID cards, would tell him to 'fuck off back to Douar Hajja', whenever he was stopped and searched outside the neighbourhood. He coped with drugs. Youssef, in Maâdid, preferred bodybuilding. He stressed the need for self-control, to avoid repeating the mistakes of others in his neighbourhood, who had made 'wrong choices' to 'overcome poverty'.

If one demonstrated the right mentality (a term adventurers also used), one could be rewarded by God and not fall into the 'bad path'. Pointing to his heart, he added: 'You have to be strong. … You have to keep everything in here. One day, it might explode, and you will do something crazy, steal, kill someone, go to jail, and then it is over.'

Illegal neighbourhoods like Douar Hajja and Maâdid have been associated with the historical division in 'pre-modern' Morocco between places of dissidence and places associated with the state (*l-makhzn*) (Waterbury, 1970). Taxi drivers from other neighbourhoods would advise me against going there, warning me against 'the Africans' and some of the Moroccan inhabitants. For Youssef and his friends, such neighbourhoods were first and foremost '*shʿbī*' (popular, working class): a term imbued with positive connotations, pointing to the constant bustle in market streets, clogged by neighbours and friends chatting outside, and the cheaper living costs for inhabitants, who readily referred to themselves as more generous and unassuming than in other places. It was a warm place where people knew each other's families and kept an eye on the children playing in the alleyways. Youssef and his friends associated growing up in hardship with life lessons that wealthier people could not afford.

Although marked by poverty and migration from rural areas, Douar Hajja and Maâdid host heterogeneous socio-economic categories of Moroccan inhabitants. Several of the young men I spoke to in the neighbourhood came from families where the father was unemployed, and the mother was the only source of a meagre income, working as a cleaner. But there were artisans and shopkeepers, as well as civil servants and members of the army and the police, living there. The mix of poor families from rural Morocco and lower-middle-class Moroccans is not surprising, since such 'illegal settlements' (Navez-Bouchanine, 2003: 7) have provided opportunities for those who did not benefit from state distributions to accede to property. While they remain peripheral, the continuous integration of such neighbourhoods within the city has pushed some of the most marginalised populations further away.

The chapters

Chapter 1 traces the construction of the 'sub-Saharan issue' in Morocco from the 1990s to the mid-2020s. It outlines how the governance of migrants from sub-Saharan Africa is a site of transnational politics of migration in the Mediterranean region. Morocco has been a key but ambivalent actor. Hostile and violent bordering measures are grounded in (pre)colonial understandings of race, that construct Black people as undesirable.

Chapter 2 examines migrants' articulation of their adventurous journeys as a quest to reach 'the objective'. Morocco has been described as a country of transit to Europe for migrants from across the African continent, with often simplistic accounts of mobility patterns in this region. The notion of transit, which has become dominant in migration studies, exposes the deep-rooted Eurocentrism within the field. Old and new forms of mobility, with historical ties across Africa, are deeply entangled with the social, cultural, and political development of Moroccan society. Exploring migrants' imaginaries of the adventure debunks the fallacy of a fixed destination as adventurers recounted tortuous and uncertain journeys driven by the impetus to reach a better life.

Chapter 3 explores an apparent mobility paradox amongst irregular migrants in Douar Hajja and Maâdid. The heroic tales of adventure amongst young men from Western and Central Africa contrasted with their stuckedness in windowless ghettoes, which some were reluctant to leave, for fear of being assaulted or arrested. Daily life was marked by boredom, waiting for their future success in the borderlands. The chapter explores how these young men sought to avoid '*devenir fou*' (going mad) and sustained hope by emphasising the necessary interplay of courage, strength, and 'chance' in the adventure, acknowledging their own agency, but also its limits, amidst wider forces at play.

Chapter 4 examines diverse living arrangements amongst adventurers in Douar Hajja and Maâdid, highlighting the move away from large, derelict, and overcrowded ghettoes to smaller housing arrangements, for those who could afford it. Many sought to leave overcrowded accommodations, that were targeted by police raids, and involved exploitation by unscrupulous landlords. In examining precarious forms of home-making amongst adventurers, the chapter highlights how migrants sought to make their everyday lives and present more comfortable, but were ready to pack up and leave for the borderlands at short notice. Chapter 4 is followed by a photo essay with a series of nine photographs shot in the ghettoes inhabited by adventurers in Douar Hajja and Maâdid. The photographs, taken with permission from these young men, echo the book's overall exploration of how adventurers faced boredom, violence, and suffering while striving to carve up a better future and a life more bearable for themselves.

Chapter 5 examines the socio-economic anchoring of adventurers, through a focus on work, especially the businesses they set up (e.g. restaurants, hairdressing salons, etc.). Work for irregular migrants was marked by abuse and exploitation in the informal economy, but also by entrepreneurial ventures, that echoed adventurers' imperative to be resourceful. Migrants' economic projects were embedded in their uncertain and (im)mobile quest for a better life and future. Businesses further anchored migrants into the neighbourhood, but they regularly opened and shut to fund border-crossing attempts.

In exploring issues of trust and the moral conundrums faced by adventurers, Chapter 6 sheds light on the tension inherent to the adventure as an individual project to realise one's life, but also as a collective endeavour. The relationships forged amongst adventurers were tenuous but essential. Migrants in Douar Hajja and Maâdid did not form a neat community, founded on a transformative rite of passage where all became equal. Neither were they merely atomised individuals, taking advantage of one another to reach their migratory and life goals. The chapter examines how a recognition of a shared suffering and common '*mentalité*' (mentality) were both the basis and the limit of migrants' relationships. They needed one another to continue the journey but would have little hesitation in crossing alone, given the opportunity.

Chapter 7 examines the interaction between bordering regimes and race and its impact on the targeting of Black migrants. The chapter focuses on relationships between adventurers and their Moroccan neighbours, who shared structural experiences of suffering and abandonment, and often the same hope to leave Morocco for better opportunities. Amidst the interplay of both racism and mutual help, Douar Hajja and Maâdid were the loci of acts of violence and kindness, sometimes enacted by the same people.

Chapter 8 tracks the development of a small organisation set up by adventurers in *l'ambassade*. The chapter explores what kind of political subjectivity and organisation is possible for people deemed 'illegal'. The 'three dimensions' of this organisation (i.e. supporting migrants wanting to return, stay, and move on) mirrored the ambiguity of adventurers' lives and migratory projects. The chapter outlines how examining the political agency of irregular migrants requires accounting for the complex, and sometimes contradictory, demands of trying to address pressing everyday issues, while seeking to carve out opportunities for a better future.

Notes

1. These terms are loaded and controversial. They point to social and political processes that categorise mobilities differently. I will omit the inverted commas in the remainder of the book. As outlined in this introduction, I contribute to such political and etymological debates through a focus on my informants' own terms.
2. It is not possible to provide accurate numbers for irregular migrants from Western and Central Africa across Maâdid and Douar Hajja. Fabien, who was prone to hyperbolic statements, often repeated there were at least two million of them. In their study on the area, Edogué Ntang and Péraldi (2011: 37)

give a figure of approximately 1,500–2,000 migrants. This seems a plausible if conservative estimate, especially for the winter period when more people came back from the forests in the borderlands to escape even more arduous living conditions.
3. Although Morocco is a signatory of the 1951 Refugee Convention, the rights of asylum seekers were barely upheld, as NGOs and migrants regularly complained that police and military forces would tear asylum seekers' papers before deporting them. Even passports with a valid visa were confiscated and destroyed.
4. Migrants and NGO workers, such as those from the catholic relief agency Caritas, located a short walk from Douar Hajja, stressed that women and families tended to seek accommodations, independently or with the support of humanitarian organisations, in other neighbourhoods, reputed to be less dangerous and hostile. The number of women in Douar Hajja and Maâdid was visibly rising during fieldwork. Especially as a growing number of migrants, including women, left the informal forest camps in the borderlands to escape increasingly brutal treatment from the Moroccan authorities.
5. Researchers at the Institut National d'Aménagement et d'Urbanisme (INAU) explained that the names Douar Hajja and Maâdid likely come from two families of landowners. Officially, the two neighbourhoods are named Hay El-Farah and Hay Errachad. 'Douar' originally refers to a rural village but also designates 'either rural peripheries more or less integrated in the urban network, [or] peri-urban informal settlements' (Navez-Bouchanine, 2003: 26).
6. Douar Hajja and Maâdid were the recipients of the first Urban Development Plan (UDP) in 1976 (INAU, 1984). The UDP is the classic example of a new approach to urbanism in the 1970s, which gave emphasis to restructuring in situ, combining 'spatial and physical upgrading on one hand, and social, economic or institutional improvements on the other hand' (Navez-Bouchanine, 2003: 17). However, it was deemed 'a total fiasco' (Belfquih and Fadloullah, 1986: 426). Analyses agree in judging negatively 'the spatial effects (architectural, urban, technical) …: excessive density, lack of public spaces, minimal garbage dumps, "slummy" and even "ruralised" aesthetics and landscape, sometimes aggravated by tortuous or difficult sites' (Navez-Bouchanine, 2003: 18). This worry over a permanent '*bidonvilisation*' (Navez-Bouchanine, 2002: 169) amid poor access to public services, was accompanied by the authorities' concerns over security and difficulties in monitoring such spaces.

1

The making of a sub-Saharan issue

On 24 June 2022, dozens of migrants perished while attempting to enter the Spanish enclave of Melilla, near the Moroccan city of Nador. Harrowing footage of the Moroccan authorities piling up the still or barely moving bodies of Black migrants, with no medical assistance in sight, quickly circulated on social media. In their report on this 'tragedy' (AMDH Nador, 2022), activists from the *Association Marocaine des Droits Humains* (AMDH) (Moroccan Association of Human Rights) denounced the 'cruel' treatment of migrants as the result of 'criminal' migration politics across Morocco, Spain, and the EU. The tragedy cast further doubt on the unfulfilled promises of progressive migration policies in Morocco. Authorities have been profoundly preoccupied by the country's international standing and have introduced reforms since 2013. Besides enhancing Morocco's reputation as a champion of stability and progress in the region, such reforms partake in ensuring the 'transitional continuity' of the regime (Naguib, 2020). The violence at the border sparked international outrage, echoing another set of dramatic events when eleven migrants were shot dead, and hundreds more wounded, trying to climb the fortified fences of Melilla and of the other Spanish enclave, Ceuta, in September 2005 (Yene, 2010; Khrouz, 2019). For many researchers, activists, and practitioners supporting migrants, brutal practices at the Morocco–Spain border are symptomatic of a 'war against migrants' (Migreurop, 2007).

Before focusing on the lives of adventurers in Douar Hajja and Maâdid throughout the rest of the book, this chapter traces the development of a so-called sub-Saharan issue, as it is commonly and uncritically referred to in Moroccan media. The chapter examines how a wide array of state and non-state actors has partaken in crafting this racialised figure of the clandestine, 'sub-Saharan' migrant as the privileged target of transnational politics of migration, fearmongering discourses, and violent bordering practices. Such dehumanising, depoliticising, and dehistoricising depictions of migrants in Morocco from across Western and Central Africa are at the heart of security-focused border regimes that seek to deny – through deadly measures enforced by border guards, police forces, and other Moroccan and European authorities – the mobility, rights, and aspirations of those deemed undesirable and rendered illegal.

Migration as a security problem

The documented deaths and other acts of violence against migrants in the borderlands around the Spanish enclaves of Ceuta and Melilla, along with the many instances that go unreported, expose the deadly consequences of bordering regimes that selectively organise and impose the forced (im) mobility of racialised Black migrants. As objects of fear, Black migrants are deemed undesirable (Agier, 2011, 2022). Their lives are treated as ungrievable (Butler, 2016). They bear the cost of violent politics of migration negotiated across the Mediterranean region – a region once understood as a space of interaction and migrating cultures, of which migrants, 'however feared, despised, and victimized by racism and social economic injustice, are the historical reminders' (Chambers, 2008: 39).[1]

A rising death toll is continuously met with contrite speeches from politicians promising tougher measures after each tragedy.[2] Indeed, many politicians, journalists, and other pundits regularly call for urgent measures to manage, stop, and deter migration flows, in the name of preventing the suffering of migrants and addressing the root causes of migration. Public debate routinely overlooks how policies and practices which target irregular migration often compound suffering and inequities. This includes humanitarian interventions legitimising bordering practices that violate the rights of migrants and threaten their lives (Pallister-Wilkins, 2022). At the heart of a world order where mobility is celebrated but encouraged and facilitated only for a happy few, the containment, control, and expulsion of migrants through bureaucratic, militaristic, and technological measures is anything but incongruous and tragic. This realm of barbed wire, reconnaissance drones, fingerprinting, and migration quotas is the 'the price of the supposedly unified world of capital' (Badiou, 2008: 38).

Within the EU, migration has mostly been approached as 'a security problem' (Bigo, 2002: 63). Complex socio-economic, cultural, and political issues and concerns are channelled into a ubiquitous migration 'problem' (Boswell, 2003: 623). Dominant narratives and depictions reduce migrants to criminals, or a sea of humanity chiefly marked by vulnerability (Malkki, 1996). In parallel to the dismantling of Europe's internal borders introduced by the 1985 Schengen Agreement and the 1986 Single European Act that created an area of free circulation for people, goods, capitals, and services, European institutions and member states have deployed measures targeting the external control of Europe's border (Cross, 2009), notably through efforts to establish partnerships with southern Mediterranean countries such as Turkey, Libya, Tunisia, and Morocco (Cherti and Grant, 2013; Stock *et al.*, 2019). The 'more powerful' states (Menjívar, 2014: 357) request the cooperation of countries labelled as 'origin' or 'transit' to selectively control, stop, and deter the movement of (some) migrants. Migration scholars exploring the externalisation of Europe's migration policies have highlighted the mechanisms (e.g. financial incentives, immigration quotas, etc.) by which the union and its member states, through a 'carrot and stick approach' (Schuster, 2005: 18), delegate the promotion and imposition of a range of bordering practices on to other nation-states 'to prevent unwanted arrivals at their international borders' (Casas-Cortes *et al.*, 2015; Cuttitta, 2020: 2). Neighbouring countries have increasingly been pressured to readmit and retain their own citizens, while being required to organise the control, dissuasion, tracking down, marginalisation, blocking, and deportation of other migrants (Belguendouz, 2005). As well as taking part in joint border control operations, capacity-building programmes, and negotiations over readmission agreements and offshore processing centres, Europe's neighbouring countries are encouraged to negotiate and establish their own agreements with other southern countries, to ensure that migrants stay even closer to their countries of origin.

These collaborations have significantly contributed to the intensification of policing and militarisation activities in the Mediterranean region – notably with the creation of Frontex in 2004 (Wolff, 2008), the European Agency for the Management of Operational Cooperation at the External Borders, revamped, with an extended mandate, as the European Border and Coast Guard Agency in 2016. This has generated a lucrative industry, delivering copious profits and opportunities for a wide array of (private) actors (Rodier, 2012; Andersson, 2014). Other effects of these collaborations include the growing involvement of human smugglers, to broker passages along constantly shifting migratory routes (Lutterbeck, 2006). Solemn announcements about respecting the rights and dignity of migrants, while maintaining a tough stance on illegality in the name of values such as security, protection, and fairness, are a regular preamble to intergovernmental declarations about (illegal) migration. But this race forward to negotiate with countries where the rule of law is weak or not respected points out the impossibility of reconciling the entanglement of securitarian and humanitarian agendas (Fassin, 2011; Willians, 2015; Pallister-Wilkins, 2022) with Europe's self-image as a human rights' defender in the region (Kausch, 2009). The treatment of migrants by Europe's southern Mediterranean partners, acting as auxiliaries of repression and harnessing migration as a form of political rent (Bensaâd, 2005), is often 'at best inadequate, at worst profoundly inhuman' (Baldwin-Edwards, 2006: 312).

Morocco and its ambiguous partnership with Europe

Since the 1990s, Morocco has been a privileged, yet ambiguous and not fully amenable, partner in the management of (irregular) migration, collaborating especially with Spain, where migration from Morocco has been portrayed as an invasion, bound up with the memory of Al Andalus and Muslim rule before the Reconquista in the fifteenth century (Gillepsie, 2002; Zapata-Barrero and Witte, 2007). The Spain–Morocco frontier, which had previously been relatively porous, underwent profound changes, driven by a rise in immigration in Spain during an economically prosperous period, and by the Iberian Peninsula joining the European Economic Community in 1986. With the multiplication of irregular crossings in the 1990s, Spain deployed new bordering measures, based on prevention, coercion, and dissuasion (López-Sala, 2015).

Visas were introduced for Moroccans in 1991. Following a friendship treaty, Spain signed a readmission agreement with Morocco in 1992. The latter was mostly applied to Moroccan nationals. The readmission of other nationals (including from sub-Saharan Africa) has mostly been an informal practice, marked by profound irregularities, which have preoccupied human rights defenders (Groupe antiraciste d'accompagnement et de défense des étrangers et migrants *et al.*, 2015; Alpes *et al.*, 2021). Spain, under the Aznar government, was instrumental in the drafting of an Action Plan for Morocco, in 1999, by the EU's High-Level Working Group (HLWG) on Migration and Asylum – a group tasked with coordinating the criminalisation of clandestine migration with a select group of countries of origin and transit (Collyer, 2010).

From 1993, Spain initiated the progressive fortification of Ceuta and Melilla, its enclaves in North Africa, retained under Spanish rule following Morocco's independence in 1956 but disputed by successive Moroccan governments. This evolving set of tall fences, adorned with surveillance technology and crude barbed wire, has become a symbol of hostile migration politics in the region (Carling, 2007; Aris Escarcena, 2022). The monitoring of the border has necessitated considerable resources from the EU and member states. The Spanish government allocated 106 million euros, between 2001 and 2006, for the launch of its Integrated External Surveillance System (SIVE). This is a high-tech system of surveillance and interception that uses militaristic expertise to detect and stop fishing boats carrying clandestine migrants. Operated by the Spanish Civil Guard, SIVE was first implemented in the Straits of Gibraltar (only 14 kilometres) but was quickly deployed across the Mediterranean and along the coasts of the Canary Islands. Cooperation over bordering processes has been intensified and expanded through numerous bilateral and multilateral programmes of information sharing, surveillance, and interception, jointly deploying policing forces from Spain and Morocco, as well as other European and African countries (Andersson, 2014; López-Sala, 2015). The border between Morocco and Spain, an 'open wound' (Anzaldúa, 1987) between Europe and Africa, has seen an escalation of bordering measures, which has led to increasingly dangerous journeys, along shifting migratory routes.[3]

Since the 1990s, there has been a rise in the number of young Moroccan and other Maghrebi *l-ḥrāqa* (literally those who burn in Arabic), the people who seek to 'expand their living space' (M'charek, 2020: 419) by crossing clandestinely into European territories in defiance of bureaucratic and visa regimes. Fleeing not just economic poverty, these young people have burned the border (along with their identification papers, to avoid deportation), driven by a deep *mal de vie* (wretched living conditions) in Morocco (and across the region), where they faced *l-ḥgra* (contempt, injustice): rampant abuses of power, generating feelings of powerlessness and frustration, amidst widespread precariousness, social and cultural scarcity, and the absence of spaces for freedom and exchanges that could foster and guarantee the fulfilment of their lives and futures (Pandolfo, 2007; Arab and Sempere, 2009; Souiah, 2012). Restrictive immigration policies and the rise of clandestine migration in the wider region also coincided with an increasing demand for cheap labour in agriculture, service sector, and other industries across some European countries (De Haas, 2007). Those young people who mobilised financial and social capitals to make the dangerous crossing met with a labour market where 'opportunities', in the form of established models of exploitation, were ready to capture undocumented migrants. As well as movement, borders regulate and structure complex 'relations between capital, labor, law, subjects, and political power' (Mezzadra and Neilson, 2013: 8). The management of labour and migration in Europe are closely entangled through bordering processes that target racialised individuals and selectively foster different degrees of precarity and mobility (see Arab, 2018).

Migrants from Western and Central Africa

The number of nationals from Western and Central African countries attempting to cross the Moroccan–Spanish border clandestinely rose from the late 1990s and early 2000s, notably via the fences around the enclaves of Ceuta and Melilla (Bredeloup and Pliez, 2005; Goldschmidt, 2006).[4] Early studies identified Nigeria, Republic of Côte d'Ivoire, Cameroon, Senegal, Guinea, Mali, and the Democratic Republic of Congo as the main sub-Saharan countries of origin (AMERM, 2008; Faleh *et al.*, 2009).[5] Those who arrived by land usually entered Morocco clandestinely across the closed border between Maghnia in Algeria and Oujda in Morocco.[6] There have also been arrivals by plane, including amongst nationals (e.g. from Senegal) for whom a visa is not required to enter and stay in Morocco for ninety days. Visas are time-limited, and even those still in possession of the correct documents have not been safe from brutal enforcement of borders since illegality, as explored below, is deeply entangled with imaginaries and politics of race. Together with places such as Gao in Mali, Agadès in Niger, and Tamanrasset in Algeria, Maghnia and Oujda have been important staging posts (Alioua, 2011) along a wide network of hazardous migratory routes connecting Western and Central African countries to Morocco and beyond (Andersson, 2014).[7]

In Oujda, migrants could rest after journeys which had taken months or years. They stopped to work, wait for help from families, and collect other resources, before resuming their journeys.[8] Once in the Moroccan city of Oujda, migrants could find further contacts and information (especially around the university campus). Some prepared to jump on the back of trains, to cities hosting a growing population of migrants in peripheral neighbourhoods, such as Fez or Rabat. Others made their way on foot or on buses (when drivers did not refuse to take them, following pressure from the authorities) towards the informal forest camps in the vicinity of Melilla and Ceuta (respectively 130 and 500 km away from Oujda). There migrants could attempt to scale the network of fences around the Spanish enclaves partially funded by EU funds for regional development (Tyszler, 2015). The fences, jointly patrolled by Moroccan and Spanish security forces, have been regularly updated since the 1990s with sharp blades and high-tech equipment (e.g. thermal cameras). Migrants often attempted such crossing en masse to increase their chance of success but faced brutal, and sometimes deadly, repression from Spanish and Moroccan authorities (and illegal refoulement). Other dangerous possibilities entailed crossing into the enclaves on rubber dinghies or swimming aided by air chambers. Crossing directly towards the Spanish peninsula could also be attempted with those same unseaworthy rubber dinghies nicknamed zodiacs by migrants, or on motored boats (e.g. pateras) for those able and willing to negotiate with smugglers. Another route into Morocco cut across Mauritania and the Western Sahara towards cities such as Laayoune – where migrants could attempt to reach the Canary Islands by boat or continue northwards towards Ceuta and Melilla.

Most migrants crossing irregularly into the Moroccan kingdom throughout the early 2000s were young, single men (AMERM, 2008), often with some level of education, and access to the social and economic capital to start their long and costly journey (see Faleh *et al.*, 2009). Migratory projects are often the result of a familial investment, requiring the mobilisation of significant resources, even if contact and support are not easily maintained during journeys (Belloni, 2016; Stock, 2016). International mobility has been restricted for the poorest, but, increasingly, it has ceased to be limited to the wealthier middle class, notably thanks to technological changes, such as faster and cheaper communication channels and money transfers (Collyer, 2010). Importantly, as reported in the Introduction, studies have noted shifts in the profile of irregular migrants throughout the first decades of the twenty-first century, notably its increasing feminisation.[9]

Studies have highlighted a significant number of migrants from sub-Saharan Africa, stuck for long periods and likely to remain there indefinitely, who nevertheless continue to harbour the hope of entering Europe (Cherti and Grant, 2013). The top-down construction of (irregular) migration from sub-Saharan Africa as a national public issue by the Moroccan authorities (Natter, 2014) has led to the lengthening of migrants' stay. While it only took a few days in the 1990s (Goldschmidt, 2002) to cross to Spain, studies in the 2000s reported an average of thirty months (AMERM, 2008). In addition to the exploration of clandestine migration amongst Moroccan and other North African nationals, the violently restricted mobility of nationals from sub-Saharan Africa became an object of study for scholars from Morocco and beyond in the first decade of the twenty-first century (e.g. Alioua, 2005; Goldschmidt, 2006; Bensaâd, 2009; Pian, 2009). This growing concern amongst decision-makers, scholars, and other observers was focused on a small population, estimated in the 2000s and the first half of the 2010s to be between fifteen and forty thousand.[10] In view of changing migration patterns, a consensus emerged amongst observers: Morocco, a country of emigration with a long-standing reliance on remittances from its citizens living abroad (Collyer *et al.*, 2009) and where authorities actively encouraged outward mobility to relieve discontent (McMurray, 2001), had become an important place of transit and was increasingly becoming a country of immigration (if often by default). The growing relevance of immigration, however, was not publicly acknowledged by Moroccan authorities, who continued, in the early 2010s, to portray Morocco as a transit place 'victim of its geographical position' (Natter, 2014: 20).

However, it is crucial to nuance generic statements about such shifts in Morocco by stressing how migration patterns were already characterised by more than simply outward mobility until the late twentieth century. The Eurocentric narrative surrounding Morocco's shift overlooks how, long before and throughout the colonial period of French and Spanish protectorates, important shifts in population (both voluntary and forced) have taken place in, across, and out of Morocco, notably as part of trans-Saharan trade and circular migration to Algeria (De Haas, 2007; Gross-Wyrtzen and Gazzotti, 2021). The mobility of migrants in the region is woven along established trading and pilgrimage routes across the Sahara: a thriving medieval crossroad which remains today an important site of exchange (see Scheele, 2012; Berzock, 2019). New forms of mobilities have emerged, notably the rise of a significant community of international students, many originating from across the African continent (Berriane, 2015).

Brutal repression

The brutal repression and targeting of Black migrants from sub-Saharan Africa, seeking to reach Morocco or continue their journeys towards Europe, has been facilitated by legislative developments. In 2003, in the wake of the Casablanca suicide bombings, Morocco adopted Law 02–03 on the entry and stay of migrants in Morocco (Khrouz, 2019). This law was Morocco's first piece of legislation on migration since its independence and was largely influenced by repressive 1945 French legislation on migration. The law criminalises irregular migration, notably unauthorised entry and stay, with the provision of measures to detain and deport irregular migrants (Belguendouz, 2003; Jiménez-Alvarez et al., 2021). Some of the measures criminalise emigration, with the threat of fines and prison sentences, in contradiction with article 13 of the Universal Declaration of Human Rights (Khrouz et al., 2009). The law also contravenes protective provisions for migrants, contained in treaties signed and ratified by Morocco, notably the International Convention on the Protection of the Rights of All Migrant Workers and Members of Their Families (Elmadad, 2009).

At first glance, this new law further establishes Morocco's status as Europe's border guard (Belguendouz, 2005). However, it is crucial not to portray Morocco as simply executing directives from the EU, which it unsuccessfully applied to join in 1987. Eurocentric analyses of bordering in the Mediterranean region, focused on Europe's externalisation of migration politics, may overlook complex, if asymmetrical, negotiations between Europe and southern Mediterranean countries, who adjust their degree of collaboration and pursue their own interests (Berriane et al., 2015; Cherti and Collyer, 2015; El Qadim, 2015; Natter, 2021). Moroccan authorities have astutely entwined migration and bordering with socio-economic and political issues (e.g. fishing agreements, energy contracts, 'advanced' status with the EU, territorial disputes).[11]

Black and irregular 'sub-Saharan migrants' have suffered the devastating consequences of tightened bordering measures, as they sought to make a life for themselves in Morocco or pursue their journeys towards Europe (Bachelet, 2019; Stock, 2019; Alexander-Nathani, 2021). Throughout the 2000s and early 2010s, an increasing number of studies and reports documented the violent consequences of these politics of containment (Wender *et al.*, 2004; Migreurop, 2007; Amnesty, 2014; APDHA, 2014). The medical humanitarian organisation Médecins Sans Frontières (MSF) (Doctors without Borders), which had been present in Morocco since 1997, extending its support services to migrant communities in the early 2000s, released a damning report in March 2013. The report highlighted how 'violence remains a daily reality for the majority of sub-Saharan migrants in Morocco … The period since December 2011 has seen a sharp increase in abuse, degrading treatment and violence against sub-Saharan migrants by Moroccan and Spanish security forces' (MSF, 2013: 3).

The brutal treatment and the infringement of migrants' rights across the borderlands with Spain and Algeria, as well as across Moroccan cities (e.g. Casablanca, Rabat, Tangier, Fez, etc.), have fluctuated in intensity, depending on negotiations between Morocco, Spain, and the EU. In parallel to these shifting transnational negotiations over bordering, ruthless 'migrant hunts' (GADEM, 2006) have regularly taken place in the forest encampments and urban neighbourhoods across Morocco. The repression by the auxiliary forces and other security corps in Morocco has regularly targeted pregnant women, minors, asylum seekers, and refugees, in breach of Morocco's commitments to international treaties but also to its own legislation (Khrouz, 2019). In 2013, a group of civil society organisations based in Morocco launched a campaign (GADEM *et al.*, 2013) to denounce the return and intensification, since 2011, of violent practices by Moroccan forces (e.g. arbitrary arrests and deportations), on a scale not experienced since the 2005 Ceuta and Melilla events. The campaign called for the opening of an independent investigation into the circumstances surrounding the suspicious deaths of migrants, especially in the borderlands with Spain (Bachelet, 2013). Their report documents numerous violations of migrants' physical integrity, dignity, and rights: violent beatings, the destruction and theft of their belongings (e.g. phones, money), the confiscation of their identification documents, refoulement from the Spanish to the Moroccan side of the border, deportation (outside any judicial process) to the no man's land at the Algerian border. These violations are part of wider efforts of displacement and dispossession to contain migrants into 'a state of deprivation and unsettling uncertainty' (Gazzotti and Hagan, 2021: 929; see also Alexander, 2019).

2013 and the new politics of migration?

Despite the escalating brutal repression targeting migrants, including leaders from established and emerging migrant associations, during the late 2011–2013 period, civil society organisations in Morocco persevered in their vocal and daring advocacy work. They continued to document and denounce the abuse at the heart of the security approach prevailing within Morocco and across its borderlands (Bachelet, 2014a). In summer 2013, several NGOs submitted reports articulating detailed criticisms of the endemic violence and infringement of migrants' rights, to counter the submission from the Moroccan State to the Committee of the International Convention on the Protection of the Rights of All Migrant Workers and Members of Their Families (Jiménez-Alvarez et al., 2021). Notably, a dozen NGOs based in Morocco contributed to a report, compiled by the Groupe antiraciste d'accompagnement et de défense des étrangers et migrants (GADEM) (Antiracist Group of Defence and Accompaniment of Foreigners and Migrants), denouncing the significant escalation of institutional violence against migrants from Western and Central African countries. The report highlighted important shortcomings with regards to fundamental guarantees provided by the convention: the right to life, security, work, education, healthcare, and justice, especially migrants in an irregular administrative situation (GADEM, 2013: 1). On 9 September 2013, the Moroccan Conseil national des droits de l'Homme (CNDH) (National Human Rights Council), a state agency with limited independence, but a vital channel for Moroccan civil society's advocacy work (Üstübici, 2016), also released a major report, echoing demands from organisations supporting migrants, in parallel to the committee meeting taking place in Geneva. In a disavowal of Morocco's approach, so far dominated by security imperatives, the CNDH, led by former exiled dissident and leading figure from Moroccan civil society Driss El Yazami, called for a 'radically new politics of asylum and migration' (CNDH, 2013). The report was quickly endorsed by a joint communique from the royal cabinet and several ministries, as Morocco hastened to put on a good show in Geneva (Benjelloun, 2021).

King Mohamed VI gave instructions for the elaboration of 'a new vision for a national migration policy, that is humanist in its philosophy, responsible in its approach and pioneering at a regional level' (Royaume du Maroc, 2013). The royal directives triggered a series of quick changes and promises (Benjelloun, 2021). A new government department in charge of migration matters was launched in October 2013 with the revamping of the Ministry overseeing Moroccans Residing Abroad, renamed as the Ministry of Moroccans Residing Abroad and Migration Affairs to emphatically mark the inclusion of immigration matters into its portfolio. Morocco also adopted a Stratégie Nationale d'Immigration et d'Asile (SNIA) (National Strategy on Immigration and Asylum) on 18 December 2014, to facilitate a better management of both migrants' integration and migratory flows (Lemaizi, 2022). This led to collaboration within civil society and the Moroccan authorities, and to important developments with regards to access to education and health for migrants. The authorities announced new legislative projects: three laws on immigration, asylum, and trafficking. Although they were all drafted by the end of 2014, the only enacted piece of legislation has been Law 27.14, on 25 August 2016, relative to the fight against human trafficking (Natter, 2021). Morocco carried out two operations of regularisation in 2014 and 2017, which benefited around fifty thousand irregular migrants and required close collaboration between the government and civil society organisations, notably to call for the regularisation of all women (Benjelloun, 2021). Some civil society organisations focused on migration, including those run by migrants, which had, until then, operated without legal recognition, were officially acknowledged by the Moroccan administration, and joined by newly created ones. An increasing number of organisations working on development, education, health, and other relevant issues reoriented their activities to include migration matters. This sudden surge in organisations working on migration was the result of a promising window of opportunity to take part in the reform agenda, as well as the attractive prospect of receiving funding from Morocco and abroad (Natter, 2021; Gazzotti, 2021a).[12]

Without belittling the efforts and achievements of civil society actors, this so-called radical shift in migration politics, for which Morocco has been profusely congratulated in diverse international forums (Norman, 2020), is not simply the result of sustained advocacy work in Morocco and beyond. A broad range of socio-political, economic, and diplomatic factors have contributed to set sudden changes in motion. This shift emerges from what Natter calls an 'illiberal paradox' (2021) in Morocco: the performance of human rights through liberal migration reform has contributed to ensure the continuity of the regime in the face of both international and domestic pressures. Since independence, and despite some reforms after the start of King Mohamed VI's reign in 1999, the central authorities in Morocco have responded to dissent and challenges through brutal forms of repression (e.g. Years of Lead, Hirak), as well as careful management of spaces of dissent: co-optation of challengers, systems of patronage for rural and urban elites, and efforts to divide opposition movements, notably within weakened political parties (see Maghraoui, 2009; Daadaoui, 2010; Linn, 2011; Buehler, 2015; De Smet and El Khalaoui, 2021; Badran, 2022; Rhani et al., 2022).[13] With regards to migration, the regime has allowed some advocacy work to exist and be visible, even though the activities of civil society perturbed its security agenda. This nurtured Morocco's portrayal as a liberal monarchy, where dissenting voices could be heard. This dynamic has been strengthened after 2013, through the involvement of established organisations and activists, notably to lend legitimacy to and ensure the success of the regularisation processes. Amidst a fraught democratisation process, marked by the arbitrary arrest of vocal critics (e.g. journalists, academics), Morocco has sought to co-opt civil society into a more humanitarian management of migration matters, while silencing dissent, especially on other important issues pertaining to equality and rights (Natter, 2021; Human Rights Watch, 2022).

Morocco has been particularly concerned with international shaming (Norman, 2020) and sought to construct and consolidate not just its image as a liberal and progressive monarchy, but also its standing and role on the international political scene, deploying migration reforms in support of foreign policy. The shift in migration politics has partially been motivated by national economic interests and relationships with other African nations. King Mohamed VI undertook several visits to Western Africa from early 2013, signing economic agreements that promised a significant increase in exports and foreign investments across the African continent. In this evolving economic environment, Morocco has been attentive to human rights issues relating to citizens from Western and Central Africa (Cherti and Collyer, 2015).

A few weeks after the announcement of the second regularisation process, Morocco rejoined the African Union, where Mohamed VI was designated as the union's champion of migration (Benjelloun, 2021). Morocco announced that it would host the African Union's Migration Observatory in Rabat in 2018. That same year, it successfully hosted two major global events focused on the management of migration: the Global Forum on Migration and Development, and the Intergovernmental Conference to Adopt the Global Compact on Safe, Orderly and Regular Migration, a non-binding cooperative framework to cover, in a holistic and comprehensive manner, all dimensions of international migration (UN, 2018). The conference was organised under the aegis of the United Nations, but the pact has been associated with the name of the city (Marrakesh) where it was adopted in December 2018, affording Morocco further prestige and recognition for its influencing role in the global governance of migration. Yet, it is not clear to what extent Morocco can play this game of balancing interests. It is difficult to reconcile pressures from Europe for the containment of migrants with seeking to become a member of the Economic Community of West African States (ECOWAS), where efforts to support social and economic integration include measures for free movement (Benjelloun, 2021).

Cracks in Morocco's new approach to migration have revealed continuities with past practices, notably in terms of violence and infringement of migrants' rights. Activists in Morocco have widely shared with me their 'disillusion' with the SNIA, as it has failed to deliver 'necessary structural changes' and foster the 'real integration' of migrants. Even issues (e.g. access to education) where there had been clear 'gains' and some form of consensus had stalled by the early 2020s. As illustrated by the lack of progress on legislative texts on migration and asylum, the implementation of Morocco's ambitious new politics is only 'incomplete' (Benjelloun, 2021). Morocco has made little progress to ensure the integration of migrants in the country. The 2021 survey by the Haut-Commissariat au Plan (HCP) on refugees, irregular migrants, and those recently regularised notes a long average in the duration of stay (over six years). It highlights that around a quarter of those who took part in the quantitative study want to leave Morocco but not return 'home', stressing that while Morocco is not always a final destination, transit turns into a more or less lengthy forced stay within the kingdom. The obstacles impeding migrants' attempts to cross into Spain have effectively turned Morocco into *'une terre d'escale durable'* (a lasting stopover) (HCP, 2021: 62). Even those who have benefited from the regularisation process find themselves in limbo, facing further difficulties to renew their residency card in Morocco (Lemaizi, 2022). Migrant leaders from associations in Rabat have regularly complained that there is 'no work' for migrants in Morocco, besides the informal sector. Despite a moratorium on raids and deportations to the Algerian border at the time of the first regularisation process, violence and forced displacement towards migrants by Moroccan security forces (especially in the borderlands with Spain) have continued. In February 2015, one day after a news conference announcing the end of the first regularisation process, at least 1,200 migrants around Nador were rounded up and dropped off by bus hundreds of kilometres away in the south, in cities such as Errachidia, Agadir, and Tiznit (GADEM and FIDH, 2015).

As Morocco prepared to host the Intergovernmental Conference in Marrakesh and in the context of a rise in the number of irregular crossings into Spain, summer 2018 marked the start of a new period of intense repression against Black migrants (Alami, 2018). GADEM released two major reports documenting in harrowing detail the resurgence of violence and abuse targeting migrants from sub-Saharan Africa, following the end of the second regularisation process (GADEM, 2018a, 2018b). Between July and September 2018, over 6,500 migrants were forcibly displaced as part of discriminatory police operations without a legal framework. Migrants were picked up on the street or taken from their homes by Moroccan security forces and brought to local police stations, to be boarded on to buses that dropped them off in the south. NGOs documented the sweeping arrests of Black asylum seekers, pregnant women, and people with regular visas. At least two people died during this operation. Raids on migrant communities continued well into 2019 and were extended to other cities further away from the borderlands (e.g. Rabat, Casablanca). In 2023, the number of migrants in working-class neighbourhoods, such as Douar Hajja and Maâdid, but also along the ocean (e.g. Yacoub El Mansour), had visibly decreased. Leaders of migrant organisations blamed this on regular arrests. People elected to stay in the south and work in agriculture, rather than risk arrest in Rabat again. Some moved to the nearby city of Salé, where authorities were said to conduct fewer arrests. Others travelled towards Tunisia, to try different routes.

2018 is also widely seen as a turning point in the relationship between Moroccan authorities and Moroccan civil society. Some organisations agreed to engage in a sustained dialogue and to collaborate with authorities, notably during the regularisation processes (e.g. appeal commissions), lending credence to the shift in Moroccan politics of migration. This relationship deteriorated when the Ministry of Moroccans Residing Abroad and Migration Affairs removed immigration from its portfolio and was downgraded to a Delegate Ministry to the Ministry of Foreign Affairs, African Cooperation and Moroccan Expatriates. In this process, civil society lost a clear interlocutor. Individuals and organisations have apprehensively followed such developments, amidst a climate of fear and suspicion fostered by direct and insidious forms of repression against those who continue to document and call out abuses against migrants by the authorities (Hagan and Bachelet, 2023).

The targeting of migrants and those who support them by Moroccan authorities has continued into the COVID-19 pandemic, facilitated by securitarian measures to contain the virus. The June 2022 events demonstrate that the vision laid out by the Moroccan authorities and their humanitarian posturing have not been realised. Violence and repression continue to be a dominant modus operandi and efforts to integrate migrants have stalled. Irregular migration remains a central issue in negotiations with the EU. In March 2023, the EU Commissioner for Neighbourhood and Enlargement, Olivér Várhelyi, announced new cooperation programmes, worth 624 million euros, under the Neighbourhood, Development and International Cooperation Instrument – Global Europe (NDICI – Global Europe). These programmes provide support for Morocco's ambitious reform agenda in key areas such as climate policy, judiciary systems, and irregular migration management. The largest of the five programmes is focused on irregular migration (152 million euros) '[to] strengthen Morocco's border management actions in the fight against smuggling networks, the National Strategy of Morocco on Immigration and Asylum, as well as the voluntary return and the reintegration of migrants to their countries of origin, in accordance with international standards in terms of Human rights' (European Commission, 2023).

Race and migration

Transnational movement into Morocco from across the African continent is not a new phenomenon but increasingly the focus of fearmongering discourses and violent border measures that single out the mobility of racialised Black migrants. Yet, overall figures for international migration in Morocco have remained relatively low. In 2020, the United Nations Department of Economic and Social Affairs estimated the number of (both regular and irregular) migrants to be 102,358 (UN-DESA, 2020). This figure needs to be contrasted with the overall population (around thirty-six million in 2020) in Morocco but also the large number of Moroccan citizens living abroad and estimated at over five million (HCP, 2020).

The construction of the 'sub-Saharan issue' as a privileged site for bordering practices and the construction of illegality are deeply entangled with politics and imaginaries of race, ordinary as well as institutional forms of racism, the legacy of trading enslaved people, and the racial dynamics of the colonial period, such as during the French Protectorate (El Hamel, 2013; Hannoum, 2020; Menin, 2020; Perl, 2020; Gazzotti and Hagan, 2021). Race stands at the heart of inequities that bestow only to certain bodies the ability to cross national boundaries with little if any friction. Others, such as those racialised as Black and sub-Saharan, are left to risk their lives to overcome the physical and legal restrictions that do not fully obstruct their mobility but that maintain their vulnerability to manifold forms of exploitation and expose them to ordinary forms of racism in the places where they live (see Chapter 7).

Black migrants from Western and Central Africa have been widely stigmatised in media and other public discourse across Morocco (Khrouz and Lanza, 2015). In a September 2005 headline, *al-Shamal*, an Arabic-language Tangier newspaper, described the events around the Spanish enclaves as 'Black locusts are taking over Morocco' (Goldshmidt, 2006: 1). Similarly, in November 2012, the weekly magazine *Maroc Hebdo*'s headline caused controversy, as it warned its readers of the 'black peril' (Bachelet, 2014a): 'thousands of clandestine sub-Saharan migrants' were deemed to constitute a humanitarian as well as a security problem for Morocco. One year later, the same magazine reused these racist tropes, with a headline announcing that Morocco was trapped and a cover featuring a mass of Black migrants. Politicians' and the media's treatment of migration from sub-Sahara has peddled discriminatory tropes, associating migrants with a wide range of socio-economic issues, such as drug-smuggling, AIDS, terrorism, and prostitution (Cherti and Grant, 2013).[14] The purity of the Moroccan kingdom, as well as its sovereignty, are portrayed as under threat from Black migrants, who have been a privileged target of the ultra-nationalist 'Moorish' movement, especially present on social media.

Civil society organisations have called out forms of institutional violence, such as *contrôles au faciès* (racial profiling). Moroccan authorities have targeted Black people on the basis of their skin colour, as it is commonly associated with undocumented migration (GADEM, 2013: 65). Police raids against migrants are denounced as *chasses aux noirs* (hunting of Blacks) by activists and scholars, who have continuously stressed how race features prominently in the violent practices deployed by Moroccan authorities against migrants (Alexander, 2019; Gazzotti and Hagan, 2021). Activists and researchers, such as sociologist Mehdi Alioua (2015), have warned that the violence and racist logic inherent to the security approach to migration in Morocco not only cast stigma on all migrants from sub-Saharan Africa, but contribute more widely to encouraging and developing xenophobia and negrophobia throughout Moroccan society. The daily discriminations faced by migrants, such as Black people being excluded from renting some apartments in advertisements, have been abundantly documented (Errazzouki, 2013). They have also included deadly violence, fuelled by racism. Prior to the new politics of migration, the year 2013 especially saw an escalation in institutional violence and racism against migrants, but also numerous documented cases of brutality from Moroccan citizens, including gruesome murders (Bachelet, 2014a). Prominent cases include the murders of Charles Ndour in Tangier and Ismaila Faye in Rabat. Scholars have highlighted the link between European pressure on its Moroccan partner to contain migration and the rise in (institutional) racism against Black migrants (Law, 2014). Without neglecting the ramifications of EU bordering regimes, it is important to account for the local dynamics of race in Morocco, which are much older.

Along with other social markers (e.g. gender), race is key to understanding how structures of domination, which are deeply intersectional (see Sahraoui, 2020), are reproduced at the border and rooted in multiple colonial histories that have informed a normative 'geography of race' (Hannoum, 2021: 235; see also Mayblin and Turner, 2020; Gross-Wyrtzen and El Yacoubi, 2022). During the colonial period, 'the North–South migration of Europeans from the metropole to the colony also durably reinforced whiteness as the incarnation of privilege' (Gazzotti, 2021b: 284). Yet, across the Maghreb, notions of race, discriminations, and racism have been shunned amidst a wider refusal to see supposedly Western preoccupations and models applied to Algeria, Tunisia, and Morocco. There is no race, so there is no racism (Pouessel, 2012). In the Moroccan context, as in neighbouring countries, migration is 'undoubtedly racialized' (Hannoum, 2020: 17), entangled with the historical stigmatisation of Blackness and its particularities across the

Maghreb, from before and during the colonial period, which remain largely taboo in public debates (Chekkat, 2020; Sadai, 2021).

The presence and mobility of Black migrants in Morocco have fuelled wider debates over Morocco's embeddedness into a plurality of overlapping cultural areas (e.g. Maghreb, Mediterranean region, Africa, etc.) which are not equally valued (Pouessel, 2012). They also foreground significant omissions in the memory and recognition of important historical phenomena related to race that resonate in contemporary Morocco and beyond. Chouki El Hamel's work warns us against the shortcomings of local historiography and the traditional portrayal of Morocco as 'a racially and ethnically homogenous nation, defined religiously by Islamic doctrine and linguistically and politically by Arabic nationalism' (2013: 2). He sheds light on the historical marginalisation of Blackness in Morocco, notably by articulating how seventeenth-century Morocco provided the context for a division of society by skin colour and then race.[15] The treatment of migrants from sub-Saharan Africa is rooted in the legacy of the trade of enslaved people and Morocco's pivotal place in this racialised system, which continued well into the twentieth century (Alexander, 2019).[16]

Racism and violence against Black migrants are entangled with important shifts in the governance of migration and the increasingly prominent role of countries such as Morocco in the violent containment of undesirable, undeserving, and threatening racialised bodies (Menin, 2020: 182). Scholars have stressed how European discourses surrounding a migration 'crisis' in the Mediterranean and efforts to contain migrants thanks to punishing border regimes demonstrate the critical relevance of race in processes that foster privileged forms of mobility as well as illegality (De Genova, 2018). In Morocco too, 'racialized forms of prejudice' (Gazzotti, 2021b: 278) partake in the construction of illegality. Violent bordering measures 'rework blackness to mark certain people as illegal and fundamentally out-of-place, impacting migrants but also interpellating black North Africans' (Gross-Wyrtzen, 2023: 651). Bordering across Morocco and the Maghreb more broadly is then intertwined with wider issues pertaining to race and ethnicity. These are not limited to Blackness but notably entail forms of marginalisation for other citizens such as Amazigh people (El Guabli, 2023). Mobilisation by civil society, in Morocco and other North African countries, against acts of racism targeting Black migrants (e.g the campaign 'My name is not *'zzi'*') has been instrumental in bringing increased visibility to such issues in the region (Alexander, 2019).[17] Yet, in the absence of legislative developments around racism (and a wider reluctance to confront imaginaries and politics of race), everyday acts of abuse and the institutional racism in the policing of migrants have perdured, casting doubt, for many migrants, on the possibility of leading a meaningful and worthy life in Morocco.

Conclusion

This chapter has traced the construction of the 'sub-Saharan issue' in Morocco from the 1990s to the mid-2020s, and the devastating consequences for migrants facing precarious living conditions and multiple forms of violence. It has outlined how hostile discourses and practices have targeted racialised citizens from (especially Western and Central) Africa as dangerous and threatening subjects. While the EU and its members states have been key actors in such transnational politics of migration across the Mediterranean region, Morocco has also played an important role, pursuing its own diverse set of economic, political, and diplomatic interests. Its collaboration with Europe in the selective management of migration from sub-Saharan countries has been marked by ambivalence. Yet, the shift in Moroccan migration politics initiated in 2013 largely failed to deliver grand promises and entailed the continuation of a strong security focus which has continued to foster suffering and uncertainty. The analysis of bordering practices targeting racialised Black migrants shows how the construction of illegality in Morocco (and across the Maghreb) is deeply entangled with politics of race, ordinary as well as institutional forms of racism, the legacy of trading enslaved people and the racial dynamics of the (pre)colonial period, and wider debates about Morocco's belonging to political and cultural areas.

In the remaining chapters, the book counters dehumanising narratives and violent practices partaking in the construction of the sub-Saharan issue by examining the complexity and existential depth of racialised Black, irregular migrants' lives, journeys, and stories in Morocco. As explored in Chapter 2, a focus on migrants' discussion of the adventure deconstructs common depictions of their journeys as unidirectional which are centred on deceptive notions such as transit migration.

Notes

1. See, for example, the work of historian Fernand Braudel (2000) for an account of the Mediterranean region as a space of cultural and economic exchanges.
2. It is difficult to provide accurate figures for the number of deaths amongst migrants attempting to cross the Mediterranean Sea as not all incidents are reported. Numerous independent reports highlight that the Mediterranean Sea and its surroundings are effectively migrants' deadliest border (Jones, 2016; Panebianco, 2022). Bordering measures can harness difficult landscapes for their cruel and hostile ends (see De León, 2015).
3. Available statistics about the number of migrant interceptions along sea and land border points (Frontex, 2023) are indicative of the fluctuating prominence

of key routes between Morocco and Spain (as well as across the whole region). Such figures should be taken cautiously. What the European border agency calls the Western African route, which connects Morocco and Western African countries to the Spanish Canary Islands, saw a sharp rise in the number of interceptions, following the Ceuta and Melilla events in 2005 (31,600 interceptions in 2006) and the tightening of the border in the north. Numbers quickly dwindled (170 in 2012) but started seeing a significant increase in 2015 (874), with a sharp peak in 2020 (23,029).

4. Overall figures for 'irregular' border crossings across the Mediterranean region are often estimates at best and refer to attempts rather than actual crossings by a definite number of people. Publicly available reports from the European Border and Coast Guard Agency (Frontex) provide some useful indication. At the Western Mediterranean route (sea and land crossings into Spain from northern Morocco), Frontex reports the following figures: 2008 (6,500), 2009 (6,642), 2010 (5,003), 2011 (8,448), 2012 (6,397), 2013 (6,838), 2014 (7,183), 2015 (7,004), 2016 (9,990), 2017 (23,063), 2018 (56,245), 2019 (23,969), 2020 (17,228), and 2021 (18,466). Amidst constantly evolving migratory routes between Morocco and Spain, the proportion of migrants from different North African and sub-Saharan countries crossing the different land and sea border points varies over time depending on the deployment of specific bordering measures, as well as wider socio-political processes. Overall, Morocco has consistently remained at the top of the list of migrants' nationalities along the Western Mediterranean route (Lemaizi, 2022). However, migrants from sub-Saharan nations have usually been the most numerous amongst those crossing the land border around the Spanish enclaves. There are also reports of migrants from Asia (e.g. China) and the Middle East (e.g. Syria) crossing irregularly (Alioua and Ferrié, 2017).

5. Proportions vary in the studies, depending on both methodology and fluctuating patterns in migration across this border and the wider region. These statistics are impacted by several issues, notably the potential concealment of 'true' nationalities by respondents for fear of being deported. Documents are also frequently destroyed, lost, or confiscated (Faleh *et al.*, 2009).

6. Though trade and other exchanges still officially take place between Morocco and Algeria (albeit via air and sea), this border has been closed since 1994 – a landmark date in a long history of tensions and rivalry between the two Maghrebi countries that have threatened the stability of the wider region (Rachidi, 2022). This closure and the overall strained diplomatic relationship have been the source of displacement and other forms of hardship and vexations for local communities (e.g. deportation of Moroccan agricultural workers from Algeria). Amongst the people making the crossing at the Algerian border are nationals of sub-Saharan countries who could not afford to fly but would have been eligible to enter Morocco legally for three months, thanks to agreements between Morocco and other African countries allowing visa-free travel. This is another example of how illegality is produced, not only by immigration policy, but by wider socio-economic, cultural, and political (in this case diplomatic) processes (Samers, 2004).

7. One of the earliest quantitative studies on the mobility of migrants from sub-Saharan Africa (AMERM, 2008) catalogues some of the types of violence and danger encountered by migrants on their journeys: lack of hygiene, exhaustion, thirst, hunger, long waits, sickness, arrest and refoulement (pushback) by police, assault, theft, racket and other tricks by smugglers, death of a companion, accidents, and sexual violence. First-hand accounts by migrants have exposed how risky such journeys are (e.g. Yene, 2010; Traoré and Le Dantec, 2012).
8. Despite the centrality of the figure of the unscrupulous and dangerous 'human smuggler' (see Zhang et al., 2018; Richter, 2022) in public debate, journeys were often started by individuals travelling alone or in small groups, often on foot until Malian and Nigerian territories, where 'guides' organised the crossing of the Algerian border for a fee (see Faleh et al., 2009: 10). Some of those paid by migrants to facilitate sections of the journey (e.g. from Maghnia to Oujda) have also often been migrants themselves, hence blurring the distinction between those labelled as victim and trafficker (Collyer, 2006).
9. Large-scale surveys (e.g. Mourji et al., 2016; Haut-Commissariat au Plan, 2021) also note the growing number of women amongst migrants in Morocco.
10. In one of the earliest studies of sub-Saharan migration in Morocco, Barros et al. (2002) estimate the number of illegal and transit migrants from sub-Saharan Africa to be around 10,000. Subsequent studies (e.g. AMERM, 2008) estimated this population to be between ten and fifteen thousand. Around the main fieldwork period for this research project, the consensus amongst most journalists and researchers was that there were between fifteen and twenty thousand irregular migrants from sub-Saharan Africa. Moroccan authorities estimated the figure to be forty thousand in 2014. Figures about illegal migration ought to be taken with great caution. In the aftermath of the regularisation of around fifty thousand migrants (not all from sub-Saharan Africa), estimates about irregular migration from Western and Central Africa have remained relatively stable – usually between thirty and fifty thousand (Stock, 2019; Benjelloun, 2021; Lemaizi, 2022).
11. Financial assistance from the EU to support economic transition in Morocco (MEDA aid programme) has been tightly entwined with bordering measures. 115 million euros (out of 426 million for the 2000–2006 period) were allocated for rural development programmes and tackling illegal migration. Cooperation between the EU and Morocco on migration issues has been consolidated by the signature of the Mobility Partnership Agreement in 2013. Between 2014 and 2022, the EU devoted 1.5 billion euros to bilateral collaboration with Morocco, notably through the EU Emergency Trust Fund for stability and addressing root causes of irregular migration and displaced persons in Africa (EUTF for Africa). Out of the 234 million euros committed between 2015 and 2021 to projects on migration via the EUTF for Africa, 179 million were directly focused on 'integrated border management and [the] fight against smuggling and trafficking in human beings' (DG Near, 2023: 1). During interviews, members of Moroccan civil society organisations have stressed to me the 'opacity' behind the distribution of such funds and the 'lack of accountability', claiming that money

intended for other issues has been 'redirected towards the issue of control in the borderlands'. A report by the European Court of Auditors highlights the limited added value and ability of such funds to support reforms in Morocco 'due to a sub-optimal focus, weaknesses in design and insufficient monitoring' (2019: 4).
12. Including 101.7 million euros from the EU to help Morocco manage migration as part of the EUTF for Africa.
13. The 2011 constitutional reform maintained this myth of Moroccan stability, in a context marked by social and political discontent, internally and across the whole region (e.g. Arab Spring), without significantly redressing power imbalances.
14. Not all media coverage of migration has fed xenophobia and racism. Media reactions to migration issues have sometimes been more ambiguous (Alami M'Chichi, 2008), and it is important to note the establishment of key and reliable journalists in Morocco, who have sought to provide independent and critical coverage of migration issues, notably the Réseau marocain des journalistes des migrations (RMJM), co-founded and presided by Salaheddine Lemaizi.
15. Under the rule of Sultan Mawlay Isma'il (1672–1727), the words deployed in dominant Moroccan culture to refer to this marginalised population 'became fused' (El Hamel, 2002: 48): *labd* (slave), *aswad* (Black), and *haratin* (a problematic term referring to free Black people, including formerly enslaved people).
16. Morocco was 'the largest single market for imported black slaves in the Arab Maghrib' (Wright, 2002: 55). In modern terms, enslaved people were purchased or raided from as far afield as 'the southern Sudan Republic, the Central African Republic, mid-Nigeria, and the countries around the headwaters of the Rivers Niger and Senegal: Guinea, western Mali and the Republic of Senegal itself' (Wright, 2002: 54). The trade of enslaved people began to dwindle in the 1840s across the Sahara but continued to flourish in Morocco well into the twentieth century (Becker, 2002).
17. '*zzi*' translates as 'negro', 'slave', or 'Black' in Moroccan Arabic. The term is derogatory (Menin, 2016: 13).

2

Reaching the objective

During idle afternoons spent sheltering from the heat in Idrissa's room in Maâdid, my Burkinabé friend would share his anxieties and indecision over what to do next and, especially, where to go. He often asked me for advice, which I was at a loss to give. More than appeals for material help, it was my informants' occasional requests for guidance about their journeys that I was most uncomfortable with. Did I think the weather was good enough at sea to try crossing? The stakes were high, and my own experience of navigating borders was far more privileged than theirs.

In Douar Hajja and Maâdid, young men from Western and Central Africa traded information about border-crossing tactics and stories about the lives they imagined for themselves, away from the decrepit migrant ghettoes. Resting in the narrow and humid room he shared with other migrants from Burkina Faso, Idrissa regularly enumerated what he wished for: becoming a professional footballer, resuming his studies, working for an NGO, becoming an actor, or a combination of all of those. In the same sentence, without catching his breath, Idrissa would express the simultaneous, and seemingly contradictory, wish to stay in Morocco if he could find opportunities for employment or education, attempt the dangerous crossing into Europe, and return home to Burkina Faso. What adventurers wanted to become, and the more dignified lives they aspired to, existed in a not-too-distant future, outside of Douar Hajja and Maâdid (and usually outside of Morocco altogether), that seemed so close yet almost unattainable in the face of violent bordering regimes. Still, they hoped for something else, a better life, usually imagined in Europe, even if this was often not a clear destination for their journeys when they first set out.

Idrissa never made it to the borderlands. He was scared and still undecided over what to do next. Reflecting on his journey, Idrissa explained to me: 'It is to prepare my future, this is what threw me into the adventure, my future. ... Because we are born poor does not mean we need to remain poor and dans *la galère* [in adversity].' Narratives of the adventure contrast with public discourse over (illegal) migration in Europe but also across the

Maghreb, which features push and pull factors as dominant concerns. This reduces complex motivations for migrating to economic rationales, driven by the assumption that, for migrants, 'money is the name of the game' (Vigh, 2009a: 92). References to the adventure emphasise migrants' own aspirations and imaginaries, revealing migration 'from the point of view of dreams' (Schielke, 2020: 112) and not simply as the mechanical movement from areas of economic deprivation to areas of abundance. Adventurers in Douar Hajja and Maâdid were adamant that they could only break away from the yoke of social forces confining their existence to hardship by taking the road, even if that entailed further violence and suffering along the way. I could only answer affirmatively when Idrissa asked me, 'Is it not true that an illegal migrant can bring into the world a child that will become president?' He laughed when I nodded and added that he could become president himself. Idrissa was constantly making ambitious plans for his life, despite seemingly insurmountable obstacles.

This chapter moves away from the labels (e.g. transit) deployed to categorise migrants in policy, media, or even scholarship. Rather, it focuses on the articulation of the adventure as the quest for 'the objective'. In doing so, the chapter foregrounds migrants' efforts for self-emancipation (and the search for justice) rather than simply a linear journey towards Europe. Discussions of migration are often structured around dichotomies such as forced/voluntary migration, with significant consequences for migrants whose levels of protection and opportunities depend on classification processes and their adjoining hierarchical sets of rights. Between people who migrate as a result of rational calculations to maximise interests and those who have no choice but to escape persecution, there is a majority who have a limited degree of choice (such as timing of movement), despite responding to social, economic, and political situations they have little control over (Richmond, 1994; Erdal and Oeppen, 2018). The chapter outlines how a focus on the adventure foregrounds the complex aspirations of migrants rather than abstract flows, hence decentring the (putative) needs of nation-states.

To critically engage with the 'politics of bounding' (Crawley and Skleparis, 2018: 48), I argue that one must examine how migrants understand and articulate their own journeys, taking seriously the terms they ambiguously use. Young men from Western and Central Africa in Douar Hajja and Maâdid referred to themselves as adventurers sharing a common 'objective' (*objectif*): 'to exit' (*sortir*) and reach 'the outside' (*le dehors*), where they hoped to escape the political, economic, and social constraints which had impeded their quest for self-fulfilment and self-realisation. Adventurers like Idrissa explained they were ready to face dangers and obstacles 'to reach the objective' (*atteindre l'objectif*): they narrated their uncertain and perilous journeys as epic quests to reclaim their future, amidst violence and suffering.

The 'outside' cannot simply be equated with Europe as a fixed destination, even if this was a place most of my informants were hoping to reach. Sat on old mats and broken crates, Idrissa and my other informants discussed with me the conundrum they found themselves in: Morocco turned out to be 'a prison'; crossing into Europe was difficult, scary, and potentially deadly; and returning home 'empty-handed' was a prospect marked by shame and failure. In the ghettoes of Douar Hajja and Maâdid, adventurers were constantly reassessing whether to stay or leave Morocco, whether to go home or push forward towards Europe, as part of their striving to reach the objective. They monitored development in the northern borderlands and pondered over information they could collect about neighbouring countries, especially north of the Mediterranean Sea.

Their tortuous journeys included dangerous and violent border crossings but also long periods of immobility during which adventurers would consider and plan their next moves. When I left in late summer 2013, most of my close informants had been stuck (notwithstanding regular but usually short trips to the borderlands) in Douar Hajja and Maâdid for a long time (often over two years). The notion of transit in public discourse about migration and the Eurocentric maps showing migrants in a unidirectional and incessant movement towards European shores are misleading. These straight arrows obscure complex and often haphazard journeys, marked by both movement and stasis. They also assume a predefined destination when many explained that they had 'no plan' when they left. They dreamed of a better life and felt the urge to leave and take the road. They often did so with little money and their first aim was usually to reach a neighbouring country. Although migrants' aspirations were very often projected northward of the Mediterranean Sea, it is important not to reify the link between their journeys and Europe as a predefined destination. Doing so only reinforces the fallacious depiction of all migrants as en route to Europe.

The notion of transit migration is 'a political fiction' (Péraldi, 2011: 17), a trope that has become dominant in discussions of migration. Often endowed with negative connotations, the notion of transit glosses over migrants' varied legal status, journeys, and intentions. It also belittles the range of forces and obstacles migrants have to confront in pursuit of their migratory and life goals. Transit emerged as a dominant concept in migration policy in the 1990s, but, despite its widespread use, it lacks a clear definition and is subjected to incoherent interpretations (Düvell, 2012). The notion of transit serves a convenient function within EU discourse on migration, as it allows for the collective portrayal of all migrants in the southern Mediterranean region as a 'migration liability' (Collyer and De Haas, 2012: 477). The chapter contributes to such scholarship by examining how adventurers articulated and acted on their quest for the objective in ways that transcend the notion of transit, highlighting instead serendipitous journeys in which migrants sought to retain some control over their lives and futures despite the violent enforcement of borders.

In his early twenties, short, and slim-built, Idrissa could easily pass as a minor when useful, especially during encounters with the police or NGO workers. Idrissa was usually cheerful and loquacious, but he remained vague, like many of my other informants, about life before he arrived in Morocco, and some of his personal circumstances. He explained that part of his family, including his parents, had moved from Burkina Faso to the Ivory Coast, where he also lived for some time. He stressed that his departure had nothing to do with unrest in the Ivory Coast and that his family never suffered any harm, despite acrimonious debates over Ivoirité and the place of foreigners that led to violence (Marshal-Fratani, 2006; Babo, 2017). In 2011, Idrissa was awarded a scholarship to pursue Islamic Studies in Egypt, but this fell through because of the revolution in the country. He decided to travel to Morocco by himself and study there. After a few months, he reached Morocco in August 2011 but, with neither visa nor money, he could not enrol in a university, and he looked too frail to get work as a daily labourer in the informal economy. He subsisted thanks to his roommates, occasional help from NGOs, and gifts from his Moroccan neighbours, with whom he could easily converse. Idrissa, whose father was an imam, spoke fluent Arabic and several other languages. He quickly adapted to Moroccan Arabic.

After months of sharing his anxieties over what to do next, he suddenly announced his departure for Burkina Faso in late 2012, telling me he was due to travel to Mauritania the next day. Two days after his departure, Idrissa rang me, distressed, explaining that, along with at least twenty other people, he was stuck in the no man's land between the Moroccan and the Mauritanian border posts. He had obtained a laissez-passer from the authorities in Rabat, prior to his departure, which was enough to allow him to leave Morocco, despite having entered without a visa. The Moroccan guards warned him he needed a visa from the Mauritanian embassy to enter Mauritania, adding that other travellers were stuck at the border because they did not have one. They advised him to destroy his laissez-passer and pretend to be a Mauritanian citizen. Idrissa ignored the advice and the Mauritanian border guards did not let him pass.

Idrissa remained stranded there for weeks, along with a growing number of migrants from Western and Central African countries. Like Idrissa, some had been stopped at the border after deciding to return and had no passport or visa for Mauritania. Others had been forcibly displaced by Moroccan authorities to the southern border, in a move that departed from the usual deportations to the Algerian border, ostensibly to send migrants much further away from the border with Spain. This practice became much more common in the following years, especially after the two operations of regularisation. Mauritania, which had previously turned a blind eye to returning migrants entering its territory without a visa to travel south, refused to let them pass; a border guard told Idrissa they did not want 'Morocco's garbage'. Such change in practice may have stemmed from renewed diplomatic tensions between Morocco and Mauritania at the time.

The number of migrants stuck in very difficult conditions rose to about fifty, including refugees recognised by the United Nations High Commissioner for Refugees (UNHCR) in Morocco, amongst whom were pregnant women and very young children. With my friend Pierre and a few other activists, we distributed leaflets to drivers queuing outside the Mauritanian embassy for a visa, asking them to spare some food, water, and blankets on their way through the two border posts. Idrissa sometimes sounded delirious on the phone, complaining that there was not even a tree around for shade. He eventually befriended some of the Mauritanian guards, who spoke Fula, like him, and allowed him to sleep in their barracks, rather than the abandoned truck where most other migrants were sleeping.

The diplomatic authorities from Western and Central African countries reacted with various degrees of concern and urgency to the plight of their citizens. Ivoirian diplomats quickly secured the release of their nationals. Following pressure from Morocco-based civil society organisations, the Senegalese diplomats eventually intervened too. Things only changed for Idrissa once myself and a small group of European and American citizens mobilised to contact Burkinabé media, launch a petition, and solicit the help of diplomatic representatives in Ouagadougou. A Burkinabé official, based in Dakar, eventually flew to Mauritania, shortly before New Year's Eve, to release Idrissa, two other Burkinabé men, and a Gambian man. By then, many of the migrants stuck at the border had grown impatient and desperate. Contact was lost with a group of people shortly after they decided to re-enter irregularly back into Morocco, through the arid no man's land, despite the presence of land mines. I spoke to Idrissa once he crossed to Mauritania, but we lost touch when he got on to a bus to cross conflict-stricken Mali, on his way to the Ivory Coast.

Fragmented journeys

Fabien, a kind but taciturn and quick-tempered Cameroonian man I befriended in *l'ambassade*, and one of the men who came along to the Golden Sands trip recalled in the Prologue, seldom spoke to me about his journey to Morocco. Whenever I approached the topic, he would grow sombre and laconically reply that he had 'seen things', before changing the subject. I preferred not to cause upset by asking him to recall harrowing experiences. In hushed tones, some of my informants in *l'ambassade* shared they had witnessed beatings and rapes (targeting both men and women) by border guards along the way. They seldom discussed this in detail and almost always talked about such episodes of violence as having happened to their travelling companions (including other people living in *l'ambassade*) rather than themselves. Instead of dwelling on past harrowing experiences, where they had often been hurt and humiliated, adventurers preferred to discuss information coming from the borderlands, assess whether it was a good time to travel, share tactics about crossing, or trade stories about how they imagined their future. If the success of ethnographic research relies on curiosity and a degree of intrusiveness, as discussed in the Introduction, it also depends on 'a willingness to leave some stones unturned' (Malkki, 1995b: 51). The only journey-related stories these young men liked to recount were trickster stories demonstrating adventurers' wit and cunningness. They liked to boast about their daring feats, fooling border guards and other dangerous people. Idrissa amused himself and others by retelling time and again how Algerian police stormed the ghetto where he was staying in the Algerian town of Maghnia. As he pretended to be a Black Algerian from the Sahara, a policeman challenged him to sing the national anthem. Idrissa improvised by humming a random melody, occasionally inserting words in Arabic, like 'nation', that one could expect in a national hymn. They arrested everyone but him. Idrissa joked that the policeman did not know the Algerian national anthem either.

While adventurers were reluctant to dwell on some of the details of their journeys, they shared their complex itineraries and some of the decisions they took, which seldom entailed a clear destination from the start. Alain, a Cameroonian man I first met in *l'ambassade*, explained he left home in early January 2012, after the small business he worked for shut down and he became unemployed. He quickly reached Algeria, where he stopped for a few months. He took on some manual jobs, because he had no more money: 'When I left home, I had no programme. I thought Algeria would be good for work. I needed money for my family. But there were too many problems. Some friends told me to come to Morocco. I saw it was the same thing, and now people tell me about Spain.'

Stories like Alain's highlighted the lack of a clear and definite outline for adventurers' journeys, as well as the importance of encounters with other migrants. For some, the trip to Morocco took years rather than months or weeks, as they got stuck on the way and had to work to pay for the subsequent leg of their journey (e.g. transport, bribes, smugglers, etc.). Others stopped along the way, with the intention to settle for a while before returning (e.g. Mauritania, Algeria, Libya), but after more or less long periods of working hard for little money, they became disillusioned with the living conditions and continued their journey towards Morocco. Once in Morocco, living in marginal neighbourhoods such as Douar Hajja and Maâdid, they were actively trying to cross into Spain, but they talked about other countries like Germany, France, and the UK. Moussa, whom I also introduced in the Prologue, wanted to go to the USA. He succeeded, but not until the late 2010s, when he obtained refugee status and was resettled through the UNHCR.

Yvan, another man from *l'ambassade*, left Cameroon in early March 2006. He had tried hard to get a visa to travel to France but was cheated by people who promised to facilitate the process for a fee. Disillusioned, he decided to leave Cameroon anyway: 'I said "Mum, I want to get out, I need to leave Cameroon. I cannot live here anymore."' His mother gave him some money. After speaking to a middleman, who could facilitate his journey and who suggested he go to Mali, he decided to head that way. He bypassed the middleman's services and sought advice from Malian friends for his itinerary. He finally reached Nigeria, after a number of scams and helpful encounters on the way:

> I met people going to Algeria, but I told them I was going to Mali. I was not thinking of going to Algeria and Europe; my destination was Mali. But it changed when I got to Ghana. People told me: 'you have done audio-visual studies, go to the Ivory Coast'. So, I did.

Once in the Ivory Coast, Yvan started working in radio stations and was, by his own account, quite successful professionally. He stayed a few years. When he travelled to Malta for a short trip because of his job, his mother pressed him to find a way to cross irregularly to Italy. He decided not to. He was confident his application for a German visa would soon be successful. However, he found himself in some financial and professional difficulties and had to return to Cameroon in 2011. After a year, during which he tried but failed to get a decent job, despite his work experience, Yvan returned to the Ivory Coast. Things did not work out and he applied for an Australian visa. This was refused. His childhood friend, Alex, who was already in Morocco, advised him to come and join him, stressing that there were opportunities there. Yvan took to the road again but found himself penniless in Mali. He had to stop for a while and sell his laptop, as well as other valuables. After reaching Algeria, he had to stay there for a few weeks, again to make some more money to be able to keep travelling. Finally, in late spring 2012, he reached Morocco. He had entered illegally and could not find a job where he could use his skills. Eventually, he gave up trying and focused on crossing the border into Spain: 'I tried five times but, by the grace of God, next time will be the right one,' he told me, shortly before he was successful in crossing to Spain. He continued towards Paris, where he started work as a night security guard, hoping to get papers to be able to stay and find a better job.

The journeys of Yvan, Alain, and others in Douar Hajja and Maâdid were neither linear nor unidirectional. They were fragmented (Collyer, 2010). Getting to Morocco, which was not always intended as part of the journey from the outset, could take a long time, as adventurers stopped, for lack of resources, before moving on to another place, where they hoped to find better opportunities. There was a degree of preparedness and planning (e.g. getting genuine or fake documents, finding money, etc.), but the journeys were not neatly planned out from one point to another. And when they were, there was no guarantee that they would reach this destination or that their expectations about that place would be met. Later segments of a journey sometimes arose from serendipitous opportunities, from fortuitous encounters with other migrants who shared their experiences and advice, or from failures to follow an intended itinerary.

Being an adventurer relied on an ability to quickly react to uncertain and volatile circumstances. Adventurers referred to this process as '*débrouillardise*' (resourcefulness). The verb *se débrouiller* means to disentangle oneself. In Douar Hajja and Maâdid, young men were constantly talking about 'monitoring the terrain' (*surveiller le terrain*), paying close attention to developments in the borderlands (remotely, via phones and the internet), in the neighbourhood where they stayed (e.g. police raids), but also in Europe and in their home country, where political changes could affect them and their prospects. Their vigilance and quick responses to volatile circumstances were necessary to be able to continue 'moving within a moving environment' (Vigh, 2009b: 420–25). Migrants were tentatively feeling their way amidst situations that could quickly change and that offered both dangers and opportunities, as they strove to reach a point beyond the horizon. In *l'ambassade*, where my Cameroonian informants preferred metaphors about football, they talked about the need to have a good '*jeu de jambe*' (footwork). One had to stay vigilant and monitor 'the terrain', otherwise it would be the terrain 'managing' the migrants ('*le terrain nous gère*').

In Douar Hajja and Maâdid, adventurers expressed bitter disappointment with their living conditions and future prospects in Morocco. They complained that television in Cameroon and the Ivory Coast displayed the new tramway system in Rabat, the mix of art deco and modern buildings in Casablanca, and the luxurious riads in Marrakesh, but not the 'tramp' neighbourhoods (*quartiers clochards*), like Douar Hajja. Even for the few I met who had intended to reach Morocco from the outset of their journey, like Idrissa, getting there entailed a profound sense of disenchantment. In Douar Hajja and Maâdid, most of these young men had their eyes set on Spain and the rest of Europe. In Rabat, they were preparing their next attempt (*tentative*) to cross the border: resting, healing, looking for money, and buying materials (e.g. dinghies, paddles, etc.).

Fabien and others in *l'ambassade* explained that most of the Cameroonian '*anciens*' were gone from the neighbourhood. The past generations of Douar Hajja adventurers had either gone to Europe, returned home, or relocated to different neighbourhoods in Rabat (or elsewhere in Morocco), deemed more comfortable and less dangerous. Yet, there were older migrants in these neighbourhoods who had been there for up to ten years and more, and who were still actively trying to cross. The population of Western and Central African citizens in Douar Hajja and Maâdid, as is the case in other marginal neighbourhoods in Moroccan cities, was overwhelmingly set on crossing the border into Europe. However, this was not always a clear intention from the start, and they were likely to remain stuck for a very long time.

Returning empty-handed

Adventurers in Douar Hajja and Maâdid's ghettoes were imagining and striving to reach 'new horizons'. Regularly, they left Douar Hajja and Maâdid, after selecting the strict minimum to take with them on inflatable boats or to carry over the fences to get to Spain, entrusting the rest of their belongings to companions, in case they returned. A few, disheartened by their repeated failures to cross and their appalling living conditions in Morocco, took the difficult decision to return to their countries of origin. Signing up for the International Organisation for Migration's (IOM) voluntary return programme was a difficult choice to make, but the violence in the borderlands and precarious living conditions compelled a substantial minority to reluctantly 'choose' to return. Several of my informants explained their decision to sign up with the IOM as a kind of insurance, 'just in case' things got really bad. This process with the IOM was itself protracted, as the organisation could not cope with the number of applications at the time of my fieldwork (Bartels, 2017), compelling many to give up on waiting for the programme's free ticket home and to take the road, despite the danger. They traced back their steps, starting with the irregular crossing of the closed Algerian border via Oujda and Maghnia.

Young men in Douar Hajja and Maâdid regularly talked about the 'shame' that returning 'empty-handed' entailed, when they were so close to 'reaching the objective'. They had been gone for 'so long'; few were ready to return home and 'start from scratch after all those years' with nothing to show for it. Whenever I mentioned returning, Fabien would laconically reply: 'To do what?' The individual stories of adventurers were entwined with expectations from relatives and friends, who remained in their home countries and whose future and livelihoods were also at stake. Some of my informants left in defiance of their families or without saying anything, but most had taken the road with some degree of support (if only some words of advice) from their close ones.

As discussed in the Introduction, the adventure was a moral endeavour. But it was not just a quest for migrants' self-realisation. Adventurers had left to reinvent themselves, seize opportunities, and bring about a better future for themselves and those they cared for. All of them stressed that they were also 'fighting' for their families. In keeping with the recurrent football-themed metaphors, they talked about being 'the strikers', on the frontline to score goals for themselves and their families. Alain, who was an orphan, confided that his responsibility to care for his younger sisters left at home weighed on him, keeping him awake at night. I had similar conversations with most of my young male informants. They talked about their duties to their loved ones as brothers, sons, and fathers and how news from people 'at home' unsettled them. They felt guilty about not being able to provide support to their families and about having to sometimes ask for help themselves (see Chapter 6).

Adventurers often had little and irregular contact with families. As I sat with a group of Cameroonian minors living above an informal restaurant, one of them received a missed call. He said it was his aunt, who was probably keen to find out how he was doing. By giving her a missed call back, he intended to say that he was well. His aunt gave another missed call right away. 'She has not understood what I meant, but I have no credit to ring her back,' the Cameroonian youth lamented. Phoning abroad was expensive, and people in home countries did not always have ready access to the internet like migrants did in Douar Hajja and Maâdid, where many could afford to spend a few dirhams in the internet cafés (cybers). Such places usually enabled migrants to keep in touch with one another, as people moved around Morocco, but it was not always effective to sustain relationships with relatives back home. Keeping in touch with close ones also entailed a moral dilemma over what details to share about the adventure (see Chapter 6).

However irregular, exchanges with their families were a source of anxiety for adventurers, as they received news about the lives and needs (e.g. school fees, funerals, etc.) of the people they had left behind, and who were sometimes still providing sporadic support to cover medical expenses or border attacks. Moussa occasionally received a little sum from his younger brother, who was studying in the Ivory Coast. Many said they refused to take money from their families, or did so with shame, since they were 'aware of the conditions back home'. Money was a sensitive matter in our discussions, and on the few occasions that I met some of my informants outside the Western Union next to *château*, they would mutter some excuse about picking up money, usually explaining it was on behalf of a friend and not for themselves.

Young men from Western and Central Africa stuck in Morocco often recast return journeys in their own moral terms (Maâ, 2023). To lessen the weight of shame and failure, those who left stressed that returning home was not the end of their adventure. Sometimes, it was important 'to take a step back in order to better jump' (*reculer pour mieux sauter*). Some delayed their return to accumulate enough money so that they could bring some goods back and avoid the shame of having nothing at all. A few people in *l'ambassade* had already returned to Cameroon and made the journey to Morocco more than once, sometimes following deportation from Europe. One Cameroonian woman, who ran an informal restaurant (see Chapter 5), had returned, with support from the IOM, to place her young child with relatives, since schooling was not possible for her undocumented daughter, and she did not want to attempt crossing with her again. She came back to Morocco with some dried goods for her business. Like getting stuck, having to return home was recast as another obstacle in the adventurers' quest, which they needed to confront to reach the objective.

Imagining the outside

After fleeing the 2011 conflict in Libya, where he had worked for many years to send money to his wife and children at home in the Central African Republic, Blaise ended up in Algeria but found no significant opportunity and ran out of money. Other migrants advised him to follow them to Morocco. Once there, he was again disappointed and thought of crossing to Europe, something he had previously never considered: 'I arrived here [in Morocco] and realized how hard it is. If there is an opportunity to go somewhere else, why not go?' When discussing his journey so far, the uncertain future, and the hardship endured, he often declared: 'This is the adventure!' Pressed to clarify what he meant, Blaise explained that 'adventure is when you leave your country for whatever destination, with all the obstacles that you may find on the way. On the road, many things happen. There is first the fact that you do not know where you are going, and you do not know the way.' When I asked what his plan was, he paused for a long time, then told me it was to 'better [his] living conditions'. Blaise explained that the setting for this plan could be Morocco, if things were better, or Libya, if the political situation improved significantly, or the Central African Republic, if Bozizé left power, or possibly Europe, though he had not tried crossing yet.

Like Idrissa and others, Blaise was undecided about what to do next and where to go. He was already in his forties and had never planned to come to Morocco.

For adventurers, everything was possible. One's range of opportunities could widen 'on the condition that one decides about one's destiny and proves willing to take risks and undergo new trials' (Bredeloup, 2013: 180). Rather than a fixed destination, a specific place, young men in Douar Hajja and Maâdid who identified as adventurers stressed that they were attempting to reach 'the objective' (*l'objectif*): a 'more comfortable life' or a 'more bearable life'. They had several scenarios of what these future dignified lives, away from Douar Hajja and Maâdid, could look like. As illustrated by Idrissa's story earlier in this chapter, they were not short of ideas and ambitions. They all pointed out the importance of mustering a sense of agency over one's life in the face of arduous living conditions and curbed opportunities. For adventurers, agency meant a readiness to face uncertainty and to risk one's life rather than enduring one's present conditions and the promised future. Ismael, a young Cameroonian in *l'ambassade*, had left Cameroon and abandoned his studies to travel because he saw his life prospects curtailed by corruption. For him, adventure was:

> the quest for a life more bearable. … If we have taken the road, it is because we hoped to find a place where we could express ourselves freely and build on our talents. That is why we have gone on the adventure. Because in our country, it does not work. A lot of things impede, kill your genius. That is how the idea to leave comes about. We do not know where chance comes from; we took the road hoping to have a better life.

'Chance' was an important feature of the adventure and entailed carving opportunities and realising oneself (see Chapter 3). Adventurers in Morocco sought to bridge the gap between the difficult and dissatisfying circumstances they found themselves in and what they aspired to become and obtain. Impoverishment points not only to the absence of income but also to 'a deprivation of opportunities to exercise one's ability' (Jackson, 2011: 38). Migrants in Douar Hajja repeatedly stressed that they needed to look for their lives 'outside'. In their 'quest for a life more bearable', they had to 'exit' their home country to escape the obstacles, such as poverty and corruption, that impeded the development of their talent and curbed their opportunities. In this quest for a worthy and dignified existence, migration – taking the road – was 'a necessity' (Vigh, 2009b: 103).

The focus on adventurers' drive to 'reach the objective' exposes their efforts to reimagine themselves, break the monotony of their lives, and, faced up with socio-economic and political challenges across the continent, be the actors of their 'destiny' (Bredeloup, 2013: 174). While sat outside *le consulat*, I was chatting with Moussa as he mended shoes next to Seydou, another Ivoirian man from the same ghetto. A middle-aged Moroccan man brought a very worn-out pair of shoes for Moussa to repair. As he was leaving, Seydou pulled a disgusted face: 'They do not even have the money to buy themselves new shoes to go to work. They are born poor and will remain poor. But you can be born poor and become a minister, is it not true, Sébastien?' As adventurers, they were striving to see their dreams realised through their migratory projects, risking their lives to bridge this 'sense of discontinuity' (Jackson, 2011: ix) between who they were and who they could become.

In Morocco, migration has affected how people understand, articulate, and project their own existence and future (McMurray, 2001; Elliot, 2015, 2016, 2021). Elliot argues that, in central Morocco, the emic notion of *l-brrā* (the outside in Moroccan Arabic), as an entity that holds a form of power over people and things, simultaneously refers to places (e.g. Europe) and opportunities for better lives and futures. Just as young men from Western and Central Africa stressed that they needed to reach 'the outside', a place where they could find and realise the full potential of their lives, many of the young Moroccan inhabitants of Douar Hajja and Maâdid used the equivalent term in Arabic.

While adventurers' journeys were usually oriented towards Spain, and the rest of Europe beyond it, many regularly stressed that they would consider staying in Morocco or elsewhere, if 'the conditions' were right. The 'objective' of looking for one's life and for better opportunities was not always strictly associated with Europe; the objective could be fulfilled somewhere else. Shortly before crossing to Spain, Yvan told me, 'What I look for is not only Europe, it is to *être à l'aise* [be comfortable], even in a poor country. If there is an opportunity in media, access to the internet to do some radio, I will be comfortable.' Similarly, while busy preparing for his attempts in the borderlands, Alain often explained that, given 'the right conditions', he would be happy to stay in Morocco and stop trying to cross to Europe. Yet, Morocco was seldom described as a place where the objective could be reached, especially not in the ghettoes of Douar Hajja and Maâdid.

Adventurers in Douar Hajja had left their home countries for complex reasons, which defied clear-cut dichotomies such as forced/voluntary or choice/constraint. To avoid simplistic push–pull narratives of migration, it is crucial to acknowledge that it involves efforts to materialise imaginaries, as much as physical movement from one place to another (Salazar, 2011). Everyday life in the ghettoes of Douar Hajja and Maâdid moved to the rhythm of discussions over how best to cross the border and get out of Morocco. In their quest to reach the outside, adventurers spent many hours stuck inside humid, windowless rooms, gathered around the television sets that enterprising migrants had purchased for their makeshift restaurants, which catered for the neighbourhood's migrants (see Chapter 4). Whatever was transmitted on the TV screen – usually the news, football games, reality programmes, or telenovelas dubbed in French or Moroccan Arabic – fuelled animated discussions about their future life and how to reach it. While eating some Cameroonian doughnuts in an informal restaurant run by a Cameroonian couple, the regular customers and I were distractedly watching a programme about a millionaire putting young female candidates to the test before choosing whom to marry. One activity involved taking turns to do a few laps with him on a jet ski. My neighbour on the worn-out sofa placidly mused:

> With one of those, I would go straight on to *Grande Espagne* [mainland Spain], *nīshān* [straight in Moroccan Arabic]. I would just speed over the sea. I would not even stop at the shore. This kind of engine would carry me over land for at least two hundred metres. Then, I would jump off and rush though the forest. The Guardia [Spanish border guards] would never have time to catch me and send me back.

Some nodded; most people laughed. We disregarded the rest of the programme to argue over how far a jet ski could really carry someone over land on a sandy beach. A mere allusion to Europe or borders in the programmes aired on TV was enough to spark long discussions. One popular Mexican telenovela, aired around lunchtime, was *La Reina del Sur*, a programme dubbed in French and centred on a Mexican woman who flees Mexico and becomes a major drug trafficker in Spain. Some of the scenes even involved depictions of migrants from sub-Saharan Africa crossing into Spain. In the informal restaurants of Douar Hajja, migrants would comment on the plausibility of the script with regards to border-crossing attempts and the obstacles faced by the (minor) characters in the show. These conversations, which entailed the sharing of fanciful fantasies about border crossing (imagined as great, cunning, adventurous heists) as well as of practical information and tactics amongst migrants with various experiences, were crucial in a place where migrants were busy preparing their next 'attacks', and constantly reimagining their future lives.

In the narrow rooms of the Douar Hajja and Maâdid ghettoes, adventurers articulated their imaginaries not just about how they would cross borders but about what kinds of lives they imagined for themselves once they reached the outside. They often described how their decision to take the road had been, in part, spurred by seeing other 'successful' migrants return home on holiday or to settle, bringing fancy gifts and money and purchasing houses and land. Seeing the material goods displayed by returning migrants fed the imaginaries of those who had not yet taken the road, strengthening the 'mimetic desire' (Jackson, 2011: 79) to possess what others did. Television and other media were also often mentioned as a source of inspiration. Gathered in informal restaurants in Douar Hajja, migrants would often watch rolling news channels like *France 24* and passionately discuss current affairs in France and across other European countries. Immigration policies and other relevant socio-political issues were obviously of particular interest as many intended to reach and live in Europe, at least for some time.

Migration always entails forms of knowledge, even if these might rest on misinformation, strange rumours, or plain fantasies. No matter how many times I challenged him, Fabien would vigorously insist, and seek to convince me, that, in Europe, 'everything is built', that there is no need to build anything else, such as houses, as 'everything is there already'. Imaginaries about what life would be like for the migrants once they had reached the outside (e.g. in terms of work, family life, income, documents, etc.) were the topic of lively and often humorous discussions, to fill the boredom of everyday life in the ghettoes. Amongst the young Ivoirian men living in the downstairs rooms of *le consulat*, discussions over technical issues, like the Schengen Area, would very often slip towards a topic that interested everyone in the room: relationships with 'white women' once they would be in France. They speculated about the dynamics of gender and relationships there, and about how they would deal with it. They copiously teased each other.

Imagining life ahead was an all-consuming activity that permeated not only the daily lives of migrants but was also omnipresent in their dreams. In the ghettoes of Douar Hajja and Maâdid, migrants sometimes slept with their heads resting on the small buoys and pillows sold with the inflatable zodiacs used by migrants to make the crossing to Spain. In a room inhabited by Cameroonian teenagers, who had travelled together, the buoys were scribbled with the names of their girlfriends from home. One of them explained that, at night, with his head resting on the buoy, he often dreamed of his life in Europe. Dreams and imaginaries amongst my informants who were actively trying to cross into Europe often stretched in time to their eventual return home, thinking about the businesses they might set up after their success in Europe. Rather than just the 'myth of return' amongst migrants longing for their home countries, discussions in the ghettoes of Douar Hajja illustrated an even more remote 'myth', that of getting to a place (an outside) in the near future, from which they would eventually return successfully in the distant future. Yet not all adventurers discussed returning to their home country and what it would be like – some deemed it impossible or undesirable.

Aside from mass media and returnees, migrants' imaginaries were also fed by the tales and images of travelling companions, who had successfully made the crossing and rushed to take pictures of themselves under the Eiffel Tower. But the portrayal of their lives in Europe, like the images adventurers shared of Morocco, could be deceitful (see Chapter 6). In his analysis of well-being in Sierra Leone, Jackson notes the existence of contemporary avenues for becoming a person of substance (e.g. acquiring money, travelling abroad, etc.) amongst young people who 'feel they have been locked out of a world where one's worth depends on purchasing power and the conspicuous consumption of foreign goods' (2011: 2). In Douar Hajja and Maâdid, adventurers sometimes spent money on (counterfeit) designer clothing, large sunglasses, watches, and fancy mobile phones. As signifiers of success, these objects were often prominently displayed on pictures shared on social media. One popular activity amongst migrants was the digital alteration of pictures, that they would then post on social media. Ali, an Ivoirian man from *le consulat*, posted a picture of a lavish villa with a large swimming pool, and an image of himself on a gigantic flat-screen TV alongside the pool. Because of his skills in digital alterations, he was sometimes commissioned by other migrants to modify their pictures, for a fee. One popular type of photomontage was the insertion of migrants' pictures (and also sometimes of their own children back home) on a large screen, next to images of politicians, such as Barack Obama, who were seemingly video-conferencing with the migrants.

These pictures and objects displayed during the adventure were 'symbols of [the] modern status' (Ferguson, 1999: 235) to which many of my informants aspired. This status was associated with a more 'comfortable' life in Europe, a life that would bring not just better education and opportunities, but also the fame and respect they aspired to and that they imagined could be achieved once they reached the 'objective'. Denied the privileges afforded to certain passports and nationalities, they needed to cross to Europe irregularly to reach 'the promising world out there' (Salazar, 2011: 589). For adventurers, migration was akin to a 'technology of the imagination' (Vigh, 2009b: 94) as they imagined better lives for themselves and, in the face of hostile migration politics, undertook perilous journeys to reach 'a viable life' (Hage, 2009: 97). This entailed bridging the gap between their present selves and imagined futures. Many explained that they expected '[their] struggle [would] continue in Europe', despite the tales they had constructed about their future lives. They had friends and families living in difficult conditions in Europe, but migrants nevertheless associated Europe with notions of progress and material wealth. Observing on the news the diverse socio-economic issues affecting the EU and its members states, migrants would stress that, in any case, life there could not be worse than being stuck in Douar Hajja. Trying to cross was still worth it.

Discussions of transit migration often obscure global inequalities. A focus on migrants' imaginaries and desires brings them into sharp relief. The digital alterations of images and the aspiration to purchase certain goods, many of which (e.g. mobile phones) were in any case necessary tools for the adventure, are not simply mocking or mimicking. Rather, in a global society marked by profound inequities, the articulation and pursuit of the adventure amounted to a striking and persistent 'claim for equal rights of membership' (Ferguson, 2002: 565). By 'exiting' their countries in search of 'the objective', adventurers sought to reclaim their place in a deeply unequal world, where the ability to move and cross borders with few constraints was not evenly distributed. This unequal distribution of mobility was just one conspicuous reminder to adventurers of the disconnections, immobility, and exclusions that globalisation entails. By embarking on dangerous and irregular journeys, young men from Central and Western Africa were defying a 'global apartheid structure' (Hage, 2016: 43), organised around race and class, which regulates differing qualities of life and regimes of mobility: the masters can roam the world and the enslaved circulate according to the needs of capital.

Adventurers were deeply aware of those wider frameworks affecting their everyday life and the conditions under which they could build their future. They readily discussed them, contrasting their opportunities and prospects with the ones afforded to me as a French and European citizen. Adventurers often stressed that their border-crossing attempts were entangled with multiple overlapping frameworks of domination and exploitation: corrupt elites in their home countries, economic and political interventionism from former colonial powers, such as France, unfair immigration policies, etc. Adventurers' storytelling, which was concerned with both their restricted mobility and their imagined futures, were efforts to modify 'the balance between actor and acted upon' (Jackson, 2002: 16). Tales of adventure from Idrissa and others were imbued with references to trickery, but migrants regularly talked about their journeys in terms of fairness and justice too. Moussa, from *le consulat*, described himself as a rebel, fighting injustice wherever he went, from politics in the Ivory Coast to migrants' rights in Morocco. Like many of my informants, he took an active part in one of the migrant associations (see Chapter 8), which forged links with Moroccan and international NGOs to denounce the consequences of hostile politics of migration for migrants.

A striking, yet unsurprising, feature of conversations in Douar Hajja and Maâdid was the reference to (post)colonial histories when discussing unequal regimes of mobility. My Ivoirian friends in *le consulat* often teased me, exclaiming '*à chacun son Français*' (to each their French), a slogan denouncing French interventionism during the Ivoirian electoral crisis and associated with pro-Laurent Bagbo supporters. Ivoirian migrants in *le consulat* stressed that, since the French government constantly meddled in their country's political affairs and secured lucrative contracts giving it access to the country's resources at the expense of Ivoirian citizens, it was only fair that they should take the road and go to France.

Conclusion

Examining the lived experiences of young men from Central and Western Africa calls for a critical engagement with the emic notions (e.g. the objective) deployed by them to make sense of their restricted mobility in Morocco. Exploring adventurers' imaginaries and desires exposes some of the pitfalls in the concept of 'transit', such as the fallacy of a fixed destination in depictions of migration. Adventurers' tortuous and fragmented journeys illustrate how navigating hostile migration policies and violent border regimes is not akin to 'a mechanical practice' (Vigh, 2009a: 432). Their efforts to 'reach the objective' were a quest for self-fulfilment and self-realisation, defined as 'looking for oneself' and 'looking for their life'. Unable to access visas and safe travel, they needed 'to exit' and reach the outside, where their imaginaries projected a better life and future. From Douar Hajja and Maâdid, my informants often sought to reach Europe, either by crossing the sea or the fences around the Spanish enclaves. Yet, many had not intended on crossing the Mediterranean Sea when they left their home countries. In discussing their journeys, adventurers ambiguously asserted that the 'objective' did not equate with Europe and could be realised elsewhere, if they found the 'right conditions'. Focusing on migrants' emic notions challenges prevailing categories in dehistoricised and depoliticised narratives about migration in the Mediterranean region, that centre on a putative crisis and on European countries' efforts to selectively deter and control the movement of migrants. Europe is routinely portrayed as the final destination, and Morocco is reduced to a place of transit. Activists and NGO practitioners often pointed out that this representation further enabled Moroccan authorities to avoid implementing the necessary changes to meet the needs of a growing population of migrants within Morocco, who were unlikely to cross into Europe and were staying in the country for increasingly long periods.

In Douar Hajja and Maâdid, most migrants living in the dilapidated ghettoes were trying to cross into Spain, usually as a first step to reaching other countries, such as France and Germany, depending on the information they had collected about these countries. The imperative to be successful in their journeys was tied to the expectations and needs of friends and family in their home countries and elsewhere, which these young men felt a duty to honour. Returning 'empty-handed' was widely associated with shame, and adventurers would recast this decision as a tactical retreat rather than the end of their adventure. Those who took the decision to return often kept this secret until the last minute. For irregular migrants from Central and Western Africa, the range of constraints placed on their lives and futures required them to throw themselves fully into the adventure, courageously facing more obstacles in order to achieve an elusive objective, rendered even more difficult to attain by hostile migration politics. Their next border-crossing attempt might be the last, but often it ended in failure, and sometimes injury or worse. As explored in the next chapter, young men from Western and Central Africa stressed that the success of their adventure required them to display courage and strength in the face of hardship, but also depended on whether their efforts were met with 'chance'.

3

Taking a chance

'What are you going to do with women anyway?' Alpha taunted his roommate, Idrissa. We were sitting together on mattresses in their bedroom in Maâdid, a few days before Idrissa announced his departure. The two young Burkinabé men were copiously teasing one another about relationships with Moroccan women, while watching a lunchtime Mexican soap opera. The programme was dubbed in Moroccan Arabic. Alpha, who had been out of work for a while, was assiduously following it. Idrissa half-heartedly provided approximate summaries of what was going on in French. Alpha, despite speaking no Arabic, seemed to have little trouble understanding the plot, which revolved around a stolen stash of money and an unfaithful married couple.

'Look at those *clochards* [tramps] there,' Alpha sneered at the TV, as his favourite programme gave way to the midday news broadcast. The first item was about Moroccan emigrants returning from Spain, because of the European debt crisis and rising unemployment. There had been many news stories about these returns in the Moroccan media, along with articles about Spanish citizens working irregularly across Morocco, on construction sites or in hotels. 'What are you going to do in Morocco?' said Alpha, standing up to harangue the returnees, filmed driving cars with suitcases trussed to the roof out of Tangier's harbour. 'There is no work here! King Mohamed VI needs to fasten his seatbelt,' he giggled. I asked him whether this turmoil within the Eurozone would have consequences for adventurers. He shrugged. 'We are not the same as the Moroccans,' Alpha retorted. 'We are not the same colour. They return from the crisis. For us, it will work out.' Did he really think so? I asked him. 'I hope so,' he replied. Uninterested in the next news item, Alpha turned his attention back to Idrissa, teasing him for washing himself with Omo washing powder instead of soap. The powder was cheaper, but Alpha pointed out that this would not help him find a girlfriend.

Like my other adventurous informants, Alpha was often defiant when discussing his uncertain journey or the prospect of violence attached to his pursuit of the objective. Young men from Western and Central Africa stuck in Douar Hajja and Maâdid often bragged about their own abilities to overcome the hostile enforcement of migration policies. They remained hopeful that they would one day manage to '*boza*' (to be successful, to cross into Europe), despite the adversity they faced.[1] They could be boisterous, but they were also conscious that success did not simply depend on their manly efforts to 'fight the fences' around the Spanish enclaves. In this chapter, I explore the gap between these young male adventurers' epic renditions of their journeys as a quest and the boredom of their everyday lives, to examine how migrants in Douar Hajja and Maâdid expressed their own ability to act and remain mobile, in defiance of borders and despite the prospect of failure, death, and madness. This hopeful attitude relied on the display of dispositions that they defined as essential for (male) adventurers (e.g. courage and strength), but also on an acknowledgement that success was uncertain and involved greater forces.

Striving to reach the objective in an unequal world, adventurers embarked on dangerous journeys in the hope that 'geographical mobility might translate into social mobility … in the right direction' (Narotzky and Besnier, 2014: S11). As explored in Chapter 2, taking the road, despite the violence of contemporary regimes of mobility, was the only viable means to break away from 'a sense of enduring crisis or marginalization … experienced as a permanent life condition' (Kleist, 2016: 4). In the humid and dark ghettoes which offered paltry protection against the many dangers they faced, adventurers traded heroic tales about their perilous journeys to reach the objective and become men. They discussed their tactics to 'shock' the border, exhibiting confidence in the future and boasting about their abilities to outwit the authorities and confront egregious acts of violence. But adventurers were stuck in windowless ghettoes and often fearful of getting out. Many had repeatedly experienced failure in the borderlands. Rather than sinking into despair, they stressed the need to '*tenter la chance*' (take a chance). This chapter contributes to wider discussions of migrants' fragile agency amidst difficult journeys violently hampered by greater forces they had little control over, with a focus on how the adventure required another kind of precarious struggle: demonstrating strength and courage in the face of adversity, recognising that success was not guaranteed yet attainable, and maintaining that balance without becoming mad.

Their border-crossing expeditions were described as '*tentatives*' (attempts) because they could not be sure whether they would succeed or not. Uncertainty was a productive social resource (see Cooper and Pratten, 2015) amongst migrants, giving rise to fears and hopes, indeterminacy and potentiality. Adventurers eagerly anticipated, and actively strove to bring forward, the future they aspired to. Unpacking how adventurers expressed and acted on hopeful journeys requires a dynamic approach to hope, as something which can vaporise or materialise, grow or diminish, since confidence in the future nevertheless holds the possibility of failure (Kleist, 2016). Hope was a powerful mantra amongst adventurers, as illustrated by the refrain in a poem, titled *Espoir* (Hope), by Ismael, a young Cameroonian migrant who spent his free time in *l'ambassade* writing: '*Demain, pourquoi ne pas y croire*' (Tomorrow, why not believe)?[2]

Hope is not evenly distributed (Hage, 2003), but its absence (i.e. hopelessness) is 'downright intolerable to human needs' (Bloch, 1959: 5). A feeling of being stuck in motion burdened adventurers entrapped in Douar Hajja and Maâdid, yet they remained hopeful. Like Alpha, they displayed an obstinate hope that their crossing attempts might one day end in success, despite the odds. Contrasting hope and expectation, Lingis argues that 'hope is *always* hope against the evidence' (Zournazi and Lingis, 2002: 23–24; original emphasis). An ethnographic exploration of these fraught but hopeful journeys provides insights into the performance and affective resonance of hope and into how it is produced and socially embedded (Jansen, 2016), including how it is constantly rearticulated in the face of contrary 'evidence'. Throughout this chapter, I focus more particularly on how young male adventurers remained hopeful they would succeed in reaching the objective by highlighting their ability to act and their own limits.

Firstly, the chapter examines my informants' epic rendition of their lives and journeys and discusses adventure and its quest for the objective as an expression of and a means to realise masculinity. I then explore how migrants sustained hope by recognising the necessary interplay of courage, strength, and 'chance' in the adventure, acknowledging their own volition and agency but also the limits of what they could anticipate and bring about, amidst wider social forces they did not control. Such balance was fragile, and in the last part of this chapter, I stress how hope could slip into despair and adventurers feared '*devenir fou*' (becoming mad).

The quest to become a man

My Ivoirian informant Moussa recalled his first trip to the forests around Nador. He travelled with a group of Ivoirian migrants from *le consulat*. At night, to avoid detection, they walked through the forest of Gourougou, near the Spanish enclave of Melilla, joining other small groups. Fifty of them stopped at dawn to rest near the fences.

> Some people went ahead to *cibler* [to target, to scout], to check the barrier, to see whether there were military men. We call these people *cibleurs*. It was fine. We waited an hour to go on the battlefield. We crawled. It is a battle. You go

against military men. You are without weapons. You rush to reach over the fence. They throw stones at you. We got spotted fifty metres before the military fence. There was a guide with us, who was saying step by step what we should do. He was also in the group to cross over into Spain. He shouted to give us the signal to go for the fence.

Like Moussa and his companions, adventurers regularly travelled from Douar Hajja and Maâdid to the borderlands, to 'attack' the fences around the Spanish enclaves or attempt crossing via the sea. They saved up money to purchase materials (e.g. inflatable zodiacs) and fund bus tickets to travel north. They were in regular contact with fellow migrants in the borderlands, who could provide information about security measures. If they had been unsuccessful but evaded getting caught and deported, they would try again over the subsequent days. Sometimes, they stayed for weeks or longer in the informal forest camps, eventually returning to Rabat or other cities to tend their wounds and look for money before the next attempt.

In the borderlands and beyond, adventurers inhabited *'death-worlds'*, generated by mobility politics that define some people as disposable (Mbembe, 2003: 40; original emphasis). Living conditions in makeshift camps, from which migrants could sometimes catch a glimpse of life in the Spanish enclaves, were rudimentary at best and involved the risk of injuries from the rough terrain and clashes with authorities. Losing one's footing while running, often at night and on a treacherous terrain bordered with ravines, could be deadly. Adventurers risked being wounded or killed by Spanish and Moroccan authorities, and the razor-wire-topped fences inflicted deep cuts, despite makeshift ladders and gloves.

This first trip left an indelible mark on Moussa. He only suffered a bad cut, but he was left stunned by the violence he witnessed: 'It's then that I understood why [other migrants] said [the crossing] was dangerous. ... There are no witnesses. If you do not make it to the fence, you are hit even more by the Moroccans. I was told I had to make it at all costs.' He explained that many managed to make it to the Spanish side but could not reach the *campo*.[3] Apart from a few, who escaped, they were all arrested by the Guardia Civil, handcuffed, and beaten, before being brought back across the border, despite 'hot returns' being in breach of Spain's national and international obligations. Once handed over on the Moroccan side, they were beaten again with sticks and iron bars. According to Moussa, at least one Cameroonian man died during that attempt. Most of the migrants, including some of the wounded, were dropped off, hungry and exhausted, in the no man's land beyond Oujda. Trying to evade Moroccan and Algerian border guards, they walked back towards Oujda. 'It was my first refoulement,' Moussa said. They faced a long journey back to the forests or to cities like Rabat, walking long distances on foot. Those who had concealed money had to negotiate with bus drivers, who were often instructed by the Moroccan authorities not to take on migrants. Trying to 'jump' on freight trains bound for Fez was also extremely dangerous and could result in the loss of a limb or worse.

To talk about their lives and journeys, including episodes such as the one recalled by Moussa, adventurers often deployed an epic register ('battlefield', 'attacks'): a recurrent motif within 'imaginaries of adventure' in which 'central African lands are turned into territories where peasants' sons can be elevated to the rank of "hero"' (Bredeloup, 2008: 293–95; translation by the author).[4] My informants discussed the adventure as a 'quest', to which their own heroic drive to surmount dangers and obstacles (especially in the borderlands) was central. Their adventure is 'inconceivable without the possibility of death' (Bredeloup, 2013: 179), but it is not a morbid quest. The possibility of death was discussed to stress their readiness to defy it, as well as the legal arsenal erected along borders. In re-ascribing positive value to labels such as *clandestins* (illegal), adventurers depicted themselves as courageous young men, always ready to pack up their bags and head into the next 'attack'. Moussa presented himself as 'a rebel', emphasising that this was an essential part of his biography: from his time as an activist in the Ivory Coast to his activity as a migrant leader of an association in Morocco (see Chapter 8). Illustrating further the prominence of contestation in the narration of the adventure (Bredeloup, 2008), many of my informants sometimes referred to themselves as 'bandits' or 'soldiers'. When I asked someone in *l'ambassade* what they were fighting against, he replied: 'We are soldiers against life.' Striving to reach the objective, as explored in Chapter 2, entailed refusing one's place in an unequal order and being ready to carve out opportunities for oneself. '*On va se battre*' (we will fight) was an everyday encouragement amongst adventurers, who coaxed each other in the face of adversity.

This epic register was widely shared amongst young men from Central and Western Africa. It was an important element in the expression of their masculinity, which was often discursively tied with their adventure. Migration and gendered identities are dialectical processes, which shape and transform each other (Viruell-Fuentes, 2006; Boehm, 2008; Melly, 2011; Elliot, 2021). As an important organising principle in processes of mobility and immobility, gender determines who has the possibility and means to move or stay. In replying to my questions about what being an adventurer entailed, young men in Douar Hajja and Maâdid often substituted 'man' for 'adventurer'. 'A man must think about his future' was a recurrent aphorism, uttered solemnly when I asked why people had taken the road.

This tight correlation between being a man and being an adventurer was most prominent when discussing the imperative to face up to hardship and overcome obstacles. Ismael's poem *Espoir*, mentioned above, discusses the obstacles and suffering faced by adventurers in their search for love and glory. One of the lines reads: 'through obstacles we recognise a man'. Reflecting on his poem's meaning, Ismael described life itself as a fight, a series of obstacles that included, for adventurers, the dangers faced on the road. He explained that such dangers were intimately entangled with the hardship in his home country, his arduous life in Morocco, and the further difficulties he anticipated once in Europe. Being an adventurer was a lifelong struggle, a moral and political project that exceeded individual biographies to address wider inequalities (see Chapters 2 and 8). Facing the obstacles ahead, Ismael explained, was about 'recognizing' oneself as a man, and 'becoming' one in the process.

Constantin, a Cameroonian migrant, was one of those who had stayed in Morocco the longest amongst people living in *l'ambassade*. He remembered the exact date he left Cameroon – 19 September 2005. He was twenty-four at the time and had spent a few years after his baccalaureate training for a job in the car industry. Unhappy with their economic situation and scarce prospects, Constantin and a group of friends took the road, like others around them had already done. They hoped to earn more money and be able to support their family. When we met in Douar Hajja, Constantin had spent many years living in ghettoes across Algeria and Morocco. He affirmed that the adventure had transformed him, that it had made him a man: 'When you come out, you learn the realities of life. ... I have learnt a lot of things here. The outside has transformed me. Now I am a man psychologically and morally.' The adventure, as a transformative experience that entailed learning through hardship (see Chapter 6), shaped migrants into men, better equipping them to face the dangers and violence of transgressing borders and living clandestinely and preparing them for their future lives – whether in Europe, back in their home countries, or elsewhere.

Becoming a man and being recognised as such (by one's relatives) was a common concern amongst adventurers, regardless of their socio-economic status and of the circumstances of their departure. For these young men, migration was a well-established means to carve up one's place in existing social hierarchies and fulfil expectations. When Idrissa listed the multiple projects he was simultaneously considering for his future, he stressed that he needed 'to become a man, to make [his] family happy'. In the room next to Idrissa's, which was inhabited by Guinean men, Amadou explained that he had left home five years ago. He had been attending high school, while also helping his father in his grocery shop. Despite his parents trying to discourage him, he decided to leave, like many of his friends had already done. He stayed in Mauritania for many months, doing a few odd jobs, like washing cars, until he found better opportunities that matched his schooling. He worked for a Tunisian man, but when the revolution broke out in Tunisia, he lost his job. Things got worse for him in Mauritania, and he left for Morocco, where the 'reality' he witnessed bore little resemblance to the stories he had been told by his friends who were already there. He tried crossing into Spain several times but failed. He was focusing on work in Rabat, despite arduous conditions. He was hoping to cross in the near future, and eventually one day return to Guinea: 'My wish is to get to Europe, even if I just stay there for a week, or a month, and then return, just to go and see it. I want to show my dad that I am a man too.' Some, like Roméo, went as far as to assert that adventure was solely a male affair. According to him, if a woman took part in the adventure, it was because she was 'thinking like a man'.[5]

Discussions about the adventure as centred on becoming, and being recognised as, a man often led to the articulation of concerns and frustrations about love, sex, and family in Morocco. For some of my informants who were married or had been in a long-standing relationship before departing, being able to fulfil one's duties as a man equated with meeting their obligations towards girlfriends and wives (alongside other family members), and sometimes children, back home (see Chapter 6). Other relationships sometimes developed during long journeys, including for people who were married before leaving, even if this was not always openly discussed. When reflecting on the unfulfilled promises of the adventure, young men very often mentioned amorous relationships – discussed exclusively with reference to women. They readily associated reaching the objective with having and supporting a family but complained that, while travelling, women were only a source of 'problems' for adventurers. Relationships with Moroccan women in particular could lead to tensions with Moroccan neighbours. Alain bemoaned that approaching women in Morocco was 'forbidden' to men from sub-Saharan countries, that knives could be drawn if they spoke to them in public: 'There are women [in the adventure], but they are not for you.' Some amorous relationships developed between male adventurers and Moroccan women in Douar Hajja but did not last long, because migrants moved on to the borderlands and because of widespread racism (see Chapter 7).

Courage, strength, and chance

Narratives about the adventure as a pathway towards manhood were gilded with heroic deeds towards victory. More prosaically, everyday life for these young male migrants involved waiting for something: a phone call from a Moroccan contact to get work, a Western Union transfer from relatives, news from the borderlands, a medical appointment at an NGO, and so on. My attempts at small talk were often met with a taciturn and gloomy answer: '*la routine*'. Life in between border-crossing attempts was monotonous at best, interrupted only by sudden bouts of violence (e.g. police raids). People were 'wasting time' (*perdre le temps*) in front of the TV in informal restaurants or hanging out by the entrance of the ghettoes, in case they needed to quickly take cover. Distractions were few, besides 'cybers' (internet cafés, usually without beverages). In the afternoon, migrants from *le consulat* would gather outside. As they mingled, young Ivoirian and Cameroonian men had the same animated conversation to determine once and for all whether Yaoundé or Abidjan had the best '*ambiance*' (atmosphere). They all agreed Douar Hajja was awful.

Waiting has featured prominently in studies exploring the lives of (mostly male, urban) African youths as they grapple with neoliberalism and other structural barriers impeding their access to the necessary resources to reach social markers of adulthood (e.g. stable income, marriage) and their promise of independence and autonomy. Such unfulfilled aspirations could foster intense feelings of boredom, despair, frustration, and shame amongst young people (e.g. Schielke, 2008; Mains, 2017; Masquelier, 2019). In deploying the notion of 'waithood', Honwana (2012) points to a suspended period between childhood and adulthood that is becoming permanent for young people. Much policy and public discourse have reappropriated notions such as 'waithood' and conflated waiting with inaction (Oosterom, 2021). Conceiving such lives as simply static does not stand up to ethnographic scrutiny and ignores people's efforts to transform their own lives despite precarious living; young people wait, 'but as they wait they talk, play, plan, scheme, hustle and work' (Stasik *et al.*, 2020: 2; see also Di Nunzio, 2019). Poverty, conflict, corruption, and a range of other structural issues had thwarted the aspirations of adventurers to, as Ismael often put it, develop their talents. Hence, they took the road. But in Douar Hajja and Maâdid (as well as other places along the way), they found themselves having to wait again. Demonstrating how waiting can entail both a sense of stagnation but also highly productive activities for migrants in limbo (see Rotter, 2016), waiting amongst adventurers was a time for preparedness and action.

Shortly after Idrissa left Morocco, I went to his old flat to meet up with Amadou, the Guinean man from the adjacent bedroom. Nobody I knew was in the flat when I arrived. The three new occupants of Idrissa's former room looked at me with puzzled expressions. They thought I was sent by the Moroccan landlord to fix a long-standing electrical issue. We chatted for a few hours while I waited for Amadou. One of them, Souleyman, a Malian man, remembered seeing me with Idrissa before. As we engaged in the familiar small talk about life in Morocco and adventure, Souleyman sighed: 'We live in hazard.' When I asked him what he meant, he replied that it would be better to answer my question with a story:

> There was once a Moroccan woman working for the King's secretary. She saw a Black man and wanted him. The man was married back home and did not want to cheat on his wife. But he did not tell the Moroccan woman. He let her linger. She gave him money, but he was not really responding to her. ... She started screaming, 'Be careful not to find yourself near me or there will be trouble.' Now, he regrets it. We, Blacks, never know what we should take or leave; we live in hazard [*dans le hasard*]. We have no fixed direction; we do not have one option only. There are people who want to become professor of philosophy and they just go for that. Here, there is no such thing in Douar Hajja. We have a lot of options. You can go in any direction. You meet someone here and he tells you he will stay two months, but two days after you have seen him, he is in the forest, and he tells you he is going somewhere else.

Souleyman's reflections on uncertainty pointed to the fluidity of the notion of 'objective' amongst migrants, as discussed in Chapter 2. His reference to the unpredictable behaviour of adventurers was familiar. We were eating bread and milk together because several of my friends and informants in Douar Hajja and Maâdid were not around. I had walked to *le consulat* earlier that day to find out people I was due to meet with had hastily travelled to the borderlands. Amadou was late because he had recently found a new job as a guardian in a villa. Idrissa's departure had also been sudden. Adventurers regularly left without saying anything, or only at the last minute. There was an element of secrecy to the adventure, but life was also deeply uncertain. The precarity they faced could translate into violent acts at any time, but there could also be pleasant surprises and opportunities to seize.

Souleyman's assertion that migrants had too many options was puzzling at first. Hostile mobility regimes greatly, and often brutally, impeded adventurers' lives and journeys, forcing them to readjust their quest for the objective. '*Le Maroc nous gère*' (Morocco manages us) was a phrase I often heard, with 'Morocco' sometimes substituted by the word 'terrain'. Recalling how he set off on the adventure, a Cameroonian man from *l'ambassade* explained that his girlfriend had tried to galvanise him by calling him a lion. Both bemused and saddened while discussing obstacles to the adventure in Morocco, he jokingly exclaimed, 'A lion! But if I am a lion, the terrain is a dragon.' Adventurers faced powerful and complex social forces they needed to confront or negotiate with, but their lives were not devoid of choices. 'The terrain' always threatened 'to manage' migrants, who were acutely aware of how limited their room for manoeuvre was, and so how important each tiny decision was. Young men from Central and Western Africa had to decide when and how to get out of their ghettoes, as the threat of being assaulted, robbed, and arrested loomed large. They needed to choose how to reach the borderlands and attempt crossing the border. When they heard of successful mass crossings into one of the Spanish enclaves, they could decide to go to the borderlands immediately, in the hope that the weakness in the bordering measures (or deliberate leniency by the Moroccan authorities) might last longer. Or they could decide to delay their departure or change direction of travel, to avoid getting caught by heightened security measures. Adventurers had plenty of experience and could access more or less reliable information to guide the many decisions they could and needed to make every day, in and out of Douar Hajja. Idrissa often shared with me his reflections as he pondered whether he should attend the theatre workshop sessions, look for work despite the unlikelihood of being picked up because of his small stature, or go to the Caritas centre near *château* to check if he could get anything there. He would ponder over what 'advantages' he was likely to get from each activity. Like other adventurers, he could not know whether he had taken the right decision.

Migrants' violent and uncertain predicaments did not necessarily lead to inaction and passivity. They hoped that things would get better and that they would eventually succeed. Their sense of hope was 'on the side of life' (Zournazi and Hage, 2002: 151); it was grounded in a form of engagement that led migrants 'to want to live, no matter what' (Zournazi and Hage, 2002: 151). To some extent, imagining and hoping for a better future involve uncertainty (see Pine, 2014). Its realisation is often seen as depending on something else, such as God or fate, especially in a passive understanding of hope (see Crapanzano, 2004). But for these young men, stranded in Douar Hajja, the realisation of hope was achieved through active and persistent engagement. More than an affect, it was a disposition that required a fine balance between displaying essential attributes, such as *courage et force* (courage and strength), and recognising the limits of one's agency (*la chance*). Migrants did not know for sure which route would be successful and talked of '*tenter la chance*' (taking a chance).[6] Getting up in the morning and being able to find a job for the day was a matter of 'chance'; crossing the fence in Melilla was governed by 'chance'. In *l'ambassade*, where football was a great distraction, many Cameroonian migrants spent time and money playing football lottery. They brought their betting slips to nearby shops in Douar Hajja. Winning or losing was also a matter of 'chance'. As articulated by adventurers, chance involves a fine balance between contingency and the ability to act. Acknowledging and sustaining such a fragile balance was crucial to staying hopeful and sane.

Chance refers to migrants' constrained agency in their uncertain quest. Migrants hoped to be successful: they could not know whether they would manage to cross, but chance might be on their side so it was worth trying.

Chance was a ubiquitous idiom in conversations amongst adventurers. Moussa asserted that, although there was no clear definition of chance as such, it was a crucial dimension of adventure: 'The adventurer plays on two fundamental levels: chance, as well as strength [*force*] and courage.' Together, they formed a crucial 'combination', necessary for the success of the adventure. Moussa argued that, for adventurers, strength was 'useful but not essential': one could cross the border without 'forcing it'. While courage was essential but not enough by itself. He gave the example of a group of adventurers, six Cameroonians and one Guinean, attempting to cross the border together. They reached the fence outside Melilla but found a large presence of Moroccan forces. They decided it was too dangerous. While returning to the forest camp, they came across another group set on scaling the fence despite the presence of border guards. The group took courage and joined them. The six Cameroonians crossed the border, but the Guinean was caught. 'What was the difference there?' Moussa asked me. 'Chance!'

In the face of adversity, adventurers needed to display what they called 'the right mentality', facing up to the obstacles and dangers on the way.[7] Moussa called it a combination of strength and courage; others talked simply of 'making an effort'. What was important was to persevere and face up to adversity, in the hope of finding chance. Only by striving to overcome obstacles and displaying the right mentality could adventurers hope to obtain 'a reward': crossing the fences and being able to reach 'the objective'. Chance was not totally random, Moussa would stress. It was the opposite of 'hazard', a word he used to mean something different than Souleyman: 'Hazard is when you do something without thinking about it, like a reflex. And if you try to think about it to do it, then it does not happen. Chance is not like this. Chance is about doing something, reflecting on it.' One should not sit and wait passively, Moussa argued, but should instead '*faire son effort*' (make one's effort). Success in the adventure required active engagement and reflection from young migrants who were trying to be active agents of their own destinies. For the chance to reach a life more bearable, adventurers stress the need for men to be courageous and demonstrate their strength in the face of violent bordering measures.

In the ghettoes of Douar Hajja and Maâdid, adventurers often coaxed and praised each other for displaying the right mentality, for demonstrating both courage and strength. Yet, Moussa and many others insisted that chance could not be 'forced', it could only be '*tentée*' (attempted): 'it is God who gives chance; you do not force chance'. For Moussa, chance was something one was born with; it was a 'spiritual thing': 'I pray for God to give me a sign, not to give me chance. I cannot change my destiny.' In his discussion of 'luck' amongst Guinean hustlers, Gaibazzi argues that human existence is informed by what he calls 'a kinetic notion of destiny ... whereby the idea of a predetermined, personalized fate largely operating beyond human cognition demands that they find their route' (2015a: 239). In Douar Hajja and Maâdid, all my informants seemed to agree that it was not possible to know for certain whether one would find chance. You could only find out by trying. If you failed, you needed to be brave and try again. Adventurers could only find out whether they would be successful by returning to the borderlands.

Moussa described himself as 'spiritual', sometimes expressing the wish to become Muslim, like his grandfather, or Rastafarian, like his brother. When discussing religion, he would recall fond memories of his tongue-in-cheek, atheist father, who always teased Moussa's Christian mother. There were Christians, Muslims, and atheists cohabiting in places like *l'ambassade* and *le consulat*. Some attended local mosques, or the churches in other neighbourhoods, if they could afford transport and did not fear getting caught. Many just prayed at home or in informal churches, set up in ghettoes. There had been Pentecostal churches set up by Congolese migrants in Douar Hajja, but they were shut after neighbours complained about the music. Religious beliefs and commitments varied greatly. Some joked that adventure brought people closer to God, that some people who had never thought about religion suddenly became devout Muslims or Christians when facing the barriers or the sea for the first time. As an existential quest to find their lives, adventure was also a religious experience for migrants. '*C'est Dieu la force*' (God is strength) was a common encouragement in Douar Hajja, routinely used as a goodbye amongst some adventurers. As some pointed out to me, the adventure could also bring people further away from God, after repeated failures to cross. It also entailed the kind of trickery and deceit adventurers sometimes boasted about, such as pretending to be Muslim, by changing their names, when looking for work, or pretending to be Christian when seeking help from charities such as Caritas, even if staff affirmed that religion was not a criterion in deciding whom to help and how.

Many pointed to God and associated chance with destiny. I accompanied Idrissa on some of his visits to Abderhamid, a Muslim Malian who had been beaten by the Moroccan auxiliary forces in the borderlands and was convalescing in a Malian ghetto in Maâdid. Abderhamid and the few other migrants who were present spoke Bambara only, and Idrissa sporadically translated their exchanges. Sat on an old plastic mat, Abderhamid was holding his rosary and praying. Once finished, he stated that those who prayed and gave charity would be protected by God. One of the other Malian men then told a story about a group of Malian migrants who had 'prepared themselves very well before leaving for Morocco'. He explained that the father of one of the migrants provided them with 'powerful medicine', to ensure crossing, and warned them as follows: 'Go to the gate [at the border] and walk straight, but do not look behind you.' The four friends went to the gate and did as they had been told. All but one, who had looked behind, crossed and reached the Spanish side.

Curious about this warning against looking back and its echoes in Greek mythology and biblical stories, I asked Idrissa to probe the group of Malians about the story, asking whether it was God that would enable safe passage. Idrissa and the Malians spoke for a while. Their laughter grew more raucous. They seemed to be taking turns telling stories, each one provoking more hilarity. Abderhamid had tears in his eyes and was holding himself, as laughter further jolted his aching body. I kept smiling awkwardly and eventually interrupted, to ask Idrissa what was so funny. He gave me a very succinct translation of just one of the stories, this time attributed to a Guinean man going on the adventure. The man prayed twice to God to be let into Spain. He prayed first before approaching one of the fence's gates. He went ahead and found the gate was not guarded. He crossed and kneeled next to the fence. He wanted to pray again and thank God immediately. As he was praying, Spanish border guards came over, tapped on his shoulder, and said to him: 'If you are finished praying now, we are just going to send you back to the other [Moroccan] side of the fence.' Idrissa and the others resumed laughing and chatting, ignoring me.

For many adventurers, it was God who ultimately provided chance, but that did not mean migrants should stop staying alert. Chance could not be forced but it did not replace the need for courage and strength. I asked Fabien – who preferred to hang out on Sundays, rather than attending church service – whether it was God that awarded chance. He replied that, yes, it was God, but added, matter of factly: 'You don't just wait in bed here until God picks you up and nicely deposits you on the other side of the barrier.' As in the Russian proverb mentioned by Zigon in his discussion of hope, 'you can put your hopes in God, but you still have to act' (2009: 259). Amidst bordering processes that hampered their mobility, adventurers in Morocco needed to explore the space of potentialities, trying to find and seize their chance. For the young men in Douar Hajja and Maâdid, finding out their destiny meant carving out opportunities, through courage and strength, in order to reach their objective.

Chance was used to explain past attempts, providing a reason, a posteriori, for success but also failure, as well as hopeful encouragement for future attempts. In Douar Hajja, people who had attempted to cross the border and failed were usually on the receiving end of fellow migrants' confident reassurances: 'It was not your time; you are not dead; next time will be the right one.' As Moussa put it, 'We lift each other's spirit amongst ourselves here. Sometimes it is not easy when you have not achieved your objective and *déception* [disappointment] starts creeping up on you. You have to lift the other person's spirit, or else that person will take a blow.' Supporting one another in 'keeping the right mentality' could be beneficial amongst companions who might be attempting to cross the border together and would need to keep each other's spirits up when scaling the fence as a group (see Chapter 6). As stressed by Moussa, disappointment could do a lot of damage. Migrants sought to keep the right mentality in the face of hardship, but the search for chance could lead to madness.

Becoming mad

In Douar Hajja, adventurers sometimes complained about people they described as having lost the right mentality, people who had forgotten about the objective. Blaise had very harsh words against people he identified as having stopped behaving as adventurers should, no longer actively looking for work or border-crossing opportunities. In his words, they were doing nothing all day but going around the streets to beg for a few dirhams, then watching TV. He decried the French channel *TV5 Monde*'s broadcasting of dubbed Mexican and Argentinian telenovelas as almost as dangerous for the adventurers as the Moroccan police. Migrants needed to keep up their quest by remaining hopeful and courageously facing up to the obstacles on the way. But adventurers were always at risk of that 'slippage into hopelessness' (Zigon, 2009: 262).

Keeping the right mentality was a difficult endeavour. The balance between acknowledging one's abilities and remaining aware of one's limits was hard to maintain. If forgetting about the objective was frowned upon, migrants were also aware of the danger of 'thinking too much'. As explained by Moussa, finding chance required adventurers to be both reflective and proactive. But being hypervigilant to the 'immediate convulsions of a fluid environment' (Vigh, 2009a: 425), while remaining focused on the objective beyond the horizon, was mentally exhausting. Migrants talked of being so '*dépassé*' (overwhelmed, overtaken) by problems that they could '*devenir fou*' (become mad). They constantly ruminated over the past actions and choices that had resulted in failed border-crossing attempts or missed opportunities.

On a February morning, Alain and I went to one of the usual cafés near *château*, where I conducted interviews with migrants when more privacy than could be afforded in the ghettoes was needed. He had recently come back, with an injured wrist, from another failed attempt near Tangier. '*Le moral n'est pas là*' (I am feeling low), he told me right away, as we sat down. He recounted how the Moroccan border guards had quickly spotted the migrants from a 'watchtower', and then went on to recall previous failed attempts and what went wrong each time. He detailed how, after he first arrived in Rabat, the three companions he had befriended in Oujda, and travelled with, decided to leave for the borderlands, shortly after they arrived. They urged him to go along with them, but Alain decided against it, preferring to rest a bit in Rabat before travelling on to the borderlands. Shortly after, he received news that his three companions had managed to cross into the Spanish enclave of Melilla. 'To this day, *ça me chauffe encore la tête*' (it still makes me upset), he said.

I also heard the expression '*chauffer la tête*' from Moussa many times, as he seemed to never find himself in the right place at the right time when it came to border-crossing attempts. During the 2012–2013 winter, many migrants rushed from Rabat to the forests around Nador. The number of migrants who made the trip was surprising for the season, as conditions were usually preferable when the weather was warmer. Moussa stayed several weeks near Nador, more than on previous trips, until the harsh weather and overall living conditions in the forest camps became too intolerable. Slimmer and exhausted, he came back to Rabat, after a journey that took a few days. By the time he reached Douar Hajja, the friends he had travelled with, and who had decided to stay longer, crossed into Melilla. Moussa was depressed and inconsolable for some time.

Shortly after his return, I made my way into *le consulat* early one Sunday morning to check on how he was feeling and suggest getting the bus to the beach as a distraction. The place was quiet, even for a Sunday. I found him lying still on his mattress, his arms folded behind his head. He said he felt very low. At 5 am, a group of Ivoirians from *le consulat* had called to inform their friends that they had all succeeded in crossing into Melilla, without any major difficulties. Moussa said there was a big commotion when the news broke in the ghetto – 'a revolution'. Those who had stayed in Douar Hajja, either because they preferred to delay their departure or could not afford to go at that time, celebrated the success of their friends but entered a quick state of agitation: 'We all got up; we could not sleep anymore. I just went to brush my teeth. I did not know what else to do.' Excitement morphed into regret and frustration amongst those who were not part of the successful trip. Moussa was lying down, thinking about the series of events and decisions which led to him being in Rabat and not in Melilla with his friends. He could have easily been amongst the group that had crossed. In the ghettoes of Douar Hajja, adventurers needed to keep the right mentality but were on the brink of despair; they had plenty of failed plans and other worries to cogitate over, and plenty of time to do so.

Alpha, who lived with Idrissa and other Burkinabé men, was a talkative and usually jovial character, but every now and then, after our discussions, he would walk away and lie down in a corner, staying still with a cigarette in his hands. 'I am smoking [away] my problems,' he would say. To shake away the disturbing thoughts that laid heavy on his mind, Alpha would go on long walks, doing the same loop along the market street between Takaddoum and Maâdid, with a midway stop to sit on the big concrete slab near *château*, smoking cigarettes in the sun. One such afternoon, as we smoked some cheap Marquise, watching people returning from work and the food stalls being set up for the evening, a young Black man came over to sit next to us. He was wearing a long winter coat and many other warm layers, despite the heat. He stared in front of him and started mumbling, sometimes glancing sideways at us. Alpha occasionally nodded to him and finally just got up to leave. I followed him to enquire what the man had said. 'I don't know,' he laughed. 'He is mad; adventure makes some people mad.' Later on that day, I brought up the incident with Blaise and others who were sitting on the rooftop of *l'ambassade*, waiting to get their hair cut by a Cameroonian hairdresser who went around ghettoes for his business. Blaise mentioned other migrants who could be seen around Douar Hajja and Takaddoum during the day, eating from bins, walking about with dogs, talking to themselves, crossing in front of buses, and seemingly not paying attention to others around them. One man getting his hair done turned to me and laconically exclaimed, 'This is the adventure.'

'Becoming mad' was a serious worry and a tangible possibility for migrants. Failed attempts and difficult living conditions took a toll on their mental health, driving some to alcohol and drug addictions. I discussed mental health issues with the coordinator of the Caritas centre, near Douar Hajja, when he was also particularly low one morning in January 2013. There had been a series of police raids in Rabat, as well as numerous new arrivals of wounded migrants from the forests. Caritas was struggling to cope with the demand on their services. He explained how, throughout 2012, drastically reduced passages to Europe, the temporary closure of the IOM voluntary return programme, and increased police raids in Rabat and other cities had left many migrants 'stuck in a vice': 'You cannot go north, you cannot go back, and you get beaten up here. People break down more quickly than they would normally do.' Many migrants who came to the Caritas centre presented psychological and psychiatric problems, compounded by their living conditions as irregular migrants: 'They cannot take it anymore.' The 'difficult context' increased mental health issues for migrants:

> People are lost; they ask themselves questions and it becomes obsessional; it can lead to depression and then maybe trigger a psychiatric issue. They keep harping on the same questions. You see them, especially teenagers, they come and ask you, 'What if I do not get my UNHCR papers, does it mean that …?' And the day after they come again, and ask you again, every day.

An overall feeling of entrapment, of being stuck in Douar Hajja and Morocco, more widely triggered and deepened mental health issues amongst migrants. In a report released shortly before they ceased their activities to denounce violence against migrants in Morocco, MSF reported a deterioration of migrants' overall mental health. The report outlines how 'the precarious living conditions that the majority of sub-Saharans are forced to live in and the wide-spread institutional and criminal violence that they are exposed to continue to be the main factors influencing medical and psychological needs' (2013: 3). The disparity between migrants' expectation for a better life and their living conditions in Morocco could 'cause psychological shock and trauma' (MSF, 2013: 8), which intensified the longer they stayed in Morocco. Increased violence, including constant police raids, meant migrants had to stay constantly alert. Symptoms of depression, anxiety, and psychosomatic tendencies were described as a common manifestation of migrants' feelings of fear, sadness, loss, confusion, anguish, and abandonment.

Conclusion

Looking for the objective was a transformative project for my male informants. The heroic self-representations of adventurers were closely associated with masculinity, despite the presence of a growing number of female migrants. In searching for their lives, young migrants from Western and Central Africa sought to become and be recognised as men. They were ready to attack borders, despite the dangers associated with violent mobility regimes. Their heroic descriptions of their lives and journeys contrasted with the monotony and boredom of their everyday lives. Waiting for the next attack, migrants prepared and remained hopeful that they could transcend their entrapment. For this, they needed to keep 'the right mentality', displaying courage and strength, despite the violence and suffering they were subjected to. Uncertainty over the outcome of their actions and reflections was discussed in terms of 'chance', which could not be forced, as it was awarded by God, but needed to be taken ('attempted') through migrants' own efforts in the face of obstacles. In discussing chance, adventurers made sense of both their failed and successful attempts. Keeping the right mentality helped sustain their hope and prevent them from falling into despair. It was crucial for migrants to remain '*concentré* [focused] on the objective'. But keeping the right mentality was difficult, and migrants risked being '*dépassés*' (overwhelmed) and 'thinking too much', which could lead them to 'becoming mad'. Such a balance needed to be constantly negotiated, as everyday life in Morocco entailed a plethora of problems and violent events, as well as disappointments and missed opportunities. In the next chapter, I explore how my informants were moving away from larger ghettoes and into smaller accommodations in Douar Hajja, which these adventurers were nevertheless hesitant to call home.

Notes

1. '*Boza*' is a term widely used amongst adventurers from Western and Central Africa to refer to the act of crossing into Europe through irregular means. By extension, it is also synonym with being successful in one's adventure.
2. My translation (see Bachelet, 2014b).
3. Nickname given to the Spanish Identification Centre in Melilla.
4. My translation.
5. Most migrants in Douar Hajja and Maâdid were men at the time of fieldwork (see the Introduction). However, there were women too, including several Cameroonian and Ivoirian women running informal restaurants (see Chapter 5), who denounced abuse from Moroccans and other migrants. As one Cameroonian woman snappily put it to me: 'Of course I am an adventurer. I have left my country, have I not?' A growing number of studies, mostly conducted by women, have explored the lives and experiences of Black female migrants (e.g. Escoffier, 2008; Cheikh and Péraldi, 2009; Stock, 2019). They highlight women as 'fully-fledged actresses' (Tyszler, 2019) in the formation and viability of dynamics of globalisation and their counter-geographies (Sassen, 2000), rather than African Penelopes patiently awaiting the return of their husbands (Schmoll, 2020).
6. In French, '*tenter*' translates as 'attempting' but also 'tempting', stressing the active participation of adventurers in bringing about the necessary conditions for success – even though it is beyond their full control.
7. I return to the notion of the 'right mentality' and the balance between strength, courage, and chance in Chapter 6 to examine its importance in the relationships adventurers forged amongst themselves.

4

Life in the ghettoes

'*L'ambassade* has been attacked,' Fabien reported on the phone one morning in October 2012. There was no agitation in his voice, just a hint of fatigue. The previous evening, the Moroccan landlord had roused up a group of young Moroccan men to storm the decrepit building in Douar Hajja, a migrant 'ghetto' inhabited mostly by young men from Cameroon. Earlier that year, he had tricked the Cameroonian men into signing a lease, in Arabic, for a six-month period, assuring them that it would automatically renew. Once the period ended, he requested the tenants vacate the building. The inhabitants refused: they had always paid the rent. As the dispute worsened, living conditions deteriorated. The electricity and water supplies were cut off. The tenants had met the regular payments for the utility bills but had made them to the landlord, upon his request, rather than directly paying the energy supplier. He had kept the money instead of paying the bills for several months. Without water or electricity, already insanitary living conditions became intolerable. Weeks passed and the Cameroonian men no longer paid rent. Tension with the landlord escalated, finally culminating in a raid by people referred to as '*clochards*' by everyone in Douar Hajja. Meaning 'tramps' in French, this is a derogatory term that designates marginal figures of urban deviance and precariousness, living in and drifting around peripheral neighbourhoods.

The people who ransacked *l'ambassade* stole what they could and left everything else broken, even the doors. Some of the Cameroonian inhabitants (and visitors) were assaulted during the break-in. Two men were thrown over the rooftop's banister and fell down two storeys, but only suffered bruises. Bags containing passports and other possessions were tossed outside. Some belonged to a group of men who had signed up to the IOM voluntary return programme and were due to fly soon. They lost everything. Fabien angrily described how neighbours joined in, stealing clothes after trying them on in the small alleyway. Policemen arrived, called by the landlord, who had complained about foreign squatters and fighting in his property. They arrested three bedridden Cameroonian men, who could not flee.

When calm returned, the inhabitants of *l'ambassade* pleaded in the neighbourhood for the return of their belongings. They came back with one chair.

When I arrived at *l'ambassade*, shortly after Fabien's call, people were sitting amongst piles of broken objects and torn-out clothes. Furious and exhausted, they discussed retaliation 'against Moroccan people' but agreed this would make things worse. Yasser, the '*chef de ghetto*' (ghetto chief), Alex, a Cameroonian man from the same ghetto, Fabien, and myself went to the nearby police station. We were accompanied by Didi, a Cameroonian businessman from Casablanca, who was the recently elected leader of a Cameroonian community association. A man, who introduced himself as the *commissaire* (superintendent), welcomed us, declaring that he felt 'African'. He scolded the Cameroonian men for not coming to see him before: 'I have been working in this district for years; it is the first time sub-Saharans come and see me. You should come before there is any crisis, so I can help.' Glancing at me, and probably mistaking me for an employee of an international organisation, he added that he did not care whether people were documented or not. There were rules 'but also greater rules, which are human rights'. Didi and Alex, by far the most diplomatic compared to taciturn Yasser and quick-tempered Fabien, did most of the talking and joking with the policeman. The *commissaire* shrewdly steered the conversation away from violence against migrants and exploitation by landlords. He admonished migrants for fighting amongst themselves. There had been scuffles in the neighbourhood between adventurers and Moroccan inhabitants but also amongst adventurers themselves. A few weeks before, a Guinean man had been killed in Douar Hajja during a fight between groups of migrants from different nationalities. The police advised the Cameroonian migrants to lodge their own complaint against the landlord, and we left.

Nothing came out of this meeting, and life became increasingly harder for those who chose to continue standing their ground in *l'ambassade*. Gradually, more and more people left the ghetto. The few men who decided to stay feared another attack, and increasingly stayed away from the ghetto during the day. They were eventually evicted by the police. One Cameroonian man resisted arrest and was jailed for six months, for illegal occupation of the house and threats to the landlord. The police brought a welder to seal the front door, and *l'ambassade*, a landmark for migrants in Douar Hajja, was permanently lost. Many adventurers from the ghetto blamed Yasser for what happened, calling him a bad 'chief' who 'let disorder spread' amongst inhabitants and failed to mend the relation with the landlord before it was too late. Former inhabitants spread out across the neighbourhood, joining other large ghettoes, or renting individual rooms in much smaller groups. Others headed for the borderlands.

This chapter examines living spaces for adventurers in Douar Hajja and Maâdid, stressing their ambiguous nature: important self-organised places marking the anchoring of migrants in Rabat, but not quite homes. Adventurers lived together in dilapidated buildings, which offered scant protection against intrusions by the police or other ill-intentioned people. Living conditions were gruelling in these overcrowded and unsanitary places. Ghettoes acted as staging posts along migratory routes, amongst other forms of accommodation, such as informal camps in the borderlands near the Spanish enclaves (Traoré and Le Dantec, 2012). These derelict buildings in Rabat were often known to adventurers before they even reached the city or crossed the border with Algeria. Moroccan authorities were not a permanent presence around migrant ghettoes, but the threat of police raids and other forms of violence constantly hung over the neighbourhood, influencing migrants' housing arrangements.

Places like *l'ambassade* and *le consulat* were inscribed in transnational bordering regimes that violently constrained adventurers' migratory and life projects through a variety of sites of encampment regulating and constraining mobility. Such sites are usually managed by state agencies, NGOs, and private companies (e.g. detention centres, refugee camps, etc.), and they exist in spatial and political continuity with historical forms of confinement targeting minorities and foreigners (see Le Cour Grandmaison *et al.*, 2007; Bernardot, 2008). In contrast, *l'ambassade*, *le consulat*, and other ghettoes (as well as informal forest camps) were self-regulated spaces of confinement. Adventurers organised their own living arrangements. Although state actors were not directly involved in the regulation of such spaces, the looming threats of assault, eviction, arrest, and deportation contributed to a sense of being under siege amongst inhabitants of such ghettoes.

In migration scholarship, the Agambian trope of the space of exception has become well established to examine the inclusive exclusion of migrants (Agamben, 1998; Rajaram and Grundy-Warr, 2004). However, the socio-political and legal processes that make up bordering regimes are undetermined struggles. The 'jargon of exclusion' (Huysmans, 2008: 165) risks exacerbating dehumanising and depoliticising tropes, by reducing (irregular) migrants to bare lives, passively subjected to unbound power from above. Casting bordering regimes as an omnipotent sovereign figure fails to account for the multiple non-state practices and actors (including landlords) that contribute to the categorisation of 'individuals as citizens, illegal aliens, legal residents, asylees and so forth' (Coutin, 1993: 88). Even when state authorities play a primordial role in determining 'the conditions and circumstances of encampment at a political level' (McConnachie, 2014: 46), they may be invisible and/or irrelevant to the daily life of migrants.

Migrant ghettoes were spaces of abjection and the site of strategies that fostered forms of rightlessness. But they also call for the exploration of 'different logics and spaces of resistance' (Isin and Rygiel, 2007: 185). Studies of refugee camps have notably shed light on the precarity and endurance of displaced people who are spatially confined, a circumstance marked by exception and also by 'real life' (Agier, 2011: 86) with transformative potential. The nicknames adventurers gave to their living spaces (*l'ambassade, le consulat*) denote these ghettoes as important loci for their social (and political) lives, as further illustrated by the businesses (see Chapter 5) and political organisations (Chapter 8) that emerged from these marginal spaces. Examining living spaces in Douar Hajja and Maâdid illustrates how adventurers actively seek to shape their own lives and journeys, beyond organising border-crossing attempts, demonstrating the resourcefulness (see Chapter 1) that is articulated as central to the adventure. However, a study of spaces of exception for migrants as also spaces of life and transformation must account for the potential of oppression and hierarchy amongst migrants too. Places like *l'ambassade* were not egalitarian heavens, though they were important spaces where migrants from across Western and Central Africa could support one another.

The demise of *l'ambassade* and the scattering of its inhabitants fit within a growing trend in Douar Hajja and Maâdid of migrants seeking, if they could afford it, to move away from hierarchical and overcrowded ghettoes. They stayed in the neighbourhood but moved into smaller rooms, where living conditions were less harsh but the rent more expensive. Larger ghettoes still existed and enabled migrants (especially those with the least resources) to pay little money for rent, but the authority of leaders (e.g. ghetto chiefs) was greatly eroded. It had become easier, though not cheaper, to find less decrepit accommodation to host a smaller number of migrants. Those smaller housing arrangements were simply referred to as '*chambres*' (bedrooms) and '*maisons*' (meaning both house and home in French), though not without unease amongst adventurers who usually sought to leave Morocco and did not feel 'at home'. By focusing on housing, this chapter explores migrants' self-organisation of their living arrangements. As adventurers strove to reach the objective, they endeavoured to make their lives more comfortable, while preparing their next border-crossing attempt. The shift from larger ghettoes to smaller rooms underscores the overall ambiguous and fragile anchoring of migrants in Morocco. They sought better places to live in but did not seek to settle in Douar Hajja and Maâdid. Pointing to the manifold forms of violence they continued to face, adventurers stressed that these neighbourhoods (and Morocco more broadly) were 'prisons'.

Home is not simply a fixed and permanent place of nurture and protection but a set of material, affective, imaginary, and socio-political processes, which connect people, spaces, and places across multiple scales, and can 'constitute belonging and/or create a sense of marginalisation and estrangement' (Mallett, 2004: 84; see also Ahmed *et al.*, 2003; Blunt and Downling, 2006; Boccagni, 2017; Wilkins, 2019). A focus on adventurers' living conditions and housing arrangements in Douar Hajja and Maâdid sheds light on complex processes linking local places to global spaces. Their efforts to find better accommodation underscore the uncertainty of home-making practices and how such processes are constrained by mobility regimes and powerful actors. Adventurers stayed in Douar Hajja and Maâdid longer than they wished for. Bordering regimes not only hindered migrants' efforts to cross borders by increasing the risks, but they also discouraged migrants from imagining their lives and their homes in Douar Hajja, Maâdid, and Morocco more broadly. It is crucial to examine the complex intersection of place and displacement (Lems, 2016) and to account for the (unequally distributed) 'power to emplace' (Jansen and Löfving, 2008: 13). Ghettoes were spaces of exception and spaces of life, where adventurers stayed for what they hoped would be a short period. They were not spaces where they saw the realisation of their objective as attainable. They offered some refuge, but violent intrusions remained a tangible threat. There, migrants could foster relationships, as adventurers sharing a common objective, but exploitation amongst migrants themselves was not uncommon, especially in large ghettoes. Exclusion, empowerment, and the potential for new interconnections were all essential features of those living spaces (see Cancellieri, 2017).

L'ambassade and *le consulat*

L'ambassade was an ordinary building in one of Douar Hajja's tortuous alleyways, located a five-minute walk away from *château*. The brown metal door was often shut, but a short rope, dangling from a hole, could action the lock. The rope could be dragged back inside to prevent intrusions. Inhabitants described being under siege in this building. The first time I stepped inside *l'ambassade*, Alex, a Cameroonian man, called it '*Black Hawk Down*' and pointed to neighbouring terraces, from where bottles and stones were regularly thrown at them by neighbours, particularly an elderly woman with a notoriously good aim.[1] Nevertheless, the place offered a comforting, if fragile, sense of protection. It was described by many inhabitants as 'heaven within hell', a refuge from the multiple dangers on the streets of Douar Hajja, even though such dangers breached into the living spaces too.

Immediately behind the brown door rose the first flight of bare concrete stairs leading to a dark landing. From there, one could access two windowless bedrooms, furnished with run-down single mattresses tucked against one another and topped with thin but neatly folded blankets. The small rooms were bare except for stacked-up bags, ready to be taken to the borderlands. Some clothes were dangling from nails, and there were scribbled names and phone numbers on the walls belonging to past and current inhabitants. An even smaller third room, the only one with a door and a lock, belonged to Yasser, the 'ghetto chief'. Adjacent to this was a rudimentary lavatory: a hole, a flimsy tap, and a plastic bucket. The ill-fitting wooden door was not enough to contain a rancid stench. As ghetto chief, Yasser's first duty seemed to be to shout at people to close the door and empty extra buckets of water down the hole.

A second flight of stairs led to an L-shaped rooftop. The top of the staircase was covered with wooden planks and plastic sheets, but water trickled down inside the building whenever it rained. An old truck tyre and some junk had been put on top of this ramshackle structure to prevent it from blowing away with the wind. On the rooftop, the floor was made of bare concrete: inhabitants called it '*la dalle*' (the slab). Partially surrounded by taller buildings, the rooftop was exposed to Rabat's humid weather. In the summer, it was scorching hot. The first part of the L-shaped rooftop was crisscrossed with wires, over which migrants hung their laundry. There was some basic cooking paraphernalia (plastic cups and plates, pots, and gas bottles), scattered near a single tap. That part of the terrace was usually occupied by a cook, running an informal restaurant, and his customers, who sat on wooden crates from the market, gas bottles, and a broken bed frame. The terrace was the centre of gravity for life in the ghetto. It was most lively in the early morning, when people were having breakfast (Cameroonian doughnuts and spicy beans) before heading to *château* to look for work, and in the evening, when those who had found work returned. Migrants would gather to chat, play cards, exchange information, laugh, and argue. During the day, it could be very quiet. On the second part of the rooftop, there were some mats, a mattress, and a couple of blankets, often tucked away behind a metal sheet during the day to make space. Some of the inhabitants slept there. During the summer, many sought the coolness of the rooftop slab at night, but winter was tough, and those allocated a place on the rooftop only had a large blue plastic sheet hanging over them, to shield them from the rain.

Inhabitants came to this ghetto after entering Morocco via Oujda or after a failed crossing attempt. Some knew of its existence from word of mouth before arriving in Rabat. Others were taken to the 'Black neighbourhood' by taxi drivers, and the migrants they met directed them from *château* to ghettoes. These were usually organised by nationality, but not always. Adventurers explained that it was important for people who 'understood one another' to stay together, including across nationalities (see Chapter 6).

Most of the inhabitants of *l'ambassade* were francophone Cameroonians, but there were also migrants from the Central African Republic and Niger, as well as francophone Nigerians. Although Blaise, from the Central African Republic, was sometimes critical of 'noisy' Cameroonians, he often talked of cultural affinities amongst Central Africans. The fact that Cameroon and the Central African Republic 'shared a border' was one reason he gave for his brief stay in *l'ambassade*. A shared ethnicity could also be a reason to cohabit, as in a transnational ghetto of Fula migrants that I visited in Douar Hajja with Idrissa.

L'ambassade's building was only inhabited by migrants. Adventurers used the term 'ghetto' for spaces (a whole or part of a building) where a large number of migrants lived together. Their organisation could differ greatly. These spaces were continuously inhabited by generations of migrants staying for various lengths of time. Ghettoes can be found along migratory routes and not only in Morocco (Traoré and Le Dantec, 2012). *L'ambassade* was rumoured to be one of the oldest in Douar Hajja, continuously occupied since at least 2006. There were many people, but it was impossible to get an exact figure. The first time I visited, in early summer 2012, Alex estimated the number of inhabitants at thirty. But, in the summer, more adventurers travelled to the borderlands, for days or weeks. Ismael explained that his room on the first floor hosted around six people, but over twice this number in winter. For Ismael, *l'ambassade* was 'a place to sleep in while you wait and think about new horizons'. People rested, tended their wounds, and looked for money before returning to forests near the Spanish enclaves. People pointed to the uncertainty over the number of people living in *l'ambassade* as another sign of the overall 'disorder' Yasser was failing to keep under control.

Overcrowding was a health hazard. Migrants strove to keep their accommodations clean, but the buildings were unsanitary and in dire need of repair. Skin conditions (e.g. scabies) could repeatedly spread as people travelled back and forth to the forest camps. Repeated exposure to treatments also lessened their efficacy. There were also cases of tuberculosis, linked to health issues amongst the Moroccan population in marginal neighbourhoods. Although it was another important reason for improving migrants' living conditions, NGOs were careful not to talk of a 'public health issue', which could feed into discriminatory and repressive public discourse. Access to healthcare for the migrants overall was inadequate. Charitable organisations like Caritas could not remedy state shortcomings in the provision of healthcare (including for the Moroccan population in these neighbourhoods). Getting wounded or ill entailed expenses that migrants could often not cover alone, relying on help from friends and families, but also people they lived with.

Staying together in large numbers kept contributions towards rent low. Ismael, Fabien, and others each paid 150 dirhams monthly towards the rent. Joining the ghetto also involved an *'intégration'* fee, a one-off sum of 200 dirhams for *l'ambassade*, paid by newly arrived inhabitants when they decided to stay, *'pour s'intégrer'* (to integrate themselves). The integration money was set as a contribution towards the meagre 'materials' (mattresses, blankets, etc.) that migrants used. It bought the right to use the materials already accumulated by former and current tenants and contributed to replacing or buying new items for the benefit of all in the room. Water and electricity bills were divided at the end of the month amongst the inhabitants of *l'ambassade*.

Money was paid to the chief of ghetto. The rent was a fixed amount, but people moved in and out, so the money raised by the chief of ghetto fluctuated every month. It is not clear what the monthly rent for the overall building was exactly. A few people living there mentioned several thousand Moroccan dirhams, which did not reflect the state of the building. Prices paid by migrants to their Moroccan landlords (but also sometimes in shops) were opportunistically inflated. Discussing money matters with adventurers was more difficult than talking about border-crossing tactics. Yasser often gave confusing information or refused to answer my questions. Other men in *l'ambassade* and other ghettoes explained that being the chief was an advantageous position, from which experienced migrants could expect to draw some economic benefit. How much depended on the place, the number of people, arrangements with the landlord, and whether the person in charge was good at the job. People doubted Yasser made much money. He was seen as incompetent, but nobody seemed to envy his position. He was responsible for paying the rent regardless of how many people had paid him. This required good management skills, keeping the landlord and the inhabitants happy and regularly finding new occupants to cover the rent.

There were 'room chiefs' who reported to Yasser. Besides paying up what one owed, there was a simple set of rules. People should not steal from, or fight with, one another, or else they would have to pay a penalty, set at one-thousand dirhams.[2] Nobody remembered it being enforced: it was meant as a deterrent. Ostracising those who 'fostered disorder' was a common strategy, to avoid conflicts within the house and prevent issues with Moroccan neighbours, which could bring about more serious problems with the police. Another duty was to maintain cleanliness at tolerable levels. In other places, the chief of ghetto set up a cleaning rota, but in *l'ambassade*, Yasser could not get people to do their chores. Things got worse when the water and electricity were cut off.

The role of chief was usually the prerogative of the person who had lived in the ghetto the longest. Such people were referred to as *'les anciens'* (the elders). It was not age but longevity within the house which conferred authority to chiefs of ghettoes. This was similar in informal forest camps, where hierarchy and discipline were important features of self-organisation, especially in large settings (Laacher, 2007; Traoré and Le Dantec, 2012). Whenever the person in charge of a ghetto in Douar Hajja or Maâdid left Morocco, the next in line would take over. People fondly recalled Yasser's predecessor, a Cameroonian man described as tough but fair, unlike Yasser, who was lonesome and belligerent and started fights himself. He was not respected because he was said to not respect others. Beyond personal flaws, his loose grip on the other inhabitants of *l'ambassade* was indicative of a decline in the hierarchical and authoritarian housing arrangements typical of the 2000s (see Alioua, 2007). Back then, people often hardly left the ghettoes, and chiefs held a tighter grip on residents. But since then, the number of migrants had risen in urban centres, as they sought to escape repression in the borderlands, and in the 2010s and early 2020s, they could more easily rent houses or circulate in the city than in the previous decades (albeit not without risk).

Another large ghetto that I visited daily in Douar Hajja was called *le consulat*. The building was split into different sections. Men from the Ivory Coast, and a few from other Western African countries, lived on the ground floor, Cameroonians stayed on the first floor, and Guineans lived on the second floor, in a room adjacent to the landlords' section. *Le consulat* was located deeper in Douar Hajja, along a narrow street running uphill from the market. Behind the metal front door of the building, there was a bare concrete flight of stairs and a wooden door that opened on to the ground-floor flat. The door had been repeatedly patched up, with ill-fitting wooden panels, following violent break-ins by the police and other intruders. There was a hole big enough to fit someone's head above the useless lock. There were no windows, and it smelled of damp and humidity. The only natural light came from the bedroom at the back, where part of the concrete slab in the ceiling had been left unfinished or smashed. There were similar openings all the way to the rooftop, from which daylight filtered to the ground floor, albeit dimly.

Pipes leaked from the basic toilet, located under the staircase, into the central room, a rectangular fifteen-square-metre room with dirty tiles patterned with brown and yellow squares. The central room was littered with rubbish, soaked in a semi-permanent puddle. In the middle stood a large concrete pillar, around which were arranged some gas bottles, a few pots, and some wooden crates on which to sit. There were three small bedrooms. A fourth room, much smaller, was the only one with a padlock. This was where the Ivoirian 'chief of foyer' slept. The Ivoirian men called their flat a foyer rather than a ghetto.[3] They associated the term ghetto with noise and disorder and stressed that, unlike *l'ambassade*, they lived 'in harmony' and were 'equal'. Though there were issues too, *le consulat* was quieter than *l'ambassade*. The Ivoirian men drew a distinction, but 'foyer' and 'ghetto' were often used interchangeably to describe similar overcrowded, unsanitary, and derelict buildings.

The bedrooms contained a few small, worn-out mattresses that lined the walls. There was a broken TV and some clothing and cream lotions were tucked between the mattresses. The number of inhabitants varied. There were typically many more people than single mattresses. Moussa and others paid 200 dirhams as a one-off 'integration fee' and 150 dirhams for the rent. Aboubacar was the chief of foyer, often referred to as the '*responsable*' (the person in charge). There was a '*propriétaire de ghetto*' (ghetto owner), an Ivoirian man who lived away from Douar Hajja and was responsible for negotiating terms with the landlord. Aboubacar was responsible for the day-to-day overseeing of the foyer, collecting rent on behalf of the Ivoirian 'owner'. As is often the case, pecuniary arrangements were unclear. The migrant 'owner' was making some money from the people living in the foyer, though probably not much. It was not clear what Aboubacar was making out of it other than, I was told, living rent-free. If he made anything, it was probably little, as he spent every day working as a street cobbler outside the building.

Life became more complicated when the landlord, who had money issues, became even greedier and started interfering with the running of the foyer. He started collecting money directly. Aboubacar obtained refugee status and received support from the UNHCR to move to a different neighbourhood. Nobody wanted to take over his position and the situation became untenable, especially after inhabitants of the building were assaulted by a neighbour (see Chapter 7). All the men on the ground floor fled, as they were the most exposed to outside threats. Moussa and a few of his roommates found a smaller room elsewhere.

The permanent closure of *l'ambassade* and this forced departure from *le consulat* were a blow for their inhabitants and other migrants. *L'ambassade*, especially, was an established meeting point in the neighbourhood. In both cases, the escalation of violence, as disputes with landlords increased and relationships soured with some of the neighbours, was far from unexpected. Migrants had come to experience brutal intrusions in the places where they lived as an unsurprising, though intolerable, part of their daily life in Douar Hajja. They talked of '*clochards*' storming into their rooms, holding machetes, and of policemen chasing them from *château* all the way into their accommodations.

After *l'ambassade* was permanently closed, some former occupants, who had moved into the building opposite, continued to sit by the entrance, reminiscing about their memories of the old ghetto. Spending time together in large ghettoes and foyers, migrants faced the boredom and violence of their lives in Morocco together. They helped one another and shared what they had, within limits (see Chapter 6). The Ivoirian men in *le consulat* pulled together their resources to cook a daily meal for everyone, regardless of what they had contributed. These confined spaces entailed forms of forced intimacy. My questions about the lack of privacy amongst migrants sharing narrow mattresses were met with embarrassed laughter. Moussa stressed that it was a bit 'troublesome' to share a bed with other people, but he had to accept it. He could not afford to pay 600 dirhams to move into a room by himself. There were never any allusions to intimate relationships, besides friendships. Per their account, they laughed a lot together and talked. Migrants did not only share information and devise plans for border-crossing attacks, they shared dreams for the future and memories of their home countries. Some people came from the same cities and even from the same neighbourhoods.

But there were also conflicts and disputes. Before the intrusion, some people left *l'ambassade* complaining of 'noise' and 'disorder', fighting, arguing, and stealing. A few remembered fondly an era when discipline and order reigned in ghettoes. Most migrants were leaving those overcrowded buildings because of the poor living conditions and to escape the previously mentioned issues. While hoping for a successful crossing and a future life that would be more bearable, they also aspired to better housing conditions for their increasingly long stays in Douar Hajja.

This is not home

Souleyman and his roommates had escaped hierarchical living arrangements in a large foyer of 'Fula [*peuhl*] migrants' in Douar Hajja. Souleyman stressed how much he had 'suffered' in this 'dirty foyer'. He pointed out that the inhabitants, despite sharing the same ethnicity, came from different backgrounds. Some came from cities, others from the countryside. They did not always get along. The people who had been there the longest and were in charge ('*les anciens*') treated others 'like slaves'. Souleyman and his friends preferred 'to struggle and pay 700 dirhams' for their own room in Maâdid, rather than 'face a whole lot of problems in a foyer', where the only advantage was a cheaper individual share of the rent.

In Douar Hajja and Maâdid, migrants who could afford it often left or avoided hierarchical housing arrangements in overcrowded buildings. They rented single rooms with a smaller number of migrants, where the central figure of the chief of ghetto had usually disappeared or was limited to the appointment of someone based on their skills (and not just on longevity) for dealing with practical matters (e.g. liaising with the landlord). Living arrangements, the viability of those buildings, and the amount migrants paid for rent varied greatly. Confusingly, some migrants still referred to these smaller accommodations as ghettoes and foyers.

Ibrahima, a Guinean man who worked as a carpenter in a workshop located a few metres away from *l'ambassade*, lived in Maâdid in a well-kept but decrepit ground-floor, three-bedroom flat. One room was occupied by Malians only, another by Senegalese. Ibrahima lived in the third room with Senegalese and Guinean migrants. Ibrahima and his companions had left a large ghetto that housed mostly Malian migrants, where they had been very unhappy with the living conditions, especially the behaviour of the people in charge. He referred to the whole ground-floor flat where he lived as a 'foyer' but stressed that nobody was formally in charge, and that the Malian men had separate arrangements when it came to food and other matters. Ibrahima did not like being called 'a chief', but that title was sometimes jokingly bestowed on him by his roommates. He had more experience and could speak Moroccan Arabic, which he had learned thanks to his job where he worked closely with Moroccan woodworkers. He was the one who dealt with the landlord on behalf of the people in his own room and of the Senegalese in the other room. Because he was deemed a fair and hardworking man, the other men living in the flat looked up to him and sought his advice on many issues.

In smaller accommodations, the words 'ghetto' and 'foyer' were often no longer used, especially as people had taken steps to move away, despite the extra expense. In Idrissa's room, where there was barely enough space for two single mattresses next to each other and a TV, the three Burkinabé migrants living together would often scornfully deride places like *l'ambassade* and *le consulat*. They ridiculed other migrants, often on the basis of their nationality (especially Cameroonians), for living in dirty ghettoes where people argued constantly. Idrissa would stress that, in his room, they simply lived together, sharing the costs equally and having occasional mundane arguments over whose turn it should be to clean the room. Communication with the landlord was handled by Papou, the Burkinabé man who had been in the room the longest. When I referred to him as the 'room chief', Idrissa corrected me, insisting that there was no chief in their room. The apartment they stayed in had a second room, occupied by Guineans with whom they were usually on good terms and who had their own arrangement with the landlord. There was also a small kitchen and a shared living room. The flat was much larger than most of the accommodations I had visited in Douar Hajja and was unusual in having a spare living room which was not formally occupied by other migrants.

As inhabitants in *l'ambassade* sensed that they were about to lose the building for good, many preferred to look around for smaller rooms, if they could afford it, before losing everything in yet another raid. Alain, with his friend Roméo and two other Cameroonians, moved to a very narrow room, which they took great pains to keep tidy. It was located in a shabby building solely occupied by migrants, who lived in separate rooms. The landlord's elderly and alcoholic uncle also lived there. His room was next to the basic lavatory, with just a tap and a hole. Migrants complained that he would peep whenever female migrants, who lived in the building or were visiting, were inside the lavatory. Fabien moved with his cousin and another Cameroorian man from *l'ambassade* into a much nicer room, of about nine square metres, which could be locked, and where the walls had been freshly repainted. There were new, bright tiles, and a small window offered enough natural light. The building, owned by a Moroccan teacher who lived on one of the upper floors, had recently been refurbished. Before accessing Fabien's room, there was a metal door, with a lock, that led to a small lobby, shared with a Cameroonian woman who was living on her own. This was not uncommon: several migrants preferred to live on their own, despite the costs, especially women and older people. Blaise, for example, explained that living alone was the only way to avoid disrespect from other younger, male migrants. Small rooms were sometimes decorated and personalised, in contrast to ghettoes, which are usually littered with broken objects. Migrants installed curtains, made lampshades for the electric bulbs out of recycled materials, and put posters up on the walls to cover holes. Some had laptops and other electronics. But migrants regularly lost all their possessions because of police raids, break-ins, and evictions.

Fabien explained that it had become easier, in comparison to the 2000s, to negotiate directly with Moroccan landlords to get a room, without having to rely on one 'ghetto owner' with connections. Sometimes, migrants solicited the help of a local Moroccan *simsar* (an unregulated broker who connects tenants and owners). But moving into a place that did not look as grim and dirty as *l'ambassade* was not cheap, and the average price for smaller rooms had risen. Fabien pointed out that, in 2011, people could pay 500 dirhams a month and have a decent small room, but in 2013, although there seemed to be more rooms available, one would only get 'a filthy hole' for that price. Migrants needed to spend at least 600 or 700 dirhams. In the overcrowded neighbourhood of Douar Hajja, there was a finite number of accommodations available for migrants, but also for Moroccans who struggled to find a place to live and could be priced out, as landlords sought higher rents from migrants. In winter especially, finding a place in Douar Hajja was harder, with people returning from the forests. Staff at Caritas explained that they were struggling to find suitable places for migrants in this neighbourhood. They had criteria for the kind of housing they would help migrants secure. Adventurers looking for a place without any support were less selective, but they still struggled to find a place.

With a limited number of accommodations available, migrants often rotated between the same places. Souleyman moved into the room previously shared by Idrissa, Papou, and Alpha. Before Idrissa left, we looked through a pile of worn-out clothes and junk in a corner of the flat. We found some identity documents that belonged to other Western African migrants, who had lived there before. Nobody in the flat knew who they were, or where they could be. After Moussa and his friends moved out of *le consulat* (see Chapter 7), they brought me to their new place. It was a dingy room where Alex and some others had lived shortly following the closure of *l'ambassade*. Alex had quickly moved out, complaining that the landlords' son living upstairs had leprosy and that, following the amputation of one of his legs, his parents would bring him downstairs to stay next to the migrants' room, so that the pus dripping from his stump would not soil their house upstairs. Alex and the others, disgusted by this and by the overall unsanitary conditions in the building, quickly packed up and left. Often, leaving a place that was squalid, or where the Moroccan landlord was abusive, only made space for other migrants to move in. Adventurers complained about '*tourner en rond*' (going around in circles) in Morocco and always facing the same violence, hardship, and suffering. Migrants' crisscross movements within the neighbourhood itself, to find suitable accommodation, mirrored their overall confined and constrained mobility, as they went back and forth between the borderlands and Rabat, trying to reach 'the objective'.

Smaller rooms were often deemed safer than large ghettoes, as they attracted less attention from police raids and were often padlocked against thieves. But migrants remained vulnerable to greedy landlords, and the threat of assault by other people in the neighbourhood persisted. When Moussa moved into his next room with two Cameroonian men, at the back of Douar Hajja, he shared his relief at having finally found a place that was significantly less run down than *le consulat* and the other places he had lived in after leaving the big foyer. Half-joking, he proudly told me that he had finally started to '*prendre son indépendance*' (assume his independence). Moving into smaller and more decent accommodation, even if he was still planning trips to the borderlands, was a significant step towards the realisation of his life and migratory projects. But his joy was short-lived, and he continued to face obstacles. In 2014, on a short trip to see informants in Morocco, I visited Moussa after he had received refugee status and moved to a better flat, in a modest residential area away from Douar Hajja. His disillusion with Morocco, and with the life he led, had reached new depths, and he focused on leaving, with the help of the resettlement programme. He was eventually relocated to the USA after a few years. Leaving ghettoes and foyers did not liberate adventurers from the dangers and obstacles they had faced. Many dangers continued to lurk on the narrow 'corridors' of Douar Hajja, when adventurers walked to and from *château* in the early morning and evening. The period during which my informants moved to smaller accommodations in Douar Hajja in 2013 was marked by a significant increase in police raids on migrants in marginal neighbourhoods. Attacks by people from the neighbourhoods were common and resulted in a number of very serious (and sometimes lethal) incidents.

Adventurers referred to smaller accommodations as their bedrooms (*chambres*) but also often used the French word '*maison*', which means both house and home. However, adventurers often stumbled over the ambiguous meaning of this term in the context of Douar Hajja and Maâdid, stressing that they were not, and did not feel, 'at home' in Morocco. Standing on the street outside her informal restaurant, the 'owner', Christine, a Cameroonian woman, was chatting with Alex and I. Both of them casually referred to the restaurant as '*maison*', until Christine stopped Alex and exclaimed: '*À la maison* [at home]? Leave it, this is not my *maison*, my *maison* is in Cameroon, not here.'

As adventurers sought to reach the objective, they attempted to make their lives more comfortable in the present. In the ghettoes where they lived, they shared memories of their past lives in their home countries with other migrants, who were often co-nationals. Some voiced a desire to return to their home countries after reaching Europe, but as explored before, their journeys were uncertain and did not follow a straight line. Contrary to the pervasive 'myth of return', home was not simply associated with a fixed place, located in a distant past migrants longed to return to. Neither was home the materialisation of some rootless, cosmopolitan ideal. Indeed, nationality remained an important criterion, as migrants often sought other adventurers from the same country to share a room with.

Exploring the housing spaces of migrants in Douar Hajja underscores the uncertainty of migrants' lives and how their efforts to make their lives 'more bearable' were constrained by wider social forces, regulating who can move, where, and how. As I visited *le consulat* in spring 2013 to meet up with some of its inhabitants, I found most people standing outside after an 'attack' on their foyer (see Chapter 7). The already patched-up wooden door of the ground-floor flat laid battered and useless on the narrow street. As I approached, one of the Ivoirian men pointed to the door and asked me angrily: 'Do you call this a home?' After he left *l'ambassade*, Fabien would often refer to the room he shared with his cousin and another Cameroonian man as '*maison*' when inviting me to come over. But he would protest whenever I used the term too, sucking his teeth and calling out to me: '*Quelle maison?*' (What home?).

In July 2013, Fabien and some of his friends grew increasingly worried about the health of Doris, a Cameroonian woman who had been a regular visitor at *l'ambassade*. One of the men living in the ghetto was her boyfriend. She had been living in the forests near Nador for several months and was heavily pregnant. After much back and forth on the phone, Fabien and a few others eventually convinced her to come back to Rabat and get some help, as her health was deteriorating. Fabien's neighbour, a Cameroonian woman, offered to keep Doris in her room for just a few days, while arrangements were made for a longer-term solution, with the help of humanitarian organisations. As Fabien and I reached the building to greet Doris after her arrival, we found the Moroccan landlady downstairs, in the midst of a vociferous argument with her tenants. She wanted to kick Doris out. She stressed that the building was not a hotel and that visitors were not allowed.

Doris, Fabien, his cousin, and his neighbour pleaded with the landlady. Tension kept escalating and strong words were exchanged between the tenants, who protested at being treated like animals, and the landlady, who sternly shouted at them to step back into their individual rooms. Fabien attempted to emphasise the exceptional circumstances Doris found herself in, calling out the landlady's behaviour by implying that she would not leave a 'Moroccan sister' out on the streets that way. He explained that Doris had only just arrived after a long journey and was simply resting for a few days before moving on. The landlady insisted that she could be in trouble with the police if Doris gave birth in the building and the baby was unwell. She told a story about a migrant who had left her babies with her Moroccan landlord to purchase some milk and never came back. If (part of) the story was true, the mother may well have been arrested and deported, rather than willingly abandoning her children. Eventually, Doris left, in tears, and went to a nearby ghetto in Douar Hajja. Shortly after, she delivered the baby overnight, with the help of another Cameroonian woman, who ran an informal restaurant nearby.

After Doris left, I took Fabien away for a walk, as he was getting increasingly furious and agitated. We walked to a nearby café. There, he continued to loudly complain about life in Morocco, ignoring in his anger the Moroccan men sitting around us, staring. 'This is a fake country with fake people. We have been tied up here in Morocco. It is witchcraft.' He contrasted his inability to have a decent life and make a home in Morocco with the lives of migrants from Morocco and other 'Arab countries' who resided in Cameroon and other sub-Saharan countries: '*Chez nous* [at ours], they are comfortable.'

We were joined by Moussa, who was returning from a meeting with other adventurers. He was due to travel to the borderlands with them but their plan was no longer viable. The friends they wanted to join, along with another five hundred people, had just stormed the fences around Melilla in one large-scale attempt. About a hundred migrants were successful. Moussa was frustrated that he had not left earlier and that he now needed to delay his departure to the borderlands for a while, since he expected security would be ramped up there. As he excitedly related to us what he had heard about the crossing and clash with the border guards, Moussa burned my hand pouring mint tea. Fabien came out of his silent, angry torpor and sarcastically observed: 'it is a shame you are not Moroccan and that he has not poured the whole burning teapot on your hand'. This display of anger and frustration from Fabien was not surprising in the face of the injustice and violence that prevented him from moving freely and attaining the life he aspired to. Douar Hajja, Moussa and Fabien agreed, was not a place to call home. As we observed the comings and goings of street sellers and inhabitants returning to Takaddoum and Douar Hajja at the end of the day, Moussa and Fabien talked some more about the impossibility of getting a decent place to live and about their constantly thwarted efforts to leave Morocco. We made a plan to go to a nice beach, further south of Rabat, by bus the following Sunday, to get away from Douar Hajja. I was tired and told them I would 'go home', back to my flat on the other side of Rabat. Moussa smirked and chuckled: 'What should the *clandestins* do then? We will go back too.'

Conclusion

In Douar Hajja and Maâdid, mobility regimes had cornered adventurers into derelict buildings, where living conditions were gruelling, and migrants were subjected to exploitative practices by landlords hoping to maximise their profit on the backs of those vulnerable tenants. Such spaces offered very little respite and protection from violent break-ins by police and other intruders. Migrants pulled resources to bring down the cost of living and supported one another through the violence and boredom of their everyday lives, helping each other maintain 'the right mentality'. Places like *l'ambassade* and *le consulat* show the transformative character of social life in spaces of exception, as further illustrated in discussions of migrant businesses and political organisations (see Chapters 5 and 8). In Chapter 6, I explore in more detail how boundaries such as nationality could become porous, as adventurers forged relationships and supported one another across those boundaries. But migrant accommodations were ambiguous spaces, where exclusion and exploitation also took place. The hierarchies and discipline in large ghettoes and foyers, often justified with references to traditional forms of authority in countries of origin (e.g. the elders), could be very coercive and exploitative. But the grip of chiefs of ghettoes on other migrants significantly decreased throughout the 2010s.

Those who could afford it sought to move into smaller rooms and housing arrangements that they were often reluctant to call 'home'. A focus on living spaces in Douar Hajja sheds light on adventurers' ambiguous and fragile anchoring in the neighbourhood, and in Morocco more generally. They sought to make their present living arrangements in Rabat more tolerable, while they searched for 'the objective' and organised border-crossing attempts. As the length of their stay in Douar Hajja increased, migrants often sought to move into smaller accommodation, where they would be more comfortable. But evictions, arrests, assaults, and deportations remained constant threats. Migrants' housing and living arrangements were organised in the margins of the Moroccan state, which regulated their capacity to move and cross borders, as well as their opportunities to emplace themselves in Douar Hajja. As discussed in Chapter 2, some adventurers envisaged staying in Morocco, if 'the conditions' were right for the realisation of their objective. But home-making practices remained constrained by Moroccan authorities and a plethora of actors, such as landlords and neighbours, with whom migrants had ambivalent relationships, marked by racism but also forms of solidarity and mutual recognition (see Chapter 7). In the next chapter, I further explore migrants' ambiguous anchoring in the neighbourhood by examining the multiplication of businesses set up by some enterprising adventurers in Douar Hajja, usually in the ghettoes and rooms where they slept.

Notes

1. *Black Hawk Down* is the title of a Hollywood war movie set in Mogadishu, which was partially shot around Rabat. There was a rumour that some adventurers from Douar Hajja were employed as extras.
2. Around £72 at the time.
3. *Foyer* means 'hearth' in French and is used to refer to a family home, as well as places that house numerous people (e.g. migrant workers, students, etc.).

Adventurers in Douar Hajja and Maâdid: a photo essay

Figure 1 Buildings in Douar Hajja and Maâdid

Figure 2 Two men playing games in a Malian ghetto

Figure 3 Ivoirian migrants cooking a communal meal on the ground floor of *le consulat*

Adventurers in Douar Hajja and Maâdid

Figure 4 An inscription in the Cameroonian ghetto *l'ambassade*: 'suffering is a school of'

Figure 5 Bedroom of Ivoirian men in *le consulat*

Figure 6 A Cameroonian barber in Douar Hajja

Figure 7 Bags and an inflatable boat in a Malian ghetto

Adventurers in Douar Hajja and Maâdid

Figure 8 A Cameroonian woman in her informal restaurant

Figure 9 Makeshift gym on a rooftop in Douar Hajja

5

Adventurous entrepreneurs

On Fridays, the hustle and bustle of market life in Douar Hajja and Maâdid peaked in the run-up to the *jumu'ah* prayer. Inhabitants, especially women, scurried around the stalls to buy missing ingredients for the family meal. Groups of men chattered, on their way to and from the mosque, while hundreds of pressure cookers hissed in unison to announce couscous dishes would soon be ready. Once the scraping sounds of food getting dished out subsided, the whole neighbourhood grew quiet, its tranquillity only interrupted by televisions. Until children started to trickle outside to play, loudly reclaiming the alleyways. I often spent Fridays at Christine's informal restaurant, which she had set up in her minuscule, ground-floor flat. She lived there with her baby daughter, who was born in Douar Hajja. I waited for other informants to turn up, while Christine fried fish and cooked rice at a slower pace. Her regular customers, mostly Cameroonian migrants from *l'ambassade* and other ghettoes in the neighbourhood, came later than usual on Fridays.

Some of my informants were reluctant to disclose their whereabouts on that particular day of the week. Alain eventually confided that he, along with a few companions, occasionally hung out on the other side of Rabat, by the Chouhada mosque and its impressive cemetery overlooking the Atlantic Ocean. They picked weeds around the graves and watered plants: 'People give you money, two dirhams, twenty, or ten. Some nice people even give fifty dirhams. It depends on the day and the people, on the weather.' Adventurers called begging '*fissabila*',[1] or '*taper salām*'.[2] Black men and women begging, sometimes accompanied by children, or aided by crutches (evidence of their recent arrival from the borderlands), were a visible presence in the city. They sat along busy roads or stood by traffic lights, especially in the city centre.

Adventurers openly discussed begging as necessary to their survival in the borderlands. In the forest camps, they said they lived 'like animals' taking turns walking to urban centres to scavenge for food in the bins and beg. But in Rabat, my informants were ashamed to discuss begging, even though many occasionally resorted to it. Support from families back home (e.g. via Western Union transfers) was limited, but begging did not fit with their narratives and self-depictions as courageous adventurers. One Ivoirian man from *le consulat* stressed that he had 'never begged in [his] life, ever'. Looking embarrassed, he emphatically added that he did not even know 'how to do it'. A Congolese man in Maâdid confided that he had spent two years sleeping on the streets in Rabat and begging: 'Deep down in my heart, I was ashamed, but how can you live?' Adventurers stressed that they never imagined they would have to beg when they took the road. Alain exclaimed: 'If someone had told me in my country that I would be doing this [in Morocco], I would have refused. But here, there is no work, and with this, you can survive two days.' Highlighting the importance adventurers gave to the decisions they could take amidst uncertain and precarious conditions, he stressed that, on Fridays, he had to decide whether to look for work, with little chance of getting anything, or go into town and be almost assured to bring back a few dirhams, despite the risk of arrest and deportation.

In *l'ambassade*, my informants argued that adventurers could not afford 'to fall asleep' and 'be lazy'. They mocked those who begged, especially if they seemed healthy, for not having the 'right mentality'. Begging was said to be 'hereditary' amongst Moroccan people and not something adventurers should stoop to. Basil, a Cameroonian man who paid for his meals at Christine's with money collected by begging around Douar Hajja, was mocked by some other customers for getting 'easy money'. Basil had lost a leg and broken the other in the borderlands. In Douar Hajja, he worried about getting mugged each time he painstakingly made his way along the steep alleyways on his second-hand wheelchair, donated by a charity. Others counselled him 'to go home', but Basil ignored them, hoping to attempt crossing again once his leg healed. It was better to 'have to beg and die trying to cross the border' than to 'return home empty-handed and crippled'.

Natan, who co-owned an informal restaurant opposite *l'ambassade*, argued that those begging were 'belittling' themselves. Talking about his business, he explained that it was important for adventurers to demonstrate that they can 'succeed' if they 'fight'. Adventurers set up informal businesses in Douar Hajja and Maâdid. Such businesses (e.g. restaurants, hair salons) did not last long, as adventurers moved in and out of the neighbourhood, crossed into Europe, or returned home. They provided their owners with a source of income and were important spaces of socialisation for young migrant men whose everyday lives were marked by violence as well as boredom. For Ruben, a Cameroonian migrant who set up a cyber (internet access business), investing one's efforts and time into such informal businesses might enable migrants to reach their objective in Morocco. Yet, businesses did not thrive. Entrepreneurial adventurers dropped everything when enough money was earned to fund their next trip. Economic integration within the neighbourhood was limited, and the range of customers usually restrained to other (irregular) Black migrants with little resources.

In this chapter, I explore the precarious anchoring of migrants in Douar Hajja and Maâdid through a focus on work, especially migrant businesses. Adventurers aspired to leave the neighbourhood (and Morocco altogether) but were an important part of its socio-economic life, although their participation was marked by abuse and exploitation (see also Chapter 7). Work opportunities were usually confined to the informal sector (e.g. construction sites), on which adventurers' Moroccan neighbours were also largely reliant. Working conditions were arduous, prompting many to try and carve out opportunities for themselves. This entrepreneurial spirit was articulated as part of the adventure's moral impetus to look for oneself and goes against common depictions of irregular migrants as unskilled profiteering hordes.

Bordering processes create lucrative opportunities for numerous actors and institutions (Rodier, 2012; Andersson, 2014; Cabot, 2019), including through the absorption of (irregular) migrants into exploitative labour regimes. The border is a device which holds more than the promise to spectacularly exclude those without the right of entry or the means to prove it (De Genova, 2005; Mezzadra and Neilson, 2013). As deportable populations, irregular migrants are routinely subjected to the state and 'its sovereign power to exclude, even while it incorporates them' (De Genova and Peultz, 2010: 15). Focusing on processes of inclusive exclusion offers valuable insights into the exploitation of Black migrants. Adventurers formed a readily available pool of disposable labour. But it is important to make sense of how adventurers also developed informal, entrepreneurial ventures (Pickerill, 2011).

Focusing on adventurers' informal businesses does not minimise their economic exploitation at the hand of wider processes through which 'borders regulate and structure the relations between capital, labor, law, subjects, and political power' (Mezzadra and Nielson, 2013: 8). It exemplifies how the lives and journeys of adventurers break through labels and categories. Some adventurers presented themselves as businessmen. The literature on entrepreneurship has been predominantly elitist (Valenzuela, 2001), with a focus on innovation, ownership, and capital. Adventurers may not fit common representations of entrepreneurs as heroes targeted by preferential migration policies that seek to attract recognised forms of talent and innovation (Ojo *et al.*, 2013). Nevertheless, adventurers' discussion of '*la débrouillardise*' (resourcefulness), in the face of obstacles, speaks to wider discussions of entrepreneurship (Misra and Kumar, 2000).

In anthropology, there is a long-standing tradition of examining migrants' economic initiatives, including within the informal economy, as entrepreneurship. Hart's discussion of small-scale entrepreneurs in Ghana does not refer to 'businessmen in the Western sense ... but rather to anyone who controls the management of capital which he has invested in some enterprise in order to realize profit' (1970: 107). Entrepreneurship is not a straightforward notion, and scholars focused on this field of study have called for its extension 'beyond the mythology of Western bourgeois capitalism, beyond the image of the entrepreneur as a fixed economic actor with a most amiable character' (Rehn and Talas, 2004: 156), stressing the need for an anthropological sensitivity in the study of economic behaviour.

The existing informal economy and 'multiple forms of exclusion' (Ojo et al., 2013: 605) encouraged migrants to launch entrepreneurial ventures in Morocco.[3] The increasing visibility of cultural and economic businesses run by migrants from sub-Saharan Africa in Moroccan cities can be seen as a reflection of important mutations within Moroccan society, through the discreet but efficient mobilisation of a metropolitan Africanity with cosmopolitan intent (Infantino, 2011). This might be the case for a growing number of spaces marked by cosmopolitan connections stretching across the European and African continents and occupied by middle-class students, NGO workers, activists, researchers, and other (temporary) residents of Moroccan cities (e.g. Casablanca) meeting to drink, eat, and dance. Alongside the transformative character of migrants' ghettoes, the business ventures opened by migrants in Douar Hajja and Maâdid demonstrate the fragility of these new socio-economic and cultural connections forged in postcolonial Morocco.

Forced labour

Those who had been lucky and found work at *château* returned to *l'ambassade* in the evening to sit uncomfortably on gas bottles and broken pieces of furniture, flustered and worn out: '*Du travail forcé* [forced labour], that is all that we, Blacks, are offered here.' They massaged their aching limbs and vented their frustration, while munching on Cameroonian *beignets* (doughnuts) prepared by Hervé, who operated his cooking business from a corner of the rooftop. Adventurers' bodies were cut, bruised, and broken because of violence in the borderlands but also because of harsh working conditions. 'Work in Morocco means death for us,' people repeated in ghettoes. Adventurers discussed working conditions as akin to 'slavery'. When a Cameroonian man died from an aneurism in his sleep, others in Douar Hajja blamed working conditions on construction sites for his death.

Adventurers came out of their ghettoes and reached the crossroad by *château* on Avenue Al Haouz, a spot nicknamed *chad*, as early as 6am.[4] They waited for work until midday, notwithstanding the risk of police raids, especially in the first few hours when there were more migrants around. Their numbers varied from a handful to sometimes well over seventy, depending on wider movement between Rabat and the borderlands. They were exclusively men. Women, who sometimes found work as domestic workers or nannies in Moroccan families (Lanza, 2011), did not stand near *château*. At the sight of a car or truck pulling over, many migrants would hurriedly gather on the edge of the pavement. Looking for docile and flexible workers (Kettani and Péraldi, 2011: 70), Moroccan bosses often selected migrants based on their physical characteristics (e.g. height or corpulence). That way, according to Moussa, 'they can exploit you the way they want'. Short and skinny, Moussa, like my Burkinabé informant Idrissa, was rarely selected. Some of my informants trained at home, building makeshift home gyms with discarded materials retrieved from construction sites, to stay fit, limit the risk of injury, and increase their chances of getting work. Strength-training, they stressed, was also good preparation for border-crossing attempts.

Like in other countries, such as Algeria, along the main migratory routes (Bureau, 2020), the jobs available to adventurers were essentially unskilled labour, on construction sites in Rabat or nearby towns (e.g. Temara), and sometimes in the agricultural sector. Other jobs included removals or maintenance (e.g. gardening) in villas within wealthier neighbourhoods (e.g. Hay Riad, Souissi). Daily wages varied. My informants usually reported earning between seventy and ninety dirhams a day, sometimes as much as a hundred dirhams or more, but often as low as forty or fifty for a long day of work.[5] There was little scope for negotiation, especially during impromptu pick-ups at the crowded place nicknamed *chad*. Low wages and overall precarious working conditions were also an issue for indigent Moroccan citizens (including those living in Douar Hajja and Maâdid), but migrants often complained that they were paid less than the Moroccan employees working alongside them. Adventurers were often hired to perform the most dangerous and arduous tasks on sites, and dismissed once these were over. Sometimes, bosses refused to pay wages, requesting to see valid passports and threatening to call the police. There was 'no light work for Blacks in Morocco'. Mohamoud, an Ivoirian man from *le consulat*, described adventurers' 'forced labour' as such:

> Forced labour is when you lift bags and boxes of tiles. When you carry stones that no man has the right to lift. '*Sīr, sīr mon ami* [go, go my friend].' Sweat dribbles on your back. They urge you to hurry up with the work. You are made to lift gravel. They call you and tell you to go pick up the stones downstairs

and carry them to the fifth floor, all day long, up and down the stairs. ... They make you lift things that machines only should carry. It cuts the arms. It breaks the feet. This is forced labour, the work done by Blacks in Morocco.

One of the Malian men living opposite *l'ambassade* explained that, in the face of constant abuse, adventurers needed to 'control their heart'. They needed to think carefully before pushing back against gruelling conditions and abusive employers. There was little chance of success and much to lose. Speaking Arabic was sometimes an asset as it could lead to less monotonous tasks, but it also meant a better understanding of (racist) abuse (see Chapter 7). Migrants needed to endure suffering and keep the right mentality at work as well (see Chapter 6). In *l'ambassade*, some Cameroonian men had strong words against adventurers spending too much time watching television, instead of looking for work: 'If people are lazy here [in Morocco], they will be lazy there [in Europe] too.' Difficult working conditions were described as an expected feature of the adventure. As a Cameroonian man put it to me, working hard would enable him to one day return home 'as a hero, a freeman, and not a thief'.

Most jobs lasted a few days only, but adventurers occasionally forged relationships with employers. They waited for phone calls at home, hoping to get better conditions than those waiting at *chad*. Such relationships varied. Some adventurers described benevolent yet patronising and controlling bosses. Amadou, the Guinean man who lived in the room next to Idrissa's, had developed ties with Moroccan employers. They sometimes asked him to bring people and so Amadou could trade favours with other adventurers or provide his roommates with the means to contribute to the rent. Amadou would also let people replace him for a day or two, so he could do another, more lucrative job, or just take a day off.

Jobs in Douar Hajja and Maâdid

A few adventurers from the ghettoes I visited worked at market stalls near *château* and on the main streets of Maâdid and Douar Hajja, selling clothing, vegetables, and sandwiches. Again, conditions varied greatly. Not far from *l'ambassade*, on avenue Al Farah, stood a building occupied by a wholesale grocer selling dried goods (e.g. flour, beans, etc.). The three-storey building opposite, owned by the same Moroccan family, was used to store large quantities of products arriving daily by trucks. Guinean, Malian, and Ivoirian men from *le consulat* and other ghettoes worked there, covered all day in a thin layer of white dust. They pulled their hoods over their necks to soften the weight of the heavy bags and crates that they carried between the trucks, the storage spaces, and the main shop.

Boku, a Malian man in his thirties, had worked the longest (around eighteen months) amongst the handful of migrant employees. His former Ivoirian roommates used to work there and got him the job before crossing into Spain. Migrants usually did not stay long because the job was physically demanding. They quit as soon as they could travel to the borderlands and successfully cross into Spain. Boku had been unlucky with attempts to cross the border and stuck to the job for longer than most. He complained that migrants were only hired to do the heavy lifting, while Moroccan employees alternated between working in the shop and carrying the goods: 'It is only the forced labour we do. We are not paid the same. We get one thousand dirhams a month; the others get two thousand, even the Moroccans who are only unloading like us.'

Complaining about his boss, and Moroccans more generally, Boku begrudged that '[Moroccan people] think we have left our country without a trade, but I left with four diplomas: in painting, in metallurgy, in masonry, and I also drive cars'. Boku worked many different jobs in Mali and then in Mauritania, where he lived for two years before deciding to look for opportunities in Morocco. Disillusioned by the living conditions in Morocco, he started trying to cross into Europe. He resented the menial tasks he had to perform and wished to put his wider set of skills to use. He saw little prospect of learning new ones or thriving in any kind of job in Morocco. Many times, he considered quitting, but he never did. His job, however unsatisfying, provided him with a more regular income than most adventurers. He focused his energy on preparing to leave Morocco, which he eventually managed to do.

Connecting the shop where Boku worked and *l'ambassade* was a narrow alleyway, littered with wood dust. Ibrahima, a Guinean man in his late twenties, swept it away at the end of each working day, along with Jaouad, his Moroccan workmate in a small carpentry workshop. Ibrahima was offered the job after he spotted the owner's son sawing a plank on a set of trestles. Ibrahima, a short but robust man with a jovial face, stopped and asked the man to pass him the saw. Without trying very hard, Ibrahima showcased his skills and was offered a job. Ibrahima and Jaouad could be seen most days working outside the modest workshop, a cramped space filled with wooden windows and doors, carpeted with thick layers of wood dust and chippings. They got along, although they had no common language. Ibrahima stressed that Jaouad and himself were paid the same and treated equally. But sometimes, Jaouad kept working and Ibrahima was temporarily laid off because business was slow. When I pointed out that this did not seem like equal treatment, Ibrahima shrugged and explained that Jaouad was kept on because 'he had a family to look after'.

When asked whether he liked his job, Ibrahima replied with one of his big hearty laughs, stressing that 'a man could not live without working'. The kind of work available to him in Morocco was just enough 'to pay the rent and eat, but not enough to prepare you for your life'. Ibrahima had been learning the trade since he was twelve. After he left Guinea, he set up his own carpentry shop in Mali. He left it all to try and get to Europe, hoping he could make more money there. The job in Douar Hajja was repetitive and at odds with his ambitions (and skills), but it provided him with regular income and the means to organise regular border-crossing attempts. The Moroccan family knew about his immigration status and his plans. Unlike others, Ibrahima did not need to lie to collect his wages early if he wanted to travel. He was asked to give a week's notice to his employer, as a courtesy. Each time he returned, he was given his job back.

The Moroccan employer and his son knew the difficult living conditions for migrants. On several occasions, during police raids, the son had hidden people from *l'ambassade* inside the workshop. Ibrahima talked about how the Moroccan man even stood up for him when neighbours and customers did not address him respectfully. If anyone expressed surprise at seeing Ibrahima, Jaouad, and the son eating together from the same dish, outside the workshop, the latter retorted that they were 'all the same'. But Ibrahima kept some distance, declining some invitations from the family. He explained that the son of his boss was like a brother, but their relationship only existed because of work: 'He is a Moroccan, they are all racists.' Nothing had happened but he stressed that he feared Moroccans: 'I have not been assaulted, but I have seen *camarades* [comrades] who have. God saves me; it could have been me. In the heads of Moroccans, they have the right to attack Blacks.' As explored in Chapter 7, relationships between adventurers and Moroccan neighbours were ambiguous, drifting between forms of exploitation, solidarity, and racism.

Being one's own boss

Some adventurers initiated small-scale entrepreneurial ventures in and around their ghettoes, selling goods (e.g. cigarettes by the unit) for a thin profit margin. One Cameroonian man sold 'zodiacs', paddles, and life jackets, purchased in supermarkets. One migrant carpenter crafted and sold wooden paddles. A few people occasionally sold second-hand clothes and shoes, bought in the nearby markets. Some offered services. Jean, a Cameroonian man who had worked as a hairdresser before taking the road, regularly visited *l'ambassade* with his electric trimmer and blades, to offer five-dirham haircuts.

The most common economic activity in migrants' ghettoes were informal restaurants, often called *maquis* and *ngandas*.[6] Hervé ran his business on the rooftop of *l'ambassade*, preparing staple Cameroonian breakfast food every morning before dawn, using ingredients from shops in Douar Hajja. People from *l'ambassade* and other ghettoes ate beignets, haricots, and *bouillie* (round doughnuts, spicy beans, and porridge made of flour and milk). Hervé was a self-taught cook who learned by observing other adventurers' cooking. He had purchased cheap pots, cutlery, gas bottles, and other items needed to start off the business with money earned working on construction sites. He had a couple of 'apprentices' who worked for him during the day, if they had not found work elsewhere. They ate for free and earned twenty dirhams for the day. His earnings were not considerable, though he was reluctant, like others, to give details about money. His customers were exclusively irregular migrants, who could not always pay up front. He stressed that there could be 'no business without credit', but many customers left for the borderlands without settling their debts.

When Hervé left to cross into Spain, he entrusted the business to his apprentices. He failed and, after getting deported, stayed in Algeria to work for a few months before coming back to Douar Hajja, shortly before *l'ambassade* shut. Working as a cook had been 'advantageous,' he explained when we saw each other again in *l'ambassade*, several months after his departure from Douar Hajja. He had felt 'free', able to work or rest whenever he wanted. He had been his 'own boss', without daily exposure to abuse from Moroccan employers. But he had no intention to resume cooking, stressing that frying oil all day was unhealthy and that the hours he had to put in were too tiring. He underlined how much respect the cooks working amongst adventurers in Douar Hajja deserved. There was a disagreement over the ownership of the cooking utensils Hervé had left behind, but given the tensions around *l'ambassade* with the landlord at the time, Hervé preferred to look for casual jobs on construction sites and travel back to the borderlands as soon as feasible.

Some activities took place on the streets of Douar Hajja and Maâdid and were oriented towards Moroccan customers. A few Ivoirian men from *le consulat* sat outside all day on wooden crates, working as street cobblers. It afforded them a greater degree of 'freedom' and 'autonomy' than casual jobs on construction sites, but was time-consuming and entailed little profit and greater exposure to outside danger. Bakary, from *le consulat*, explained that he had picked up shoe-mending because there were few working opportunities at *château*, amidst increased raids. Earning a few dirhams was better than nothing. Sitting with a soiled rag spread over his legs to protect his clothes from dirty soles, he explained that he felt 'free' compared to people doing 'forced labour'. Under a few old shoes, a box of tools contained a jumble of needles, reels of black and white threads, knives, screwdrivers, glue, small nails, and a cast-iron cobbler stand. All this cost less than two hundred dirhams and was handed down to Bakary by another man from *le consulat*, who gave it to him for free ('you are my little one, take it') before travelling to Tangier and successfully crossing into Europe. Bakary later passed the box to another man from his ghetto before his own crossing into Spain.

Bakary worked up to twelve hours a day, earning around forty or fifty dirhams on a good day. Often, he earned far less or nothing. Aboubacar and Mohamoud from *le consulat* also worked the same trade nearby, having learned it from other adventurers. They explained that they usually managed to earn around forty dirhams, but some of the money had to be reinvested in materials. A small tub of glue cost about eight dirhams but did not last long, especially since a few Moroccan teenagers living nearby regularly and forcefully asked for some to sniff. As opposed to Bakary, who occasionally still looked for work at *château*, Aboubacar and Mohamoud had made cobbling their steady activity. They had regular Moroccan customers, who paid with food when they could not afford cash. Mohamoud was tired of toiling on construction sites, and Aboubacar was no longer able to lift heavy things because of a spinal injury. They were focused on making just enough money to leave for the borderlands as soon as possible. Mohamoud often stressed that it provided a steady income, however small, without having to deal with Moroccan employers. Aboubacar laughed when I asked if he would work as a street cobbler in the Ivory Coast. He was only doing this 'to survive'. It was another temporary trial to overcome, until they could get out of Morocco. There was a degree of shame attached to it, just like begging. 'If you tell my mother [what I am doing here], she will not believe you,' Aboubacar explained.

Adventurers also set up businesses in their own accommodation rather than collective ghettoes, especially restaurants operated by female adventurers, like Christine in her small ground-floor flat. When I first met Christine, she was heavily pregnant and staying with the two Cameroonian men who ran the informal restaurant on the ground floor of the building opposite *l'ambassade*. She had just returned from a forest camp near Nador, to have the baby in a city. Shortly before delivering her baby, she moved into a small flat with two Congolese women, who left for the forests soon after. Christine's windowless flat was made up of two small rooms. The back room had just enough space for two couches, a low table, and a TV. The front room, accessed directly by the front door, had a sink and a gas hob. One corner, separated by a curtain, housed Christine's bed, with just enough space for a single mattress and a couple of large plastic storage bags, filled with her belongings. In a small alcove, there was a squat toilet. Customers sat in the living room, watching *France 24* rolling news, football, or southern American soap operas.

Christine had worked as an auxiliary nurse in Cameroon, before moving to the Republic of Congo, where she operated the till at a relative's restaurant. She left, hoping to cross to Europe, and reached Morocco in early 2011. Realising there was a demand for 'African food' amongst adventurers, she set up a business in *le consulat*, after gathering 150 dirhams as start-up capital. She prepared sandwiches with beef skin, which she bought from Moroccan wholesalers. She carried the sandwiches in a plastic bucket to *château* in the morning, selling them for four dirhams apiece to people waiting for work. Exhausted, she used her small savings, built up over a few months, to go to the forests near Nador, where she stayed until December 2012. She became pregnant, but the man she was in a relationship with left her and crossed by himself. Upon her return to Rabat, she did not want to work as a cleaner, like other migrant women. She valued being autonomous and independent. A strong and outspoken woman, she was well respected by other Cameroonian migrants in Douar Hajja. It did not take her long to build a steady clientele once she retrieved the TV and cooking utensils she had left with other migrants before moving to the borderlands.

She worked hard in this enclosed space, where a thick cloud of smoke hovered most of the day, a mix of fried food and cigarettes – which Christine also sold by the unit. She occasionally hosted a few women, who had temporarily returned from the borderlands and helped her with the restaurant in exchange for food and a place to sleep. But mostly she was alone, cooking and selling the food to her customers from morning until late afternoon. In the early morning, she went out to buy food. She would haggle with Moroccan shopkeepers in Douar Hajja, or elsewhere in Rabat if prices were cheaper for fish or chicken, taking her newborn baby on her back. In the evening, she cleaned and prepped for the next day. It was relentless.

Prices in informal restaurants were low and the profit margins very thin. Christine started off by selling rice with peanut sauce and fried fish for ten dirhams a dish. When business picked up, as customers discovered the new restaurant, she started making chicken dishes too for twelve dirhams each. For a while, she stocked cans of beer and bottles of red wine, but she worried her Moroccan landlord might find out and cause trouble. She explained that, by selling around fifty dishes, she could cover food expenses and make a profit of around 150 dirhams. But she still needed to pay rent and her bills. Often, she only had around twenty customers throughout the entire day.

Restaurants were convenient for migrants, like Boku, who had a short lunch break. Adventurers pointed out that 'African food' was more 'nutritious', that they could not 'recharge' themselves as well with Moroccan food after working on a construction site. The success of such ventures relied on the establishment of spaces where migrants felt safe and could find some distraction and respite from their everyday lives. At Christine's windowless restaurant, the TV and its satellite channels provided a temporary escape from precarious and monotonous living conditions. In the hairdressing salon set up near *le consulat* by Charlie, an Ivoirian in his late twenties, people came to chat, even if they did not need a haircut. The salon was a kind of storage space: a windowless room with a door and a curtain. A few chairs were set up against one of the walls, facing the mirrors on the opposite side. There was a small TV that played music videos and films all day. Like the restaurants and the ghettoes, Charlie's hairdressing salon was a place to meet up and chat about everyday life and the future. As Charlie put it, people came 'just to pass the time':

> We chat about life here, which traumatises people. They only talk about this: how people treat them. It is everyone's intention to leave, but at first you do not know. We discuss how to go forward and backward. It is the adventure. ... You get a sense that all the Blacks are ambitious and courageous; they have objectives. So, we chat about the adventure, how to orient ourselves. Everyone has their objective.

Some of the business ventures launched by enterprising adventurers required little start-up money, especially small activities within ghettoes, but they demanded a significant input of labour. Keeping prices down was crucial, because of the clientele's limited means and the competition from other adventurers. Jean stopped carrying his trimmer from ghetto to ghetto and began working for a Guinean migrant, who had opened a hairdressing salon and was also the 'owner' of several ghettoes. The Guinean man had little experience in hairdressing. In the absence of more lucrative opportunities, Jean worked in the salon, charging seven dirhams for a haircut, cheaper than the ten dirhams charged by an established Nigerian hairdresser nearby. Jean shared the money with the Guinean man, who took more than half of the intake but was responsible for buying supplies, paying the rent and bills, and taking care of other matters.

Adventurers showed ingenuity in finding ways to attract customers. Samuel, a Cameroonian man who had lived in Douar Hajja for several years, often claimed that he had been the first to buy a large TV for the restaurant he set up with his partner Florence. This was after he saw migrants standing outside Moroccan cafés, unable to sit down to watch a game because of racist patrons and unaffordable drinks. He purchased an *Al-Jazeera* subscription so customers would come to his restaurant to watch football games. Migrants who set up restaurants insisted that they did not compete against one another, but they had to keep prices low and paid attention to how much other people charged. Finding a good location was also important. Christine's restaurant was deemed safe, because it was located further inside

Douar Hajja and police raids targeting migrants did not occur that far. But some feared being mugged on the way to Christine's because of its remote location. To provide an incentive to hesitant customers, she kept her prices lower than those at the restaurant opposite *l'ambassade*, chipping further away at her already thin profit margin.

The businesses set up by adventurers generated little income, although money issues were not an easy topic of conversation. There were the rent and utility bills to cover. Jean explained that they paid the 'Black price' for the small salon. Other Moroccan shopkeepers they had befriended only paid five hundred dirhams for similar premises – half of their rent. Some landlords objected to businesses operating in their buildings, complaining about the noise or the smells. Christine managed to convince her landlord to let her continue her restaurant, stressing that her economic activity on the premises had allowed her to pay the rent without problem. This was a risky argument, as landlords already overcharged migrants and sometimes further increased the rent when they knew their tenant ran a business.

Business ventures were also affected by the range of issues facing adventurers. Customers and adventurous entrepreneurs were Black 'irregular' migrants targeted by constant police raids, which had repercussions for businesses. Christine complained about customers staying away because of police activity or rushing out to the borderlands. She had to calculate how many dishes to prepare for the following day, to limit waste, but never knew how many people to expect. For Christine, fluctuation in the number of customers could mean '*la faillite*' (bankruptcy). Migrant businesses were marked by uncertainty. Charlie bemoaned: 'I never know. I get up and I might make twenty dirhams or sixty dirhams, you don't know. There is no fixed amount of money. You get up and you never know how many customers you will have. It depends on whether the Blacks got work or not.' He stressed that he could only 'get by' (*se débrouiller*) if and when his clientele could get by too.

One way to mitigate was to offer credit or other forms of flexible payment, like Hervé. Activities within the informal economy are embedded within a framework of trust. As explored in Chapter 7, trust amongst migrants living in equally precarious living conditions was fragile. Not getting paid by customers who rushed to the borderlands could compromise one's own travel plans. Florence and Samuel stopped offering credit to people, other than those living in the same building. It was easier to chase up creditors who lived nearby. Relationships with customers could be tense. Unhappy customers accused Christine of 'eating money', of making a living by exploiting other migrants, even though she barely made enough money to sustain herself and her child.

Migrant businesses and mobility

Using a common expression amongst young migrants from Western and Central Africa, some adventurers referred to their economic activity as the means to 'look for themselves' while in Morocco. In 2013, Ruben, a Cameroonian who had been in Morocco for two years, opened a cyber near Douar Hajja's market. He charged three dirhams per hour, one dirham less than the usual price in businesses operated by Moroccans in the neighbourhood. Ruben held a diploma in electronic maintenance and had worked in that sector before taking the road. After arriving in Rabat, he became employed by Moroccan employers in a small computer and TV business, although he had no legal right to stay or work in Morocco. Thanks to his Moroccan contacts, he set up a phone line and a cyber, with six second-hand computers connected to the internet. Ruben explained that he reached Morocco with the intention to cross to Europe. He failed twice and lost most of his money. Fed up with 'forced labour', he had looked for more lucrative opportunities: 'When you arrive somewhere and you master some technique, first you dance like the others before looking for yourself.' Like Christine identifying a demand for 'African food', Ruben looked around and observed that 'the only distraction for Blacks' was the cyber, and he proceeded to set one up, where migrants did not have to be exposed to the threat of assault by the other inhabitants of Douar Hajja.

Ruben gave up his room and slept in the cyber to save money, though he hinted that he was still not making much of a profit and could not pay the Cameroonian 'assistant' who looked after the cyber whenever he was away. Ruben said that he was, 'for now', giving up on the idea of entering Europe without a visa. He was also considering other destinations like China. In the meantime, he was 'looking for [himself]' in Douar Hajja, even thinking of branching out into opening other cybers in Douar Kora, if things went well.

I met Ruben shortly before leaving at the end of summer 2013. When I returned the following year, his business had disappeared. Like other migrant businesses in Douar Hajja and Maâdid, the cyber faced many issues. A circle of customers reduced to adventurers, who had little spare cash, and a few researchers, greatly narrowed the economic potential of business growth. Moroccans did not usually frequent migrant businesses. In informal restaurants where alcohol was sold, this was an explicit rule to avoid further problems with neighbours and the police. There were some exceptions, with some Moroccans taking advantage of the low prices in some of the hairdressing salons and 'African boutiques' (e.g. hair products).

Migrant businesses were embedded within the economic life of the neighbourhood, which was also marked by informal practices. Christine would haggle with Moroccan traders, who knew her well. Hervé was nicknamed '*le maire*' (the mayor) by the shopkeepers around *l'ambassade*. Migrants working as cobblers on the streets of Douar Hajja and offering cheap services to Moroccan customers illustrate further the economic links between migrants and the other inhabitants, some of whom lived in precarious conditions. The multiplication of some Moroccan-owned businesses in the neighbourhood 'can be read as a sign of prosperity linked to the presence of sub-Saharan populations' (Edogué Ntang and Péraldi, 2011: 46).[7] Migrants were regular customers of cybers and other businesses (e.g. telephone booths for international calls, money transfer services, corner shops, etc.). They bought food and other goods. They paid rent. They paid cash, usually without access to informal credit, and were often overcharged. However, the customers in the businesses set up by adventurers were almost exclusively migrants.

Cities in the Mediterranean region have been transformed by new mobilities. Migrant entrepreneurship has heralded a form of globalisation from below (Tarrius, 2002) which recalls the extensive circular patterns of migration and trade centred around the Mediterranean in the sixteenth century (see Braudel, 2000). For instance, Schmoll and Semi (2013) focus on shadow economies and multi-scalar mobilities to examine the making of increasingly diverse cities, reshaped by multiple encounters. Yet, exploring the economic lives and business ventures of adventurers in Douar Hajja and Maâdid shows how limited and precarious such encounters can be.

As several informal restaurants opened in spring 2013, following the arrival of many migrants from the borderlands, I asked Samuel if he was worried about the potential impact on his and Florence's restaurant. He shrugged: 'As soon as they will hear that people are crossing in the borderlands up north, they will pack up and go like the others.' New informal restaurants were regularly opened by adventurers (especially women). Some had benefited from training courses and charitable organisations' funds. Given the limited opportunities for employment, migrant entrepreneurship was seen as an important tool for economic development and the integration of migrants in Morocco. But such businesses quickly disappeared. One Cameroonian woman, who opened an informal restaurant to sell Cameroonian doughnuts in a shabby Douar Hajja basement flat, explained that she did not know how long she would stay when I visited her, days after she opened the business. She lived in the room where she cooked, with her toddler and husband. They could not cover the expenses and were looking for another person to move in. They were considering leaving for the border again: 'You never know when *mbeng* [thinking about and actively trying to enter Europe] will finish in your head.'[8] She quickly added that she was also thinking about returning to Cameroon, but 'not empty-handed, with at least five hundred euros'. The business never picked up. They headed for the borderlands a few weeks later.

A few adventurers had purposefully travelled to Morocco in the hope of pursuing business ventures. Charlie explained that he had no formal training in hairdressing but a 'gift'. Unable to set up a business in the Ivory Coast, because of elusive 'conditions and the milieu', he left the country to get 'anywhere, Europe, Africa, anywhere else'. He was initially set on travelling to Gabon, but a friend advised him to go to Morocco instead. He flew to Morocco in late 2012 and moved to Hay Nahda. In spring 2013, with an expired visa, he took over the hairdressing salon of another adventurer in Douar Hajja, who left for the borderlands and never came back. I met him shortly after he had taken over the business. Charlie's salon was a bare six-square-metre room, protected by a curtain. The only visible sign was a hand-painted inscription outside the shop advertising 'Black coiffure', with a phone number. A few months after starting, Charlie was already disenchanted with his living and working conditions in Morocco. His 'greatest concern' was 'to find a way to leave Morocco'. He pointed out that, like his customers, he could not imagine his life here: 'Settling [in Morocco] permanently is not in people's intentions. It is not in my programme either. The situation does not allow it.' He would lament that 'all the Blacks here in Takaddoum have a trade, but finding your place in the [Moroccan] society is hard.' He needed more time to consider what to do, especially as he had just 'taken the risk' of investing money into the rent for another month, spending six hundred dirhams: 'We will see what happens. In life, what you do is a risk, but I am a fighter.'

Like all adventurers, those who set up businesses were constantly reassessing their options, readjusting their migratory plans. Florence, a woman from Cameroon who had been in Morocco for two years, explained that she got scared when she first saw the Mediterranean Sea. She had paid for the crossing but did not get on the boat. She met a Cameroonian man, Samuel, who had already been in Morocco for over six years. He told me he had tried crossing 'too many times'. It was 'too late', he thought, to continue attempting crossing into Europe, just to struggle to make a living from scratch again once there. Together, Florence and Samuel set up a restaurant to save as much as they could before returning to Cameroon. Florence hoped to open a beauty salon, Samuel to buy a taxi or a piece of land. In contrast to most of the scruffy informal restaurants, they tried to make theirs 'the best restaurant in Takaddoum'. They even invested in a freezer, to keep food longer and make savings by buying chicken or fish in bulk when prices were low. They did not see themselves staying in Morocco much longer, because of the overall 'conditions', but were not ready to leave right away, preferring to save more money to be able to start their projects back home.

Having a business did not stop migrants from travelling. Adventurers invested money and time in businesses, but equipment could be sold or passed on, and weighed little compared with a successful crossing into Europe or opportunities expected elsewhere. Natan, a Cameroonian man, opened the restaurant opposite *l'ambassade* with two other migrants, one of whom managed to cross almost immediately. Natan and the other man regularly used the earnings from the restaurant to fund their travels up north and border-crossing attempts, buying equipment like life jackets and zodiacs. Whenever they travelled, they left someone else in charge. Upon returning after an unsuccessful trip, they took back the restaurant. Natan was still in Douar Hajja running the restaurant, by himself, when I visited in spring 2014 and subsequent years. He explained that some people would sell all their materials and pass on the business before moving to the borderlands. He preferred not to, especially since he had been so unlucky with border crossings. Businesses and material possessions were not holding adventurers back. They could be entrusted to someone else while attempting to cross the border. If they succeeded, not much would be lost, compared with the opportunities they imagined in Europe. If they failed, they could resume their activity.

Conclusion

For everyday life and to fund border-crossing attempts, adventurers needed money. Resources from families were limited. Begging was seen as shameful and contradicted self-depictions as adventurers, although many had some, at least occasional, recourse to it. Black migrants could find occasional jobs, which they described as 'forced labour' because of the arduous and precarious conditions on construction sites (and in other sectors requiring manual labour). Some found opportunities in Douar Hajja and Maâdid, but working conditions varied greatly. Migrants formed a cheap and disposable labour force. They stayed for increasingly long periods before managing to cross into Europe, where the informal economy would absorb *sans-papiers* (paperless) workers too.

Young men from Central and Western Africa complained about their working conditions but stressed that being an adventurer entailed facing up to all sorts of obstacles. It is crucial to explore how migrants carved economic opportunities for themselves, notably by setting up businesses in and out of their ghettoes, such as hairdressing salons and restaurants. Many sought to be more autonomous and independent by engaging in such entrepreneurial ventures, but there was limited scope to thrive (and make money). Business owners and their customers were irregular migrants who faced hardship, uncertainty, and violence.

A wide range of mobilities have the potential to contribute to the transformation of cities. But in Douar Hajja and Maâdid, the presence of migrants and their contribution to exchanges and relationships were uncertain. Businesses opened and closed, as people sought to leave the neighbourhood and Morocco, which was described as a place where nobody could find themselves. More than simply livelihood strategies, migrants' businesses were tied to their 'objective'; they were embedded within their uncertain and (im)mobile quest for a 'better life'. As means of saving money to keep moving and reach the objective, economic ventures were of strategic importance for adventurers navigating an uncertain terrain and often readjusting their 'destinations' (see Chapter 2). These business ventures also illustrated how varied and complex relationships could be amongst migrants. Business owners were often accused of profiteering, and fellow adventurers who could not afford to pay asked for credit or appealed to the owner's generosity, on the basis of a shared predicament. In the next chapter, I explore in more detail the moral conundrums and social relationships that are part of the adventure.

Notes

1. From '*fī sabīli llāh*', meaning 'in the name of Allah', a phrase from the Qur'an associated with almsgiving. Migrants who could not speak Arabic would simply utter this formula and point their index upward to ask for charity.
2. *Salām* means peace in Arabic, while *taper* means scrounging in French.
3. In Morocco, the informal economy sector is estimated to represent between 20 and 30 per cent of the overall gross domestic product indicator and is growing, as a result of factors such as rising corruption, increasing urbanisation, and levels of taxation (Bourhaba and Hamimida, 2021: 91). 'Unskilled' and 'low-skilled' Moroccans with a low level of education are predominantly employed within the informal sector, working in precarious conditions (e.g. no access to minimum wage), leaving them 'trapped in a vicious circle of poverty and need' (Bourhaba and Hamimida, 2021: 103).
4. *Chad* was a term used by most adventurers to refer to spaces where they looked for work, but nobody could explain its origin. Edogué Ntang and Péraldi (2011) point to similar spaces in Algeria, where migrants (originally mainly Chadians) waited to be picked up by employers.
5. At the time of fieldwork, one pound sterling was roughly equivalent to thirteen Moroccan dirhams.
6. In French, '*maquis*' designates a type of low vegetation in the Mediterranean region (especially in Corsica), characterised by thorny shrubs and associated with the French Resistance. According to Chappatte (2014), in the 1980s, the term was adopted in the Ivory Coast to designate clandestine restaurants.

The term was used amongst adventurers to refer to informal restaurants set up by migrants in peripheral neighbourhoods along migratory routes. Some also used *'nganda'*, a Congolese term with the same meaning (MacGaffey and Bazenguissa-Ganga, 2000).
7. My translation.
8. *Mbeng* was a term used by (mostly) Cameroonian migrants to mean entering Europe (usually irregularly). I return to this notion in Chapter 6.

6

Chacun sa route

I wished Roméo a happy birthday as he returned from work. Around us, on the rooftop, the other Cameroonian men living in this Douar Hajja building were doing their laundry. It was a sunny afternoon, in the middle of Ramadan. Alain, Roméo's friend and roommate, sat on a makeshift weight-lifting bench. Putting down the dish he was using to prepare a tomato salad for that evening's party, Alain gesticulated and gave me an awkward look. Then, he whispered I had misunderstood the invitation. It was not a birthday party but a gathering in honour of Roméo's sister, who had recently passed away in Yaoundé. Roméo smiled at me wearily and went back inside to get changed.

About thirty people attended the event, mostly Cameroonian and Ivoirian people, including a few women. Some brought hashish and beers to complement the buffet prepared by Alain and Christine. To avoid problems with neighbours observing the fast, food was served inside. But first, Alex, as the charismatic leader of a migrants' association in Douar Hajja (see Chapter 8) and one of my key informants from *l'ambassade*, made a speech and led everyone in a Lord's Prayer. A confident and inspirational speaker, Alex was fit for the job of improvised priest. He stated that all the migrants gathered there, regardless of their national and religious backgrounds, had 'come together' to support Roméo through the loss of his sister. He stressed repeatedly how important it was for migrants to support one another in the adventure.

Afterwards, the mood quickly brightened, as popular songs from Cameroon and the Ivory Coast, downloaded in Douar Hajja's cybers, blasted from speakers. There was dancing. After dark, people went up to the roof with their plates, some brazenly taking beers. A Moroccan man from an adjacent terrace cheered and tossed over a plastic bottle filled with a yogurt-based drink, as an offering for the party. People sought to have fun, but their usual concerns did not disappear. A few of the guests, including Fabien, left early to catch a night bus to Tangier. They were prevented from boarding and regularly phoned people still at the party with updates. Amidst all the fun, a guest approached me, visibly inebriated, to deliver an impromptu slam. He looked at me, and leaned very close to my face, but seemed to be addressing Europeans more broadly:

> What are you going to do for us? We are men, not animals. Do you see how we live? You have built a barrier. How are we going to make it? It is not a life here. But the barrier, we are going to eat it. I do not know the end of the world, but I am going to get there because we are men. We are a family here. I could not bring anything to Roméo because here, *je suis dans la galère* [I face adversity]. I cannot help him. But we are all a family here.

During the party, there were several references to adventurers constituting 'a family'. They were 'together', and 'doing things like home, like in Cameroon'. This feeling was common amongst adventurers. Alain always referred to Roméo as '*mon gars*' (my guy), '*mon frère*' (my brother), or '*ma personne*' (my person). They had met when Alain was still living in *l'ambassade*. Shortly before it was shut down (Chapter 4), Alain and Roméo moved to a room in the building where the party was held – a tiny room that they shared with another two Cameroonians. The two were close and often just kept to themselves: sharing food and stories, planning trips up to the borderlands, and smoking hashish in front of the TV to pass the time.

A year later, in spring 2014, I briefly visited Alain in Boukhalef, a peripheral neighbourhood of Tangier. Alain had moved there to be closer to the border. When I arrived, I expected to see Roméo too, but he was gone. Alain explained that there had been a disagreement. Alain had bought a piece of hashish from a local dealer in Boukhalef for four hundred dirhams. With its higher street value in Douar Hajja, Alain expected to make at least twice that sum by dividing the piece into smaller chunks and selling them to migrants in the ghettoes. Alain entrusted Roméo, who needed to return to Rabat for work, with the hashish. Roméo later returned to Tangier, having sold everything, but only handed four hundred dirhams to Alain. When Alain started asking questions about how much money was really made in Douar Hajja, Roméo gave vague answers and left. Alain was hurt and felt betrayed:

> Right now, I do not trust him with money. I will continue spending time with him, to discover his mentality. ... Before trusting someone, you need to discover how someone is through and through. We spend time together, we study one another. ... He took the money. That is life. You need to save yourself because you have a problem? It won't disturb me. But you are incapable of explaining to me where the money is? Then, there is no point. It was four hundred dirhams. Had it been two hundred euros, then knives would have been drawn.

This episode marks more than ups and downs in the friendship between Roméo and Alain. Adventure entails precarious but necessary social relationships, forged amongst irregular migrants during their journeys. Such relations amongst people facing similar forms of hardship, violence, and suffering can at times foster, alleviate, or hold uncertainty 'in suspense' (Cooper and Pratten, 2015: 2). In this chapter, I explore the issue of trust and the moral conundrums faced by adventurers. Exploring trust sheds light on the tensions in migrants' dangerous journeys to reach the objective. The adventure was an individual project to realise one's life but also a collective endeavour. People sought to realise themselves to help their families. In this goal, adventurers were bound by similar conditions of violence and precariousness. They were an important source of support and advice for one another, as relatives lived far away and support from charitable organisations was limited.

The relationships forged by adventurers in Douar Hajja and beyond were tenuous but essential. Many were planning 'attacks' on the Spanish border and needed to pool their resources and coordinate their actions to scale the fences around the Spanish enclaves or reach the Spanish peninsula on an inflatable dinghy. Adventurers needed to support each other to be able to 'mbeng', that is, to successfully reach Europe.[1] Migrants explained that 'the right mentality' (i.e. displaying courage and strength in the face of adversity; see Chapter 3) was not simply necessary to the granting of 'chance' in one's individual quest. It was also the basis on which relationships amongst adventurers could be forged and could endure. Nevertheless, migrants needed to be ready to seize opportunities. Being able to face up to the obstacles of the adventure could mean leaving companions behind.

In further exploring the moral imaginaries at work in the adventure, this chapter examines how cooperation, trust, and their limits were articulated in the hazardous and violent conditions experienced by adventurers. I am attentive to what Clara Han, in her analysis of care and violence in Chile, calls 'the difficulties and achievements of being in another's present' (2012: 28). Although precariousness and violence have not thrown migrants into a Hobbesian war of all against all, we must also account for 'network failures, disconnections and social frictions' (Schapendonck, 2015: 818). Marginal spaces in Maghrebi cities are places where migrants meet and cooperate but also avoid one another and argue (Alioua, 2007). Common experiences of precarious living conditions and violent repression engender both solidarity and exclusion amongst migrants (see Pian, 2009). Their everyday lives spent in enforced vicinity illustrate how (enforced) intimacy can foster both comfort and danger (see Geschiere, 2013).

To trust someone is to believe that the person is unlikely, if and when the opportunity arises, to behave in a way that is damaging to us (Gambetta, 1988). Besides their interactions with state authorities, NGO practitioners, as well as researchers and other figures, migrants embarking on perilous journeys frequently needed to decide whether to trust each other. How did migrants such as Roméo and Alain forge and sustain relationships when their everyday lives were marked by violence and the systematic infringement of their rights? How did they manage the tensions between pursuing their individual journeys and collaborating with one another?

Michael Collyer notes that collective action amongst migrants in Morocco is limited because bonds remain tenuous within 'spontaneous social networks' (2007: 682). While Collyer is right to point out precariousness, labelling such networks as spontaneous risks obscuring the fragile processes through which trust was established amongst migrants – and the fragile nature of that trust. Social relationships amongst migrants are highly mutable and dynamic, especially in the context of dangerous and fragmented migratory trajectories. These relationships require work; they may collapse. Mutual help and cooperation exist alongside betrayal. It is crucial to examine more closely how relationships are forged successfully and how they fail. Through a focus on trust, this chapter recalibrates the exploration of migrants' fragile relationships by examining the tension between individual migratory journeys and the collective endeavours necessary to face violent and hostile border regimes.

Suffering is a school of life

At *l'ambassade*, in the staircase leading to the rooftop, the wall displayed a partial inscription reading, '*La souffrance est une école de [la vie]*' (Suffering is a school of [life]). Inhabitants quipped that the word 'life' was missing or had been erased. Fabien often told me: '*On ne vit pas ici, on vit seulement les problèmes*' (We have no life here, only problems). As I took notes in their ghettoes, migrants urged me to report on their '*souffrance*' (suffering), to write down details about the violence they faced, such as forced labour (Chapter 5), squalid living spaces (Chapter 4), arbitrary arrests and deportations (Chapter 2), and racist attacks (Chapter 7). 'When you become a high-ranking executive in your country, tell them that we suffer in our countries and here too,' a young man pressed me in *le consulat*.

Many informants doubted that disclosing this suffering would lead to fairer and less brutal migration policies. Yet, this disclosure is important. Not as a voyeuristic account, centred around 'the subject living in pain, in poverty, or under conditions of violence or oppression' (Robbins, 2013: 448), which has come to figure so prominently at the heart of anthropological works (Ortner, 2016). But as part of a wider effort to understand adventurers' own experiences and how they made sense of them. In calling for 'an anthropology of the good', that would trace how people individually and collectively organise their lives to bring about what they think of as good, Robbins warns against scholarship where accounts of trauma and suffering are less about providing an account of how lives are lived elsewhere than helping readers to experience 'the vulnerability we as human beings all share' (2013: 455). Anthropologists have long warned against exploring individual biographies of suffering without accounting for how they are embedded 'in the larger matrix of culture, history and political economy' (Farmer, 1996: 272). Amongst adventurers, the good, articulated as the pursuit of the objective (see Chapter 2), was deeply entangled with facing up to forms of violence, suffering, and risk.

When discussing his numerous failed *'tentatives de passsage'* (crossing attempts), Moussa would often say to me: *'Après la souffrance, la récompense'* (After suffering comes the reward). He highlighted that there could be 'no success without suffering. Even the richest: if he explains to you how he has acquired his wealth, he will tell you how he has suffered for it. You have to suffer to deserve.' Other adventurers expressed that the horrendous suffering experienced during their journeys entitled them to a reward: to be let into Europe to live the life they imagined for themselves. They had deserved it. Hervé talked about 'karma': 'A man cannot suffer all his life. ... You pay here for the acts you have committed before. You pay before you enter [Europe].' In discussions of suffering, Christian as well as Muslim migrants would often talk of God and the need to display the right mentality, to demonstrate their courage and strength in the hope of being granted 'chance' when attempting to cross the border (see Chapter 3). As Amadou put it: 'If you believe this, you will not get tired too much, just a little, but not too much.'

Adventurers often underscored that while they had not been successful, facing up to suffering during their journeys, and in their lives in Morocco and beyond, entailed precious learnings. 'Suffering is not a bad illness; it strengthens the heart,' Samuel, who was keen on proverbs, repeated to me while working in his Douar Hajja restaurant. Ismael, who wrote poems about hope and the adventure, explained that suffering could destroy adventurers, but that it constituted 'a school of wisdom'. Sitting near *le consulat* with Moussa and a few other Ivoirian men mending shoes, I listened to Youssouf as he talked about suffering:

> With my adventure, I have learned some *ouverture d'esprit* [open-mindedness]. Even if I have not earned money, I have seen a lot of things, a lot of realities. I have touched them. In Ivory Coast, there are people who think that the world ends at the borders of the country. They should come here to see the real realities. Adventure is stuffed with teachings. *Ça te forge dans la tête* [It shapes your mind]. It makes you humble.

Like Youssouf, my other informants regularly highlighted that the adventure provided them with important lessons by exposing them to various forms of suffering, violence, and deprivations. These lessons were invaluable in helping them acquire the experiences and skills necessary to reach the objective, and would be useful well beyond Morocco, wherever next they would find themselves – including if they failed to cross into Europe. Though they were usually vague about details, one recurrent example was learning how to live with little money and make it last. Adventurers discussed learning in terms of '*débrouillardise*' (resourcefulness), of making do with meagre means.

Some even claimed to purposefully seek out difficult situations. Roméo insisted that he preferred to live in Douar Hajja, which he described as 'a school of suffering' that was 'good for the poor', rather than in safer (yet still modest) neighbourhoods, where migrants paid higher rents for marginally better conditions. 'When you are poor, you know what you have come to get. Suffering gives you the heart to do what you cannot do. You think about how to pay your rent, how to eat, and shock [the border] for *mbeng*.' Having to endure what adventurers euphemistically described as '*les conditions*' (the conditions) was intrinsic to imaginaries of the adventure. But adventurers were not morbidly seeking to maximise their suffering, as many Cameroonian informants often put it to me, by quoting this proverb when discussing suffering and the adventure: '*Tout le monde veut aller au paradis, mais personne ne veut mourir*' (Everybody wants to go to heaven, but nobody wants to die).

Being the same, suffering together

Small talk amongst adventurers meeting on the streets of Douar Hajja and Maâdid often followed a recognisable script. They would start with, '*Le Maroc, c'est dur*' (Morocco is hard), then proceed to discussions about common difficulties (work, borderlands, racism) and end with, '*On est ensemble*' (We are together). Facing difficult living conditions provided a shared sense of identity amongst adventurers of diverse nationalities living in ghettoes and collectively attempting to '*choquer*' (shock) the border. As during Roméo's party, they often asserted that adventurers from sub-Saharan countries were 'a family'. They were 'all Blacks' and 'suffered the same'.

In Douar Hajja and Maâdid, ghettoes were usually organised according to nationalities but not only these (see Chapter 4). Migrants stressed that it was preferable to stay amongst people who 'understood each other', pointing to shared languages, common ethnicity, and other socio-cultural aspects (e.g. being from Western Africa) to justify 'staying close' to other migrants. Alpha provided a striking example of migrants' complex identities and how social relationships could be renegotiated whenever necessary. Born and raised in the Ivory Coast, Alpha referred to himself as a Burkinabé because of his family's origin. When I asked whether Alpha and his relatives had suffered under the articulation of 'Ivoirity' (Marshall-Fratani, 2006) during or after the civil war, he categorically dismissed the idea. He asserted that he held an Ivoirian passport, and that, in Ivory Coast, people considered him an Ivoirian man. After living in Burkina Faso for a year with relatives, he went on the adventure. He explained how he alternated between Burkinabé and Ivoirian travelling companions:

> In Algeria, I saw Burkinabé brothers. It was me who chose to go with them. The Ivoirians there were sleeping in a hole. I am not a rat. Burkinabé consider me a Burkinabé not an Ivoirian. I am with other Burkinabé people when there are Burkinabé people around. Otherwise, I continue with the Ivoirians. I walk with both nationalities. It depends on the men. If it does not suit me to stay with some people, I move to the other community. I move back and forth between the two. People cannot prevent me from doing so. I belong to both countries; both countries belong to me.

Deploying their diverse social capital, adventurers could move from one group of people to another, as ghettoes opened or closed, people moved on, or fights broke out. They had a wide circle of acquaintances, acquired during their long and tortuous journeys. Adventure did not imply a radically new and unifying identity. Instead, it provided a space for *'débrouillardise'*, where sociality amongst Black migrants 'all suffering the same' could be renegotiated. Everyone was trying to reach the objective. When collaborating or soliciting help from one another, adventurers appealed to a wide range of ties: ethnic group, nationality, language, region on the African continent, or having travelled together along the way. In the absence of more straightforward ties, Central and Western Africans in Douar Hajja simply stressed that, in the adventure, 'all Blacks' (often using the English word) were 'the same'. They were 'together' because they faced the 'same suffering'.

In the ghettoes of Douar Hajja and Maâdid, adventurers often claimed that pre-existing tensions and conflicts in home countries (whether along ethnic lines or party allegiances) no longer mattered. On the ground floor of *le consulat*, occupied mostly by Ivoirians, there were both pro-Gbagbo and pro-Ouattara supporters, who had fled the post-election violence. Ivoirian politics was still discussed in the ghetto. There were animated conversations and humorous taunts, but migrants stressed that the divide between them had been bridged (at least temporarily) by the common search for the objective, as well as the hardship faced by all in Morocco.

At Christine's, I often witnessed good-humoured arguments between two full-mouthed Cameroonian adventurers, who were prone to teasing each other: Fabien, who identified as a Bassa man, and Murielle, who presented herself as a Bamileke woman, and who temporarily lived with and assisted Christine in her restaurant. To mock Fabien and allegedly educate me about Cameroon, Murielle mockingly described Bassa people as arrogant and constantly bragging about being the driving force behind the independence, and as dangerous people who practised witchcraft, sending monsoons and diseases to other people. Fabien, looking at me, would retort that Bamileke were stingy and were scheming to make money off other people. After one such conversation during which they taunted one another through me, I earnestly asked about tensions amongst Cameroonian migrants, given the discrimination suffered by the Bamileke minority ethnic group in Cameroon. Fabien replied that these were '*des faux problèmes* [senseless problems]. In Cameroon, yes, but here, in the adventure, it is less so. We form one family. We help one another. We get to know each other. We see that life is easy [between Bassa and Bamileke], we go forward.' Murielle vehemently agreed with Fabien and quickly resumed teasing him. Nevertheless, there were often very disparaging comments made in *l'ambassade* about Bamileke people, especially those running businesses in Douar Hajja.

Suffering was discussed as an intrinsic feature of the adventure. It was an important and recognisable element in the articulation of a collective identity amongst migrants of diverse nationalities who shared arduous living conditions in derelict ghettoes, stood side by side at *château* in search of low-paid work, organised crossing attempts in the borderlands, and faced racism (see Chapter 7). Yet, adventurers did not form a straightforward group that transcended ethnic, national, linguistic, or religious boundaries. Denouncing the uncritical use of Anderson's concept of 'imagined community' (1983) in migration studies, Hage notes that there often seems to be little community but 'a lot of imagination instead, usually the imagination of the researchers' (2005: 468). Besides frequent fighting with Moroccan neighbours in Douar Hajja, migrants were occasionally involved in violent (and sometimes lethal) fighting amongst themselves. A personal feud between a Guinean and a Nigerian in Douar Hajja led to increased tensions amongst migrants from both nationalities, and the death of a Guinean migrant in 2012. Staff in the Caritas centre near Douar Hajja explained that altercations along national or ethnic lines were not uncommon at the centre. Alex complained that migrants from Central and Western Africa could be 'more racist than Moroccans'. In *l'ambassade*, Cameroonian men complained that Malians were weak and stupid, that they were responsible for driving wages down by agreeing to work for nothing.

Adventure did not imply *ex-novo*, utopian, cosmopolitan identity, nor simply the strengthening of existing (e.g. national, ethnic) identities. The ghettoes of Douar Hajja and Maâdid were transformative and resilient spaces, where relationships and identities were constantly renegotiated rather than simply reproduced or maintained. As a more prosaic example of transformation, many of my informants were known by multiple (nick) names, some acquired during their journeys. Some of my informants pointed out that they were not even sure that the names they knew others by were the real ones. Alain underscored that he shared his real name with me and that he only did this with people he trusted. When asked how he decided whom to trust, Alain stressed that one needed to stay close to people who had '*la bonne mentalité*' (the right mentality).

Wasting and spoiling *mbeng*

Walking about in Douar Hajja on a Friday, Alain handed out a few dirhams to a migrant begging outside a mosque. I asked him why, since he had so little money and himself occasionally begged on Fridays. Alain simply replied: 'Because I know his situation. He suffers like me. It could be me asking [instead of him].' While reflecting on the support they provided to one another, adventurers euphemistically talked about sharing '*les mêmes conditions*' (the same conditions). Amadou underscored how recognising each other's suffering amidst the adventure was a crucial catalyst for cooperation and mutual help, by recalling an incident on a construction site involving an older migrant tasked with pouring cement to set up a pole:

> After the old man finished, one Moroccan came and saw that the work was not right. He started insulting the old man. He called him a son of a bitch. There was a younger Black [man] there. He knows the old man. They spent a long time in the forest [camps] together. They suffered a lot and came to Rabat together. They want to leave again soon, together. He saw what was happening and punched the Moroccan in the face.

It was not clear what happened to that young man, but the older one stayed on the construction site for a while longer. A few weeks later, once the heavy-lifting tasks were complete, the Moroccan employer, as was often the case (Chapter 5), proceeded to lay off most of the migrant workers, including the old man. Amadou, who was a very skilled and experienced worker, was due to stay. He protested that he would walk off if the old man was dismissed. The latter thanked Amadou but said that he was too tired anyway and wanted to leave.

By protesting, Amadou risked losing a job and damaging valuable working relationships with Moroccans he had known for some time. Yet, he was prepared to take a stand for a fellow migrant. Small acts of generosity and mutual help provided relief from gruelling living conditions. Cigarettes, food, mobile phone credit, money, and information passed hands amongst people who were not always well acquainted but who recognised in each other a similar suffering. There were clear incentives, as adventurers needed their roommates to be able to cover their share of expenses (e.g. rent). But there were also disinterested instances of support and help amongst these young men, not despite but because of a shared suffering.

When Christine was about to return temporarily to Cameroon, with support from the IOM's 'voluntary return' programme, I asked her whether she would keep on using one of her nicknames there. Some of the other Cameroonian adventurers in Douar Hajja called her '*marmiton*', meaning scullion in French. It is used to refer to someone for whom cooking is a hobby or a profession. The term is positively endowed with notions of hospitality. In her restaurant, Christine often offered refuge to people coming back from the forest camps and who had nowhere to go. She regularly gave food for free to people in need, stating that she did not have the heart to refuse them. She explained her nickname as meaning 'someone looking after others' and stressed that she had no use for that nickname in Cameroon, since what '*marmiton*' stood for was 'the adventure'. Back home, she added, people had long-standing circles of friends and relatives to rely on. There was no such thing in the adventure. Adventurers only had each other.

But there were also stories of thefts and mischievous acts amongst migrants. Ghettoes were sites of mutual help but also of deception and betrayal. My informants shared cautionary tales about the adventure and relationships with fellow migrants. In *l'ambassade*, Ismael, whom I often found alone writing in a corner, insisted that the adventure could bring the worst out of people. Adventurers shared stories and rumours about some of their roommates, describing them as dangerous individuals, on the run following serious crimes committed in their home countries, in ways that were reminiscent of crude anti-migration discourses. That both mutual help and suspicion of deceitfulness coexisted in the ghettoes of Douar Hajja and Maâdid was not surprising. Alain often stressed that whether migrants acted altruistically or selfishly with others was a matter of 'education' and not because of the adventure itself. The journey was a transformative experience and entailed valuable teachings, but adventurers were different people with their own backgrounds and stories. As underscored by Alberto Corsín Jiménez, 'trust and social crises are presented as natural enemies, the former rushing out when the latter draw in' (2011: 177). Migrants did not live in a world of constant suspicion and betrayal, nor did they become radically new moral agents from embarking on the adventure. Issues surrounding trust were closely linked to migrants' hampered mobility, and how they coped with suffering.

Adventurers often stressed that those sharing a room ought to 'live like a family'. However, sharing a room did not necessarily entail close relationships or trust, especially in overcrowded rooms. As Moussa pointed out to me, 'Trust comes with time, from seeing *les actes que l'on pose devant toi* [others' actions in front of you].' This could come from sharing a room, but you could also share a room with someone 'and not trust him'. Adventurers lived in conditions of enforced intimacy, especially in overcrowded ghettoes, where they shared small mattresses (see Chapter 4). There was little privacy. At *le consulat*, Ivoirian men claimed they knew who had money and who did not, since it was difficult to hide it. Whenever a communal meal was prepared, they explained that they could tell whether someone was lying or not when claiming they could not contribute. Those who lied and breached trust could be refused food at the next communal meal. Trust, as argued by Elizabeth Colson, 'rests on reciprocity' (2003: 5). Migrants, living in forced conditions of intimacy, forged relationships with one another and expected the others to share what they had. Relationships and the degree of trust involved varied. Getting to know one another was a gradual process.

As Alain put it to me, he needed to discover Roméo's '*mentalité*' (mentality). Trust is a process that requires one to remain open to evidence, 'acting *as if* one trusted' (Gambetta, 1988: 234; original emphasis) until trust can be more firmly established. My informants discussed the need to stay close to people and observe whether they displayed the right mentality. As stressed by Ismael in one of his poems, adventurers should not weasel out and 'give up in the face of suffering'. This ability to cope with suffering is what migrants discussed in terms of having '*la bonne mentalité*' (the right mentality), loosely defined as upholding a positive attitude, displaying 'courage and strength' in the face of adversity and uncertainty, and overcoming difficulties rather than giving up (see Chapter 3). As a process, trust is embedded in one's experience of life and the world but requires a 'mental leap' (Möllering, 2001: 417). Amongst adventurers, trust stemmed from seeing first-hand how others dealt with shared forms of violence and suffering, encountered as part of the adventure, and from the expectation that they would continue to behave accordingly. Mutual help was anchored in the recognition of a shared suffering as Black migrants in Morocco. Trust was built not just on this shared suffering but on the ability to cope with it and with the difficult 'conditions' faced by all in Morocco and beyond.

Trust was not needed for everything. It was not necessary to trust all the people living in the same ghetto, at least not always. But staying close to people whom you could trust was important in some aspects of everyday life and for important occasions, especially for border-crossing 'attacks'. A common example mentioned by adventurers was the need to cross the Mediterranean Sea on an inflatable boat with people who had the 'right mentality', and who could be trusted because they displayed the necessary attributes (e.g. courage, strength). More prosaically, this referred to people who, amongst other qualities, would not give up paddling in the middle of the sea (see Chapter 3). Having the right mentality was not only crucial for the realisation of one's migratory journey and aspirations, it was also a required characteristic to enable trusting relationships and facilitate collaborations. But the 'right mentality' also potentially marked the collapse of such relationships. It pointed to the tension between individual and collective endeavours within the adventure.

Moussa was unequivocal about the strength of his relationship with Bakary, whom he called '*mon gars*' (my guy), and with whom he shared everything. Following troubles in *le consulat* (see Chapter 7), they moved together to a small room. When discussing their relationship, Moussa always emphasised that they had gone through difficult times together in the forest and had attempted crossing the border together on numerous occasions. However, such relationships, based on suffering and a shared mentality, were precarious. One time, Bakary travelled to the borderlands alone, without Moussa who did not have enough money for the trip. Bakary successfully crossed into Spain, and Moussa was happy for him but visibly disappointed about having been left behind. The special bonds forged amongst migrants did not prevent people from moving on, or in the case of Roméo and Alain from breaking mutual trust.

Journeys, which often lasted far longer than expected, saw the emergence of new relationships, including romantic ones, amongst migrants and sometimes with Moroccans. Moussa, the Ivoirian man from *le consulat* who often portrayed himself as a bit of a Casanova, constantly talked about seducing women from sub-Saharan countries living in Douar Hajja and beyond. Chatting with Ibrahima, the Guinean carpenter, Moussa told us about his latest misadventures with a Gabonese woman in Douar Hajja. Busy sanding a wooden window frame, Ibrahima kept his usual jovial expression but disagreed on relationships during the adventure: 'How can you keep running and look behind your shoe at the same time?' Yet, Moussa was not alone. There were love stories in Douar Hajja and Maâdid, and like any other love stories, they sometimes ended abruptly. One of my informants, a married man with a family back home, who had been on the adventure for several years, was in a relationship with a Cameroonian woman in Douar Hajja. This relationship ended when she crossed the border. Others were more long-lasting, compelling adventurers to rethink their migratory journeys and life plans.

Adventurers discussed how their journey implied the freedom to pack up and leave at any time, alone if one preferred, in defiance of borders and authorities, to go wherever they wanted to go (see Chapter 2). People disappeared without any notice, especially as preparations for border-crossing attempts were often kept secret from those who did not partake in the outing to the borderlands. Sometimes, this was because they owed other migrants some money. Alain insisted that migrants never fully knew one another and needed to remain vigilant. He was proven right by his friend's actions. This uncertainty over people's conduct is a constitutive part of trust. Trust is relevant precisely because of 'the possibility of *exit*, betrayal, defection' (Gambetta, 1988: 218; original emphasis). It requires suspension, 'the bracketing of the unknowable' (Möllering, 2001: 417). In the adventure, as in other circumstances, making the leap to trust someone else could have unfortunate consequences. Amongst adventurers, breaches of trust were largely related to their trapped mobility.

Somehow anticipating criticism of his own future behaviour, Roméo explained to me in Douar Hajja what '*choquer son pourcentage*' (to shock one's percentage), an expression I often heard amongst Cameroonian migrants, meant:

> It means that you have to suffer alone. ... You are alone, good or bad. ... If something is good or bad, it is for yourself. You and others leave the country together, but at some point, you have to split up. Not because you want to. God splits you. The money you have in your pocket cannot be enough for three people; you are forced to leave, alone. You can come together, but *chacun sa route* (to each their own path). You have the same goal, but you each have to find your own way.

He further explained that '*l'aventure, c'est d'abord le d'abord*' (adventure is first and foremost putting yourself first). Migrants need to provide for themselves first, before helping others in similar conditions of hardship, if they can and are willing to. He added:

> We have discovered the *d'abord* [the foremost] here in Morocco. We are ten travelling together as a commando [in the borderlands but] three get lost, they walk slowly. You arrive [at the border] and have the possibility to cross [the fence into Spain]. You are not going to say, 'We have to wait for the three.' You have to *mbeng* [enter into Europe]. You need people with strength, warriors, those with energy. You have got everything ready, but three got lost. The forest is not a place for sleeping. Each morning created by God, the police turn up. You must shock *mbeng* or you get caught. You don't waste *mbeng* because of one person.

Adventure, as described by Roméo, required cooperation amongst migrants who travelled together, lived in shared rooms, and organised collective border-crossing attempts to reach the objective. But such relationships and the trust they entailed, based on a shared mentality, remained precarious precisely because one had to think of oneself and one's objective: to go '*mbeng*', to enter Europe. The 'right mentality' set both the basis and the limits of cooperation and trust amongst migrants since, faced with opportunities to overcome hardship alone, one should grab them, even at the cost of leaving people behind.

The imperative 'not to waste your own *mbeng*' (e.g. by wasting opportunities to cross alone) set the limits of cooperation amongst adventurers. Regardless of the bonds forged with other migrants, one might have to continue alone in the pursuit of one's objective. Adventurers in Rabat also highlighted the moral imperative of 'not spoiling others' *mbeng*'. When Alain discussed Roméo's betrayal, he was resentful about the lies. He would have been prepared to help his friend with money, but he had lied. Alain felt he could no longer trust Roméo with money. He also stressed that, if a more substantial sum of money had been involved, there could have been a fight. Echoing Roméo's words above, Alain emphasised that '*il ne faut pas gâter le mbeng des autres*' (one should not spoil someone else's *mbeng*). This is where my informants drew the line of what was morally permissible. Leaving others behind was understandable in the pursuit of the objective, but spoiling someone else's *mbeng*, to help oneself, amounted to a dangerous breach of trust and was described as immoral. Yet, in practice, the line was murky. Migrants had few resources, and living conditions remained marked by the constant threat of violence in the form of assault, arrest, and deportation.

After I met Alain in Boukhalef (Tangier) and he recalled what happened with his friend Roméo, we went for a walk around the neighbourhood. Alain showed me the building where a young Cameroonian migrant, known as Cédric, fell from the top floor and died in an incident which sparked further tensions in Tangier between Moroccan inhabitants and adventurers. Alain accused the police of pushing Cédric during a raid. We talked about new politics of migration in Morocco (see Chapter 1) and enduring violence against migrants. Beyond his anger towards the Moroccan authorities, Alain expressed his outrage at the behaviour of another Cameroonian migrant, Brice, who had also lived in *l'ambassade* when Alain was there. Brice moved to Tangier after the ghetto was shut by the police. One day, Alain spotted Brice leaving Cédric's building, carrying a large package. Shortly after, Cédric realised his zodiac had been stolen. Cédric and a few other migrants from the neighbourhood had to cancel their imminent border-crossing attempt. Alain was convinced Brice had stolen the inflatable boat but could not prove it. He was upset, drawing a direct connection between the theft and the death of the young man. He guessed that, since this theft occurred a few days before the raid, Cédric would likely not have been in Tangier when the police stormed his building. He would either have crossed or been forcibly displaced to the Algerian border. Alain held Brice partially responsible for the death: 'Because Brice stole his zodiac, Cédric stayed. Now he is dead.' This death, Alain concluded, should weigh heavily on Brice's conscience. Brice's reckless and morally reprehensible actions were a far cry from the right mentality expected of adventurers.

Cameroonian adventurers referred to those who betrayed other migrants as '*noka*', a term originating from Cameroonian street slang that refers to someone who destroys, spies, or betrays what others do. Another recurrent expression amongst Cameroonian migrants was '*boxer le polo*'. *Boxer* (to box in French) was used to mean spoiling or destroying, while '*polo*' was a recurrent term amongst most adventurers for a favourable situation or place (as well as a hideout in the forest). Calling someone a '*noka*' or accusing another of '*boxer le polo*' referred to behaviour and actions which could endanger other migrants (and jeopardise their migratory journeys), thereby demonstrating that person to be untrustworthy and potentially dangerous.

Constantin, a Cameroonian migrant from *l'ambassade*, recalled how, in 2007, 'two *nokas*' were identified amidst the large group of migrants (over one hundred people) that he was a part of, living in the forest near Nador. Despite careful planning, several collective border-crossing attempts were thwarted by Moroccan and Spanish authorities, in circumstances deemed suspicious by some of the adventurers. Following another violent encounter with the authorities in the borderlands, and a deportation to the Algerian border, migrants regrouped, looking for traitors. Constantin explained that, at the time, owning a mobile phone was forbidden in that forest camp. Only the leaders of the group were allowed to have one, keeping overall control over communications. The group discovered that two Cameroonians amongst them were hiding mobile phones. Messages and calls from those phones were inspected, and the two men were accused of passing on information to a Spanish officer from the Guardia Civil. They were allegedly promised safe crossing if they helped foil ten crossing attempts. Constantin described how the young men were tied up. One of them protested that he was innocent. He was beaten and his feet burned with melting plastic until he confessed. They were eventually released. Constantin stressed that others had faced harsher treatment for similar accusations, justifying such measures because treachery further endangered adventurers, who faced getting shot or beaten when crossing the border.

Families and telling the truth

Wandering around Douar Hajja, I was sometimes accused, humorously or earnestly, of being a *noka*, of collecting information on behalf of European or Moroccan authorities. There were also concerns that my work could provide unwelcome insights into adventurers' lives to their families, whom they often kept in the dark about the details of their living conditions. One point of contention revolved around the photographs I took in the ghettoes, although they were taken with my informants' consent. Other inhabitants, not featured in these photographs, were sometimes unhappy about me taking pictures that divulged adventurers' 'true living conditions'.

Truth demands are imposed on to migrants by sovereign powers requesting verifiable, linear, and authentic accounts of migrants' journeys, stories, and traumas (Salter, 2006; Good, 2007; Wooley, 2014; Bachelet and Palladino, 2024). But amongst adventurers, there were important moral dilemmas over what truth to share with family members, especially as kinship ties are often directly or indirectly involved in migratory journeys (Reeves, 2012; Belloni, 2019; Craig, 2020). Family relationships (with their expectations) were tied to the moral conundrums experienced by adventurers, who needed to collaborate with one another but were pursuing the objective for themselves and their families. This entanglement of different sets of relationships was made clear during the ceremony organised to commemorate the death of Roméo's sister, with migrants stressing the importance of their relationships with both their relatives back home (i.e. Cameroon) and their fellow adventurers (as 'one family'). This dense set of relationships, which coexisted with migrants' selves and migratory project, entailed 'different demands and desires' (Han, 2012: 20).

Although they were (physically) absent, the relatives of adventurers were affectively and morally (and sometimes financially) embedded in migrants' efforts to reach the objective. When an Italian journalist and a migrants' association (see Chapter 8) shot a video of Clément, a Cameroonian man, dying from his wounds in the forest around Nador, following a failed border-crossing attempt, they titled the video after the inscription on his shirt: 'Number 9'. Alex explained that many considered themselves the 'Number 9' of their families: the strikers out there on the uncertain and 'dangerous terrain' to 'score goals for themselves and their families'. Regardless of whether they had received help from their families to start or continue their journey, young men in Douar Hajja and Maâdid expressed a deep sense of duty towards their relatives. Reaching the objective was important for both the adventurer and those left behind, as people were striving to reinvent themselves, seize opportunities, and bring about a better future for themselves and those they cared for.

The imperative not to spoil one's *mbeng* was a response to multiple expectations and demands from families back home. In *l'ambassade*, some of my informants described how, at night, they dreamed about their future lives in Europe but were also haunted in their sleep by images of their children and relatives waiting for them at home. Several of my informants explained that they tried to stop thinking about families and their expectations to avoid 'going mad'. Talking about loved ones back home was often too painful. The shame adventurers felt about repeated failures to cross and the squalid living conditions were articulated with reference to their loved ones. For instance, Aboubacar from *le consulat* insisted that his mother would not believe her eyes if she saw him sitting on a wooden crate mending dirty old shoes for a few coins in Douar Hajja. Not that he wanted her to see him that way.

Many felt ashamed about their living conditions and what they needed to do (see Chapter 5). They were torn when it came to revealing the difficulties and hardships they endured to their families. Many did not want to 'tell the truth', often for fear of worrying family members who already had many problems to cope with, which adventurers were hoping to address once they reached the objective. Others explained how urgent and necessary it was to tell what was really happening, especially in case they one day needed to ask for help after falling ill. After Basil lost his leg, he insisted that I should ring his family to let them know. He was worried his relatives would think he was lying and just wanted some money. If adventurers did not explain what was happening to them, how could their families believe them when they needed support? Sharing the right amount of information with one's family was tricky. Because he was able to find regular work, Blaise could afford to ring his family in the Central African Republic more often than he did. He insisted that he was eager to speak to them more, but that he purposefully limited his phone calls to once a month. He was concerned about what his wife might infer about his finances, if he were able to make more regular international calls.[2]

Migrants' self-portrayals on social media were the subject of debates in *le consulat* and *l'ambassade*. Adventurers often took pictures of themselves wearing their best clothes in affluent neighbourhoods of Rabat, giving misleading accounts of their lives in Morocco. A Malian man from *le consulat* met me in the centre of Rabat, away from Douar Hajja, to take pictures for his Facebook page. Despite the scorching heat, he wore at least seven layers of clothing. He asked me to take pictures of him outside well-known tourist sites, proceeding to take one layer off after each picture, so it looked as if the photographs had been taken on different days. When I expressed my puzzlement over such misleading pictures to Fabien, he stared back, sucked his teeth, and delivered one of his usual deadpan quips: 'It is not us who invented that we should look good in nice places on pictures, it is the guy who invented photography.' Looking your best on a pretty avenue made more aesthetic sense than a picture of a shabby room in Douar Hajja. Yet, people also discussed how such pictures could be deceiving and induce friends and families to take the road with false expectations.

In *l'ambassade*, I met several newly arrived men who complained about deceiving information and images shared by their own brothers, cousins, and friends. 'Shedding light' on to the 'real conditions' migrants faced, partially to inform people at home who might be enticed to take the road by phoney pictures, was one of the main preoccupations of the association set up by adventurers in 2012 in Douar Hajja (see Chapter 8).

Conclusion

Migration and asylum discourse and practices are permeated by moral considerations. What moral obligations do European countries have towards migrants and refugees escaping poverty and conflict in their former colonies? What are fair immigration policies? Moving beyond the well-established focus in anthropological research on the entanglement of logics of control and care amidst bordering processes, this chapter expands the analysis of morality 'in practice' (El Qadim *et al.*, 2021: 1608) by focusing on social relationships amongst adventurers.

Migrants in Douar Hajja did not form a neat, egalitarian community, founded on a transformative rite of passage, whereby all became equal during the journey. Neither were they merely atomised, selfish individuals, constantly prepared to take advantage of one another to reach their migratory and life goals. Regardless of their backgrounds, migrants in Douar Hajja and Maâdid recognised one another on the basis of a shared 'suffering' and aspiration for the objective. They stressed they were 'all Blacks' and suffered similar hardships in Morocco. Adventure offered the possibility to renegotiate existing social relationships and forge new ones, although they were not always long-lasting. Adventurers often needed to collaborate with one another to survive hardship and be able to resume their journeys. They shared small rooms and lived alongside one another in forced intimacy, seeing first-hand how others endured hard-hitting living conditions. Migrants discussed how trust amongst adventurers was built on sharing the 'right mentality', displaying courage and strength to overcome ('to shock') the obstacles.

Sharing such a 'mentality' was necessary to trust other migrants to be suitable companions, at least for part of the journey. Relationships were precarious and constantly had to be renegotiated, amidst moral dilemmas compounded by difficult living conditions and violent bordering practices. Migrants were caught in a tension between 'not wasting one's *mbeng*' and 'not spoiling others' *mbeng*'. Adventurers needed one another, but they could not afford to lose sight of their own objective, which was often entangled with expectations and desires from families at home. Exploring such moral dilemmas shed light on the tensions within the adventure, as both an individual project and a collective endeavour, with overlapping sets of expectations projected beyond tortuous and deadly journeys. In the next chapter, I explore how tensions were also palpable between migrants and their Moroccan neighbours, as these relationships were marked by exploitation and racism but also mutual help amongst people who aspired to a better life.

Notes

1. *Mbeng* was a word used amongst francophone migrants from Western and Central Africa as a verb (to enter into Europe) or as a noun (meaning crossing but also sometimes as a synonym for Europe). Some informants claimed that it originated from Cameroonian 'street slang' and initially meant 'to enter'.
2. At the time of fieldwork in 2012–2013, smartphones (and mobile internet connections) were not as widely available amongst migrants.

7

Between violence and shared dreams

'I'll go up to him and say "How are you? You alright?"' Jamal, a Moroccan man in his thirties, smiled, spreading his arms wide open to show how he intended to greet Omar the next time he would see him. I flinched as Jamal used his tongue to flick forward a razor blade concealed in his mouth. Clenching it between his teeth, he mimicked cutting Omar's throat, then froze, with his head turned towards us, to gauge our reactions. Anas, another Moroccan man from Douar Hajja, and I were too stunned to be scared by Jamal's antics. When he had casually placed the blade in his mouth, five minutes earlier, while chatting with us, I had mistaken it for a piece of chewing gum.

Satisfied with his small act, Jamal laughed and resumed rolling his next joint. We were sat on wooden crates and gas bottles in the shabby building owned by Jamal's mother, which migrants had nicknamed *le consulat*. This was the central area of the ground-floor flat inhabited by Moussa, Aboubacar, and other young Ivoirian men. Jamal encouraged migrants to call him by a sobriquet he had chosen for himself: *le grand dragon* (the great dragon). Behind his back, migrants called him *le poisson* (the fish), on account of the pattern of linear scars (some apparently self-inflicted) and stab wounds that covered his upper body and bore a strange likeness to scales. One of his eye sockets was crushed in from a knife fight.

Jamal had been in and out of prison many times, including once, I was told by Moussa, for murder. I heard many things about Jamal. In one story, he was born in prison because his mother had killed her husband while pregnant. Anas, who claimed that this was a true story, looked much younger than Jamal but was also in his thirties. Originally from a different neighbourhood in Rabat, he was living in an adjacent street with his Douar Hajja-born wife and their daughter. Always well groomed and stylish, Anas worked part time as a waiter in the city centre and played percussion in a *gnawa* band in Douar Hajja. Moussa and others in *le consulat* called him '*la fouine*' because he resembled the French rapper. He was a friend of Moussa and often hung out with people from *le consulat*, to whom he occasionally brought food and clothes. I often came across him in Douar Hajja, wearing a black T-shirt with anti-racist slogans and engaged in some conversation with migrants.

Omar, whom Jamal wanted to kill, was not a migrant but another Moroccan man. He owned a cyber near *le consulat*. The previous night, Omar had attacked and wounded three migrant men from the ghetto. Staring at me through the glasses he had broken in the ensuing brawl with Omar, Jamal recalled how his mother and wife had dissuaded him from using his machete to retaliate against the man who had wounded some of his tenants and tried to break into the building. Jamal was still seething. He evoked the rural origins of Omar's family. Many Moroccan families had migrated to Douar Hajja from across Morocco: 'Omar is not from here, he is from the countryside, the mountains. He should be with cows. That's his work. He is ignorant. He is a racist, he hits *'zzī* [Black people]. ... He thinks he is a bandit. He is a *bambino* [baby]; I am a great bandit.'

Unaware of the previous night's events, I had reached the ghetto early in the morning to meet with Moussa but found the place empty. Inhabitants of the ground-floor flat, the most exposed to break-ins, were staying away. They all moved out permanently shortly after this incident. After chatting with Jamal and Anas, I walked back, passing Omar's cyber, which was still closed. Just around the corner, I met Mohamoud, sitting at his usual corner amongst shoes and tools. In his late thirties, Mohamoud was usually quite a jovial person, but that morning he looked scared. It was late April and already warm, but Mohamoud was wearing a quilted winter jacket and several other layers underneath. This was to protect himself from stab wounds, he said, nervously glancing at some of the young Moroccan men who were hanging out next to him. He muttered that some of them had taken part in the attack. Mohamoud spoke Arabic fluently and sometimes chatted and joked with these men. But he stressed that they were 'unpredictable'.

I continued towards *château* to meet with Sidy, Guillaume, and Aboubacar from *le consulat*. They had returned from the hospital, where Sidy's wounds had been checked. We sat at one of the cafés I regularly used for interviews, along the main avenue, a place where the waiters were usually respectful to the adventurers who came along with me. They gave me their account of what happened. Like most evenings, young men came out of *le consulat* to smoke and chat in the alleyway. Young Moroccan men were also hanging out in small groups, a few steps from the migrants. Sometimes, they interacted together, chatting and laughing. Omar came out of the cyber to complain that the migrants were talking too loudly. He was aggressive, apparently high on some drugs. The young men ignored him, and Omar stormed back into the cyber, where adventurers were also regular customers, to grab a machete. He first approached Sidy, a Malian man living on the ground floor, and hacked at his legs. There was a lot of blood. Panic ensued and people quickly dispersed, rushing back to the relative safety of the ghetto. Some of the Moroccan men who had been hanging out outside grabbed Sidy and robbed him of his money and mobile phone.

Guillaume, a Cameroonian man living on the first floor, was standing outside, and was hit by Omar too. Aboubacar, the Ivoirian chief of foyer on the ground floor, tried to intervene. Getting even more infuriated, Omar grabbed Mohamoud's iron cobbling tool and used it as an additional weapon to continue attacking those who had not left yet. Sidy was taken in by Moroccan neighbours, who helped tend his wounds and hid him until it was safe to go out again. Aboubacar went into the ghetto to prevent the Moroccan men from ransacking the place. This had happened several times before. A Moroccan woman, who sold homemade pastries in a shack opposite *le consulat*, warned Aboubacar not to come out, as Omar, still in a rage, was now destroying all his shoe-mending equipment, which had been left on the street. Some of the Moroccan men, including people who sometimes hung out with him during the day, stole tools and the shoes deposited by Aboubacar's customers. Jamal rushed downstairs to prevent Omar from breaking in, shouting: 'You can hit Blacks outside, but not in my house.' All this happened in the presence of a policeman in uniform, probably going home at the end of his shift. He stood by but did not intervene.

Guillaume sighed and pointed out that their lives in Morocco amounted to 'slavery'. For Moroccans, violence against Black people was 'almost a habit': 'They think we, Blacks, are worth nothing.' Guillaume's opinion was shared by many adventurers in Douar Hajja and Maâdid. Racialised as Black, illegal migrants by Moroccan authorities, they also faced everyday forms of violence and racism from Moroccan citizens, including their neighbours. On 14 May 2012, Amadou, a young Malian man, was stabbed to death in a grocery store near Douar Hajja in Takaddoum. Migrant leaders argued that the assault on the Black man was motivated by racism. Several other deadly assaults against migrants have been documented by journalists and activists, who have condemned anti-Black racism in Morocco (Alexander, 2019; Menin, 2020) and set up national and cross-Maghreb anti-racism campaigns (see Chapter 1).

In this chapter, I explore encounters and relationships between migrants and Moroccans in Douar Hajja and Maâdid. I examine how mutual help and discriminatory practices could coexist amongst migrants and 'host' populations living together in the same neighbourhoods, but often leading largely parallel lives despite experiencing similar hardship and aspirations. Scholars have explored how anti-Black racism afflicting migrants from sub-Saharan countries in Morocco stems from the legacy of slavery (El Hamel, 2013) as well as from contemporary developments, most notably the political construction of Blackness as a marker of illegality (Gazzotti, 2021b). While scholars have highlighted the anti-racism campaigns as an example of more positive relationships between migrants and Moroccan nationals (especially in civil society organisations), they mostly portray working-class neighbourhoods as the loci of violence against migrants. I outline how the ambiguous relationships between migrants and Moroccan inhabitants in Douar Hajja have been marked by tensions and racial abuse, but also by forms of support, conviviality, and solidarity, rooted in shared dreams of mobility and similar experiences of precariousness.

Anti-Black racism

During one of my first visits to *l'ambassade*, a middle-aged Moroccan man attempted to break the front door of the building with a machete. The young Cameroonians on the rooftop felt none of my nervous apprehension. Some leaned over the wall of the terrace to giggle and shout encouragement: 'Break that door, Grandad!' This was many months before the closure of the ghetto, and a sense of relative safety still prevailed. Nevertheless, violence and fraught relations with Moroccan neighbours were important concerns amongst adventurers in that ghetto and others. One Cameroonian man shook his head and sighed, pointing to the Moroccan man downstairs: 'He is even Black like us.'

As Black migrants, adventurers were privileged targets of violent muggings in the narrow alleyways, especially after dark. The police were unlikely to trouble those who targeted migrants. These regular attacks further hindered the mobility of migrants, who feared going out of their ghettoes. Blaise, who lived alone near *l'ambassade*, described to me how, on his way to work early one morning, a Moroccan man walking past him pulled up his T-shirt, revealed a large knife, and asked him to hand over his money. Afterwards, Blaise became reluctant to walk in Douar Hajja, even during daytime. Migrants feared getting hurt. Access to healthcare was limited and not being able to work, even for a few days, could have grave consequences amongst people who often lived hand to mouth.

While hyper-visible in public debates that vilified them, many adventurers sought to stay in the shadows, living in forest camps and peripheral urban neighbourhoods. Many strove to minimise exposure to outside threats by staying in their ghettoes. A young Malian man, Abderhamid, was bedridden following clashes with Moroccan and Spanish authorities in the borderlands that resulted in several broken bones. He often complained about the risk of getting attacked every time he and his companions left the ghetto to get some fresh air, look for work, or go to the shop. He also felt vulnerable inside. Because of his injuries, he could not move. He was scared, since he was often alone and there had been several break-ins by *clochards* (tramps): a term used by both Moroccans and adventurers to refer to marginal people described as poor and violent thugs and addicts. A Moroccan drug dealer, who lived next door, had intervened with the Moroccans who targeted migrants because he was concerned that violence on the street, even if against migrants, could jeopardise his own activities. But others kept coming: '*Clochards* came into the house with machetes. Whenever they found somebody alone, they attacked him. Once, one came in but there were three Malian men sitting inside. He got scared and pretended he had entered the foyer to sell an MP3 player.'

My Moroccan informant, Hassan, Idrissa's friend and neighbour, often denied that migrants suffered from racism in the neighbourhood or that there were any issues between Moroccan inhabitants and migrants, stressing that he himself had been mugged several times in his own neighbourhood: 'Moroccans have no problem with Africans.' Such affirmations amongst Moroccan inhabitants were common. People clung to common tropes about hospitality in Morocco. Someone tried to convince me that migrants returned from the borderlands to Douar Hajja because they enjoyed living there. Any mistreatment, people claimed, had to do with the Moroccan authorities, since it was the Moroccan government which had 'signed conventions with Europe' and stopped migrants from travelling onwards; it did not come from the 'ordinary people' of Morocco, as Ali called them.

Yet, others, like Anas, were willing to acknowledge and discuss the tensions that were palpable between Moroccans and migrants. Anas explained that Moroccan inhabitants blamed migrants for rising living costs in Douar Hajja, stressing that landlords were asking for higher rents because they could charge migrants inflated prices. Migrants were also accused of driving down wages for Moroccans and stealing jobs. Ali, who was homeless and unemployed, often joked that at least they could not steal his. Near Christine's restaurant in Douar Hajja, a Malian started sweeping and cleaning the streets and received money from Moroccan neighbours. This led to a confrontation with an older Moroccan, who had been performing this task for many years. Fears over housing prices, jobs, and other socio-economic issues were likely genuine, but they were projected on to migrants from sub-Saharan Africa. Black migrants were racialised, assumed to be illegal, and associated with a litany of harmful stereotypes.

Taxi drivers taking me to *château* warned me about 'dangerous' or 'cunning Africans', blaming them for criminal activities (drugs, prostitution). After discussing at length his marital problems with his two wives, one in Fez and the other in Rabat, a taxi driver joked that his problems would be solved by marrying a third one: 'a Black wife, a Senegalese'. There were plenty to choose from, he said, merrily propagating the common stereotype that women from sub-Saharan countries are licentious. Regaining his composure, he said that a Senegalese woman would be a bad idea. When I asked him why, he seemed puzzled by my question, retorting that 'all migrants' had AIDS, 'especially the women'.

Negative stereotypes indiscriminately targeted migrants from sub-Saharan African countries, but some interlocutors differentiated between nationalities in their assessment of migrants' dangerousness for the moral and physical well-being of Douar Hajja, the nation, and the Moroccan people. Nigerians, who often spoke little French and Arabic and had limited interactions with Moroccans, were usually described as the most violent and dangerous. Hierarchies of sub-Saharan nationalities were often related to assumed religious backgrounds and cultural affinities with Morocco. Senegalese migrants were better regarded than Cameroonians, with Moroccans pointing to religious and economic connections between the two countries. Many of my Christian informants adopted fake Muslim names, in the hope of getting better treatment when looking for work or interacting with neighbours and shopkeepers. Yet, those who attended the mosques in Douar Hajja complained about racist abuse there too.

As my friend Idrissa, a Burkinabé man, and I stopped near *château* to buy fried-sardine sandwiches, we struck up a conversation with a Moroccan street-seller. He asked Idrissa whether he was Muslim and jokingly tested him on his knowledge of the Qur'an. Idrissa, whose dad was an imam, had no problem passing the mock test. He had initially left his country to pursue his study of Islam. With a big smile, and speaking in Arabic, he appealed to Islamic concepts of charity, asking the man for extra food in his sandwich. The Moroccan man laughed, joking that Idrissa was probably a rich man, as he gave him more food. After he asked about the purpose of my visits to Douar Hajja, the man shared the usual stereotypes about migrants, drawing a distinction between 'Muslim migrants' and 'the Ivoirians'. When we retorted that many of the Ivoirian people in Douar Hajja were Muslim, he seemed puzzled. 'Well, Ivoirians are alright,' he corrected himself.

Walking around with Idrissa, Fabien, Moussa, and others, I saw people pinching their noses in front of my informants, even spitting in front of them. There was much consternation in *l'ambassade* when a ten-year-old boy started loudly insulting migrants walking past, even threatening them with a knife, while Moroccan adults looked on without intervening. Overcoming his initial embarrassment, Youssef, a Moroccan man in his early twenties who was friends with Idrissa, recalled some of the things said about migrants: they smelled and they neither washed their bodies nor their clothes. Some people feared that all Black migrants in Morocco were involved in witchcraft. Fabien evoked a rumour circulating in the neighbourhood about migrants: 'Blacks are cannibals, and they ate a housewife who disappeared.' We joked that if a 'Moroccan housewife' had disappeared from the neighbourhood, she had probably fled to Spain with her Cameroonian lover. Shortly after, a handbag stuffed with a wig was mysteriously found hanging in *l'ambassade*. Fabien and other inhabitants joked that a cannibal was living amongst them.

Migrants resented the disparaging words used daily by Moroccan people to address them. My informants did not like being hailed as '*camarade*' (comrade), a term I have only heard in Morocco in reference to Black migrants. They disliked being called '*mon ami*' (my friend). When I raised this, Youssef shrugged, saying that Moroccans call each other 'my friend' in Arabic and use the French word when addressing migrants. Yet, '*mon ami*' was conspicuously used in a scornful manner by many. I even heard the term transformed into a noun, with the possessive mark embedded into this neologism: '*monami*', synonymous with 'Black person'. The term adventurers complained the most about was '*ʿzzī*', an ambiguous notion which usually holds derogatory meanings and translates as 'negro', 'slave', or 'Black' in Moroccan Arabic (see Chapter 1).

The verbal abuse of migrants could escalate to physical violence. Mohamoud, who worked as a shoe cobbler near *le consulat*, felt particularly exposed. He explained that a customer once shouted at him to go fetch something for him. Mohamoud refused and the man grabbed him by the neck, shouting: 'You are Black. Where I tell you to go, you go. You do as I tell you.' A few days later, the same man returned and started ordering Mohamoud to do something for him, grabbing him by the collar of his jacket. Mohamoud left his tools and fled. He was scared as the man was accompanied by someone else, who had pulled out a knife. Douar Hajja and Maâdid were the loci of racially motivated attacks on migrants that were particularly violent and could also be lethal.

In Morocco, issues around race and migration, along with other relevant socio-cultural debates (e.g. Amazigh identity), point to the 'thorny question of Morocco's own self-positioning in the global colour line' (Gazzotti, 2021b: 287). Grounded in historical processes of subjugation and exclusion (El Hamel, 2013; Alexander, 2019; Hannoum, 2021), the exclusion of certain (Black) bodies is 'activated by racialized forms of prejudice which structure societies according to hierarchies of dangerousness, visibility and deservedness' (Gazzotti, 2021: 278; see also Gross-Wyrtzen, 2020). This is visible in the violent confrontations occurring at the Morocco–Spain border and in institutional forms of racism, but also in the everyday lives of migrants and their fraught encounters with Moroccan citizens. In Morocco, adventurers were subjected to state violence (including arbitrary arrests and deportations, violence, theft, etc.), and to 'the violence of ordinary citizens' (Khosravi, 2010: 3) in the form of (racist) attacks and muggings, sometimes leading to death (see Chapter 1).

Sidy, Guillaume, and Aboubacar, with support from the local office of the UNHCR, since Aboubacar was an asylum seeker, lodged a formal complaint with the police after the assault. Sidy even postponed his departure to the borderlands: he was worried the complaint would be ignored if he went away. But nothing came out of it. When we discussed what happened with Omar, I was puzzled by the policeman who stood idle. Aboubacar and the others did not share my surprise, stressing that they were used to Moroccan authorities ignoring violent acts against migrants – when they were not the ones assaulting them. Adventurers often complained about their belongings being stolen, confiscated without any legal basis or receipt, on the street, often in plain sight of Moroccan neighbours and passers-by, thereby sending a strong message that robbing them was acceptable, or at least free of consequences.

In the same boat

When a middle-aged Moroccan woman died near *l'ambassade*, the mourning family invited some of the Cameroonian migrants to their house for some leftover food, out of charity. The bereaved brother sat next to me. We chatted, while the Cameroonian men ate. He spoke no French and could not interact with my informants. He asked me a few questions about migrants in Douar Hajja, looking curiously at the Cameroonian men. Why were they here? Where did they want to go? The presence of migrants from sub-Saharan Africa has fostered both rejection and fascination amongst the Moroccan inhabitants of neighbourhoods such as Douar Hajja (see Alioua, 2007). The men from *l'ambassade* loudly complained that they were only invited in a Moroccan's house for weddings and funerals, as a good deed. Some laughed, fumbling for the last few bits of meat in the semolina and vegetables, joking that there should be a funeral for a Moroccan every day. That way, they would get something to eat. My friend Alain chuckled but looked uncomfortable. He asked me what he should say. He repeated the short Arabic sentence I taught him to the grieving man, who accepted it with a smile, and we made a swift exit.

Relationships between migrants and the Moroccan inhabitants were often tense. Violence and racism were intrinsic to migrants' everyday lives in Douar Hajja, Maâdid, and beyond. My informants also shared harmful stereotypes about Moroccans and Arabs which often mirrored those peddled about 'sub-Saharan people' (e.g. cleanliness, etc.). My informants amongst adventurers could grow increasingly frustrated and angry with the abuse and violence they had to face. After discussing a vicious attack that left a young migrant in a critical condition from multiple stab wounds, I went on a walk with Fabien from *l'ambassade*. He was furious. We noticed a middle-aged Moroccan man using power tools outside a shop, with no safety equipment and one foot placed dangerously close to a puddle of water. My friend, who had been silently ruminating over our discussion, stopped to stare at the worker, shouting that 'a dead Moroccan' was 'a good Moroccan'. The noise of the power tool covered the angry outburst, and we resumed walking.

But Douar Hajja and Maâdid also saw more positive exchanges, sometimes based on mutual interest, as in the relationships between Moroccan shopkeepers and migrants who had set up an informal business (see Chapter 5). Beyond encounters marked by violence and racism, there were instances of charity, help, solidarity, and conviviality in Douar Hajja and Maâdid. Moroccan inhabitants sometimes provided migrants with food, clothing, and other materials. The narrow alleyways were shared spaces of sociability for young men from Morocco and sub-Saharan Africa, even if they did not always share a common language. Adventurers and their Moroccan neighbours could be seen sat together on the rough concrete steps of buildings, sharing sets of earplugs and tapping their feet to the rhythm of Moroccan or Ivoirian music. There was also occasional banter. Alain spent part of the day hanging out with some of the older shopkeepers near *l'ambassade*, laughing and playing practical jokes on one another. One of the shopkeepers occasionally asked Alain to mind his shop on Fridays, when he went to pray at the local mosque, adding that he did not trust Moroccans to do it. Some Moroccan people living near *le consulat* sometimes stopped to exchange a few words with Moussa and other informants I was chatting with, enquiring about their travel plans and wishing them well. Yet, for the most part, migrants and Moroccans lived separate lives in the neighbourhoods of Douar Hajja and Maâdid. Many were too fearful to leave the ghettoes unless necessary (e.g. for work). Business owners interacted the most with Moroccans but, as discussed in Chapter 5, restaurants and other businesses opened by migrants almost exclusively catered for other adventurers.

In this peripheral neighbourhood, the parallels between the lives of migrants and of the Moroccan inhabitants were striking. Living conditions were difficult for all. Money was tight. I saw both Moroccans and migrants twiddling with their water and electricity meters. In a neighbourhood marked by illegal forms of habitation (see the Introduction), people shared a certain defiance against the state. Many Moroccans also worked in the informal economy and were weary of the authorities. I heard many stories from my informants about Moroccan neighbours and shopkeepers hiding them during police raids. But some people also liked to shout 'police' when there was no danger, relishing in seeing migrants run away in fear, and others still went out of their way to grab migrants and hand them over to the police.

When I discussed positive exchanges and encounters between migrants and Moroccans living in Douar Hajja, my informants argued that most Moroccans were uneducated and ignorant, which they said explained their behaviour towards migrants. But they also said that those who had been '*dehors*' (outside, here meaning abroad) were more likely to be understanding. Ali had lived in Ireland for many years and often decried the treatment of migrants in Morocco, drawing parallels with his life on the streets of Dublin as an irregular migrant. Some adventurers shared stories of Moroccans they had met in the neighbourhood, who could speak at least a few words in Wolof or another language, because they had worked in Western Africa. Anas, though, had never been 'outside', yet he was a recurring presence around migrants, bringing them gifts and spending time chatting with them in *le consulat*.

These small observations are reminiscent of what Gilroy refers to as 'conviviality', that is 'the processes of cohabitation and interaction that have made multiculture an ordinary feature of social life in Britain's urban areas and in postcolonial cities elsewhere' (2006: XI). In Rabat, people sometimes just got on. However, 'the convivial turn has also been criticised for downplaying some of the structural issues bearing down on spaces of urban diversity' (Gidley, 2013: 367). While some of these structural issues are discussed in the Introduction and Chapter 1, I wish here to stress the coexistence of acts of violence as well as generosity. Social interactions were often ambiguous, hesitant, and fragile. Relationships between migrants and the Moroccan inhabitants were rooted in shared aspirations about a better life. They dreamed of reaching a Europe that they equated with opportunities and success. They were driven by a conviction that staying in their own countries would not help them realise themselves, that they needed to carve out a path for themselves in a global economy that had left them at the bottom. Discussions with the Moroccan youth I met in the neighbourhood brought to the fore many similar preoccupations and concerns about the future and how to realise the lives they aspired to. The idioms they used were often strikingly similar. Moroccan youngsters I spoke to in Douar Hajja and Maâdid talked about the need to '*khrj*' (exit) and reach '*l-brrā*' (outside), leaving Morocco to have a chance at a better life, mirroring the adventurous imperative to '*sortir*' (get out) and reach '*le dehors*' (the outside) in search of 'the objective'. Discussing similarities in experiences and aspirations between migrants and Moroccans, Ali stressed that they were all 'in the same boat', which was sometimes actually the case in the borderlands.

I met Youssef and Idrissa shortly after moving to Rabat and joining a workshop for young people, organised by an American student in Music and French, who had secured a grant for a three-month project to foster cross-cultural exchanges between migrants and Moroccans. The group was called '*les voix d'ici et d'ailleurs*' (voices from here and elsewhere). Idrissa lived on the same street as Youssef in Maâdid and brought him to the workshop, where the group of young Moroccans and migrants met once a week over a couple of months. Participants developed songs, plays, and other short acts for a final performance in summer 2012 at the Fondation Orient-Occident in Yacoub El Mansour, another peripheral neighbourhood. Elements of the adventure featured in some of the sketches developed by Idrissa and other participants. Youssef was keen on playing a character he called 'bad boy' (in English) who was set on 'the bad path': a young man living in difficult socio-economic conditions, facing further hardship, making bad decisions (taking drugs, joining a gang), and getting stuck in a downward spiral that ends with his own murder.

I spent a lot of time with Youssef, some of his childhood friends, and other young Moroccans in Douar Hajja and Maâdid. Especially as my informants from Western and Central Africa often disappeared to the borderlands, and sometimes never returned to Rabat. We chatted about the presence of migrants, but also about their own lives and expectations. Youssef came from a very modest background, living in a sparsely furnished one-bedroom ramshackle flat, on the top floor, with his younger sister, his unemployed dad, and his mother, who worked as a cleaner for more affluent families across Rabat. We hung out with some of his friends, also from modest backgrounds but who illustrated the socio-economic diversity amongst people living in this working-class neighbourhood. There was Hassan, who lived with his three brothers, his mother, and his father, a retired soldier with a small pension, and Karim, whose dad used to work for the royal palace and was now running a small butcher shop by the main market street. Hassan and Youssef had occasionally worked on that same market street during school holidays, selling goods at a small stall during the day, and sleeping under the plywood tables at night to protect the merchandise.

When I met him, Youssef was sitting his baccalaureate exams for the third time. He successfully passed the exam that year, but it seemed unlikely he would achieve his dream of getting into a training institute to become a qualified gym instructor. His grades had suffered because he had to help his family, working during the weekends, holidays, and sometimes after school. Hassan had done much better at school. He had a diploma in accounting and was preparing for the entrance exam to become a gendarme. Together, we occasionally hung out in one of the game rooms along the main avenue, outside Takaddoum. We drank sodas and played American snooker. Besides game rooms, pirate DVD shops, and cybers, there were few other forms of affordable entertainment for young people, who struggled in education and in the labour market.

When talking about their neighbourhood's bad reputation, Youssef and Hassan were quick to underline that people were 'not bad inside them' but that the violence, the drugs, and the other issues in the neighbourhood were the result of people's '*ẓurūf*' (circumstances). They were also keen to stress that Maâdid and Douar Hajja were '*sh'bī*' (popular, working-class) neighbourhoods, depicting the majority of people as decent, generous, and hardworking. It was a welcoming place, despite the hardship, and they were proud to have been born there, even though they aspired to leave. Like the Cameroonian men in *l'ambassade*, who discussed suffering in the adventure as a school, Hassan and Youssef stressed that growing up in a poorer neighbourhood was packed with learnings that made them stronger and taught them more than if they had been born in a rich family.

They complained about political issues in Morocco, such as unemployment, inequalities, and corruption, but usually came short of criticising the government or any institutions directly. Others, like Ahmed and Ali, were much more vocal when it came to blaming the authorities. Ahmed had crossed into Europe clandestinely in the 1990s, when he was a teenager, and then crossed from Calais into the UK, where he lived as an undocumented migrant for fourteen years. He said he had returned voluntarily but was vague on the topic. Ahmed, who enjoyed practising his fluent English with me, often complained that Morocco was 'corrupt from the small guy to the top'. He shared with me his difficulties in finding employment, made worse by his lack of connections and inability to pay bribes, arguing that, in practice, human rights and democracy did not really exist in Morocco. He complained about wider inequities in Morocco, where, although there was 'enough to feed everybody', life was tough for most people: 'People starve, people cannot get treated in hospital. If you need an operation, you must buy the needle, the thread and the cotton yourself.' Ali directly pointed to the King and the Moroccan elite for the lack of freedoms in Morocco. He had countless jokes about this. 'Do you know the joke about the man who gets drunk and goes out on the street?' he once asked me in a café. 'He shouts, "Death to the King, he is a scumbag." His mother comes running out, telling people, "Spanish king, Spanish king, he means the Spanish king."'

Both Ali and Ahmed had lived in Europe and were very critical of living conditions in Morocco for 'ordinary people', as Ali would call them. Like the migrants who inhabited temporary ghettoes, young Moroccans in Douar Hajja and Maâdid aspired to a different life, often in Europe. They looked for ways to escape. Leaning against a concrete wall, near a migrant ghetto I had just visited, a Moroccan teenager waited until I walked past him to blow a big cloud of hashish smoke in my face. 'When I smoke this, I am not here anymore, I am in Miami,' he said, looking upwards and grinning. Moroccan youth's gaze was often directed towards the other side of the Mediterranean. One solution was to 'burn the border' and irregularly cross to Europe. For many, this was not feasible, and they looked closer. Youssef told me that he loved Maâdid but that he aspired to get a job and a house 'outside', even if it was just in Hay Nadha, a modest working-class neighbourhood, seen as a step-up from Douar Hajja and Maâdid and located on an adjacent hill.

Hassan stressed that, in Douar Hajja, poor Moroccans and 'African migrants' had the 'same need for money' and the 'same objective'. They cannot find work in Morocco and so they 'think about the outside'. In the imagination of Moroccan youth, Hassan explained that Europe was synonymous with 'everything which goes well. Everything which is missing in Morocco can be found in Europe … . For people, *l-brrā* means better education, culture, work, development.' Europe was a place where people could succeed without recommendations or connections, where they could reach their objective, even if they came from a poor background. For Hassan, not taking the 'bad path' of criminal activities was difficult unless you were 'born rich', but 'in *l-brrā*, if you work, for sure you will become a rich man. … In *l-brrā* … if you have the will, you will succeed.' As Youssef put it to me, echoing many conversations with migrants in *l'ambassade*, Moroccans all had some '*l-maūhiba*' (talent): 'But in this country, you cannot develop it.'

Like adventurers talking about leaving to look for their lives, Ali explained: 'Outside means Europe. We say, "I am going to the outside; I am going to look after myself." We say, "go to the outside to look after my future, to get my life, to become rich". Here, people want to *ḥrg* [burn, cross the border irregularly]; it gives them hope.' Moroccan youth often hailed me on the street, as I walked around Douar Hajja and Maâdid, jokingly asking me for papers to go to Spain. My Cameroonian friend, Alex, was always making jokes about young Moroccan women allegedly looking at me. He said that they just wanted my '*bordeau*' (burgundy – from the colour of the EU passport). The young men (and the few women) I spoke to in the neighbourhood wanted to get out, because they needed medical care and had no money, because they strived for equality or for better education and job opportunities. Europe was the place where they imagined they could achieve what they aspired to, for themselves and their families. Many Moroccans and migrants beyond Douar Hajja and Maâdid share these hopeful aspirations, embedded in this imaginary 'outside'. As Elliot puts it, in Morocco, migration to Europe has affected not only the GDP but 'also the very way in which existence, future and possibility are spoken about and understood' (2015: 1; see also McMurray, 2001; Elliot, 2021).

But Ali and Hassan knew very well the dangers that crossing clandestinely and living in Europe undocumented entailed. Ali had a difficult life as a homeless man in Ireland and was dismissive of equating the outside with paradise: 'It makes people live in *l-ḥulm* [dream] not *l-ḥaqīqa* [reality, truth]. Some think you can just go to Paris and find money behind the cafés and bring it back. They say I am stupid [because] I was in Europe eight years, and I did not learn how to make money.' Ali would laugh about this. He pointed to migrants back from Europe on holiday and ostentatiously showing signs of wealth, enticing young people to make their way to Europe: 'Migrants here give fake stories. They come with a car, but maybe that is all they have; they have hardly anything to eat. Maybe he has to go back to work right away because he might be losing his job.'

Yet, Ali described the outside and going to Europe as a solution to inequality and a lack of freedom and opposed it to '*l-ḥgra*' (oppression): 'If you stay here, you go to prison. Here, it is *l-ḥgra*, but if you go to *l-brrā* [the outside], you can have your *droits de l'homme* [human rights]. You get respect. Here, you cannot get respect.' He complained that his marginalisation translated into a loss of mobility within Rabat itself, that policemen often kicked Douar Hajja kids out of more affluent neighbourhoods if they were caught walking there. 'Being illegal [in Europe] is better than being legal [in Morocco]. Here, you are legal only in your pocket,' Ali often joked. He described people like himself as outcasts: 'In Morocco, we might have nice food and lovely weather, as they say, but we are like strangers in our own country. That is why we run away.'

Though many of the youths I met talked about Europe, few had attempted the crossing. There was more awareness about the dangers of crossing the Mediterranean Sea. Ali claimed that a reduction in activities in the adjacent industrial zone meant that there were less opportunities for hiding on trucks to reach the harbour in Tangier and other hubs from which to cross into Europe. Pointing to people that he knew had attempted crossing by sea, in the market of Maâdid, Youssef stressed that people of his generation were 'cleverer'. They looked for help in getting a visa or sought to marry a foreigner. He was hopeful that he would manage to get out and be able to help his parents once he was 'outside' of Maâdid, even if he only made it a few minutes away.

Like adventurers from sub-Saharan African countries, he talked about the importance of not giving up in the face of hardship. Youssef and his friends talked candidly about the efforts required of them to carve themselves a better future, given their modest background in a deeply unequal society. Youssef stressed that, for poor people like himself, it was necessary to demonstrate a certain '*l-raghba*' (willingness) to keep away from 'the bad path' and strive to succeed despite the many obstacles: 'It is impossible [to give up] if you have this willingness. ... You need to take the good path and never give up. God will help you if he sees you doing the good things. If you have a good mentality. God willing.' Giving up meant taking the bad path and possibly ending up dead, as in Youssef's theatre play. But keeping the right path, not giving up, was not easy. Youssef shared how heavy that burden of keeping 'the right mentality' was: 'You have to be strong. ... You must keep everything in here [pointing to his heart]. It is not good. One day, it might explode, and you will do something crazy: steal, kill someone, go to jail, and then it is over.'

Unpredictable

During Ramadan, shortly before I left Morocco at the end of summer 2013, Anas, Moussa, and myself went to a café in Douar Hajja. Anas talked about how people he knew were resentful towards migrants, blaming them for a rise in living costs, especially the rent. He added, 'A clever person will know that the problem is not really about the sub-Saharans, but about poverty here.' As always, we talked about life in Morocco for migrants and Moroccans. Anas was knowledgeable about adventurers' living conditions and their tactics in the borderlands.

After a while, we were joined by Osni, who played the violin in the same *gnawa* band as Anas. He spoke almost no French, but he and Moussa quickly befriended each other, laughing and smoking hashish together. They started singing a song, 'Un Gaou à Oran' by Magic System and 113. Moussa sang the parts in French and Ivoirian dialect, and Osni the Algerian Arabic lyrics. A few minutes later, they were both high, their faces pressed against one another, singing Khaled's raï hit 'Aïcha'. Then, Osni started singing some of the lyrics from Ivoirian Alpha Blondy's 'Multipartisme (Médiocratie)' song. When he reached the line, '*Les étudiants sont fâchés, ils veulent plus de liberté*' (The students are cross, they want more freedom), Moussa stopped him and sang: '*Les mounamis sont fâchés, l'Espagne est toujours fermée*' (The *mounamis* [my friends] are cross, Spain is still closed). They all burst out laughing and the evening continued like this.

Fabien was always suspicious of Anas. I could not understand why he insisted that migrants should be wary of people like Anas. He seemed to be a nice man, especially compared with Omar, or the landlord Jamal. The latter, despite his reggae-coloured, Africa-shaped pendant, and all his talk about being a 'brother' to the migrants, was exploiting migrants. Fabien told me how Jamal was once 'tied up and whipped for days', for abusing the Cameroonian migrants who lived in his house on the first floor. Jamal was forced to flee the neighbourhood for a few months, and, as another man from *l'ambassade* put it to me, came back 'converted', self-identifying as a 'brother' to migrants from sub-Saharan countries. For the migrants who lived in his building, being on good terms with Jamal, or at least engaging in some friendly banter with him, could be useful. Rather than genuine friendship, Moussa stressed that this was about 'security'. Keeping on his good side could be useful to protect them against other Moroccans. People did not fear Jamal as they did before, but they remained cautious, since he was unpredictable and could turn aggressive, especially when high on tablets.

The week before I left Morocco, not long after that evening singing in the café, I was surprised to find that Anas had cheated a group of Cameroonian men. They had bought a zodiac and some other materials from him, to organise a border-crossing attempt. Fabien revealed that this was the reason behind a recent fight in Douar Hajja, involving some migrants and Moroccans. I had no idea that Anas was involved in the business of zodiacs. As I shared my surprise, Fabien shook his head and chuckled dryly. He said he had known all along that this would happen:

> Why are you surprised? He is from Takaddoum; he is poor. We went to ask for the 3,500 dirhams back. The whole family came out with knives and told us to get lost. A Moroccan there explained to us that they had used the money for Ramadan. The police came and asked what was going on. They said it was the Blacks. So, they told us to go, or they would arrest us. I said, 'Let's leave it' to the others. But I had told them [the other Cameroonians] before: 'What are you doing, dealing money for zodiacs with a Moroccan man living in Douar Hajja? He also needs money. It is better to avoid problems.'

Adventurers often shared stories to underscore how relationships with Moroccans were *'imprévisible'* (unpredictable). It was deemed difficult and dangerous to get too close. For Yasser, who was the last, unpopular chief of ghetto at *l'ambassade*, the long scar running across his face was a reminder of this. As he sat outside on the front step of the ghetto, a Moroccan neighbour he said he had no quarrel with unexpectedly pulled out a knife and slashed his face. Unpredictable was also how Mohamoud, an Ivoirian man, described Moroccans, especially those who hung out on the street where he repaired shoes. There had been incidents in the past, and he always worried that the casual chitchat and joking could turn into something threatening. Mohamoud spoke Arabic before getting to Morocco and had become quickly proficient in the Moroccan dialect. Language skills helped, but it was not sufficient to establish durable relationships. In playing down the advantages conferred by his fluency in Arabic, Mohamoud stressed that being able to speak Arabic mostly meant that he could understand the abusive and threatening language aimed at Black migrants on the streets.

Mohamoud often said that there were bad and good Moroccans. But, when asked if he had any Moroccan friends, he would shake his head: 'No, it is just chitchat and that's it.' He stressed that making friends with Moroccans was 'both easy and not easy', because living conditions were difficult for migrants and not always much better for their Moroccan neighbours. Working from 8 am to 8 pm on the street as a cobbler, he had repeated encounters with Moroccans. He added that there could hardly be any reciprocity in relationships with Moroccans. Like relationships amongst adventurers (see Chapter 6), relationships with Moroccans were entangled with family ties, and their sets of expectations and responsibilities. He explained that if a migrant became close to a Moroccan person, they may benefit by getting help from that person, but they are unlikely to reciprocate: 'When it is you who gets money, then you will leave, or you will want to send it to your family.'

Idrissa was wary of Youssef. I had met them together and initially assumed them to be close, but it seemed that their friendship was sustained by the relationships I maintained with each of them independently. Idrissa lied about his migration status, telling Youssef that he was a student. Youssef grew suspicious and asked me several times if it was true. I gave vague answers, and he looked slightly disconcerted by the prospect of being friends with an undocumented migrant. When asked, Idrissa ambiguously asserted that yes, Youssef was his friend, but then he quickly corrected himself: he had 'no friends', only 'acquaintances', in Morocco. Youssef was not welcome in Idrissa's flat, because of the other migrants, who did not want any Moroccans to come in. Youssef also confided that Idrissa could not come to his place, because of his parents. When I told Idrissa that I did not understand why he kept Youssef at a distance, Idrissa frowned and whispered that 'one never knows': all Moroccans were 'unpredictable'.

Ali stressed that migrants too were very unpredictable. They kept disappearing. He expressed his solidarity with migrants over their difficult living conditions in Morocco, but he often also voiced some frustration, arguing that they were in denial over their migratory journeys. Some had been in Douar Hajja for years: 'They say they are *passagers* [passengers]! Five years here is not *passsager* [temporary]!' He lamented that migrants stayed 'close to themselves' and that they never made any effort to get to know Moroccans around them. He criticised migrants for not speaking any Arabic or not trying to learn. He drew on his own experiences, but he had learned English thanks to state-sponsored programmes in Ireland. Adventurers in Douar Hajja and Maâdid had no access to such initiatives. Their focus was on gathering the necessary resources to try crossing the border again.

Conclusion

The politics of race in Morocco, marked by the legacy of slavery and by contemporary migration policies, shaped the lives and journeys of adventurers from Western and Central Africa in the borderlands, but also in marginal neighbourhoods like Douar Hajja and Maâdid. There, migrants forged ambivalent relationships with Moroccan inhabitants. Everyday life, in and out of the migrant ghettoes, entailed the threat of racism and other forms of violence. Migrants were easy targets for assaults and exploitation by cunning landlords and employers. The police were more likely to arrest and deport irregular migrants than to chase up those who abused them. Adventurers stayed in Douar Hajja and Maâdid not because of some inherent hospitality amongst its inhabitants, but because it was affordable. The rent was cheap, and they could focus their attention and meagre resources on their 'objective', trying to organise trips to the borderlands.

But relationships between the adventurers and their Moroccan neighbours were not limited to violence and racism. There were stories of Moroccans providing much-needed help to migrants, who received food, clothes, and other essential items from people in the neighbourhood. Beyond generous acts, driven by charity, there were signs of conviviality amongst people who lived in precarious conditions, felt left out of a range of socio-economic opportunities, and defied authorities. People of different nationalities in Douar Hajja and Maâdid shared dreams of an elsewhere, an outside, where they could carve out the lives they aspired to. For young men from both Morocco and sub-Saharan Africa, Douar Hajja and Maâdid were an 'open-air prison'. The idioms they used to talk about their lives and (aspired) journeys were strikingly similar (e.g. to exit). The themes and topics of discussion with the 'original people' of Douar Hajja and Maâdid sketched in this chapter (e.g. keeping hope, lack of opportunities, finding oneself, etc.) echo the similar experiences amongst adventurers explored in previous chapters. There were striking parallels between the desires, expectations, and hopes (as well as their limits and constraints) of disenfranchised Moroccans and irregular sub-Saharans.

In focusing on some of the encounters between adventurers and their Moroccan neighbours, this chapter has underscored how wider relationships between migrants and the 'host' populations cannot be reduced to either racism, violence, or exploitation. There were forms of help and conviviality. Relationships were ambivalent and some individuals, like Anas, showed how both abuse and support could coexist, and even be enacted by the very same people. In Douar Hajja and Maâdid, young men from sub-Saharan Africa and from Morocco lived in precarious conditions and were eager to escape their predicament. Under a set of analogous pressures and striving to redirect the course of their lives, migrants and Moroccans saw each other as 'unpredictable'.

While reflecting on the challenges faced by people of all nationalities in Douar Hajja, Ali cried out: 'Imagine what would happen if the sub-Saharans came close to the Moroccans in Douar Hajja!' He marvelled at how their lives could change, how much they could achieve. He fantasised that they could face up to the government together and compel the authorities to address the conditions they lived in. But for this to happen, Ali sighed, there should be a 'new Morocco', a place where people were not running around just to feed themselves. Ali was quite pessimistic. He was a homeless man, who shared his astute commentary on Douar Hajja and Morocco with few people. Moroccans and migrants often thought that the drugs had gotten to him, and that he had become a bit mad. Yet, adventurers were already collaborating with the wider Moroccan society, to bring about changes in Morocco with regards to migration and other human rights issues. In the next chapter, I examine the birth and development of a migrant association in Douar Hajja.

8

Fighting illegal migration

'We lived like kings in Oujda. Everyone enjoyed the setting and the debates. Now, it is just back to Hervé's *beignets* [doughnuts],' Moussa bemoaned, toying with a piece of fried dough. It was early October 2012 and we were on the rooftop of *l'ambassade*, the Cameroonian ghetto which doubled up as the modest headquarters of *Association Migration sub-Saharienne au Maroc* (AMSAM) (Sub-Saharan Migration Association in Morocco).[1] Most members of the young association, set up the previous summer, lived there. We had returned from a two-day gathering focused on migration, which had taken place in Oujda, near the Algerian border. It was organised by the *Forum Social Maghrébin* (FSM), as a preparatory event for the 2013 World Social Forum in Tunis. It was the first time that associations of migrants from sub-Saharan countries living in Morocco had been invited to such an event.

The overall enthusiasm amongst AMSAM members, sparked by their participation in lively debates with delegates from civil society organisations, who had travelled from across Morocco, the rest of the Maghreb, and beyond (e.g. France), was plummeting. We were ill, because of faulty air conditioning on the night train back from Oujda, and my informants grumbled about the return to their morose everyday lives in Douar Hajja, having spent a few nights in hotel rooms with running hot water. Many were already late with paying their share of the rent. The time spent in debates about migrants' living conditions was time spent away from construction sites. Finding money was still a pressing worry.

We had returned in the early morning and met in the late afternoon to debrief about the exchanges with activists and practitioners from human rights organisations, including more established migrants' associations such as *Conseil des Migrants Sub-Sahariens au Maroc* (CMSM) (Sub-Saharan Migrants Council in Morocco, also known as *Le Conseil*) and *Collectif des Communautés Sub-Sahariennes au Maroc* (CCSM) (Collective of Sub-Saharan Communities in Morocco, also known as *Le Collectif*). AMSAM members had shared insights about their lives in Morocco and listened with interest to other participants (including more experienced migrant leaders), who talked about migrants' rights and called for the 'regularisation of all *sans-papiers* [irregular migrants] in the Maghreb' – something they had never discussed in their weekly Sunday afternoon meetings in *l'ambassade*.

People were excited to discuss these ideas with other migrants who had not been able to attend the Oujda forum. They also reflected on the reception of their new migrant organisation, especially its stated objective of '*lutter contre l'immigration clandestine*' (fighting against clandestine immigration). This had confused many forum attendees. Moussa, the Ivoirian man from *le consulat*, commented: 'My combat [battle] is about regularisation. It is to fight inequalities and injustice. Regularisation is an important idea, which we did not master before the forum. Some people told us, "AMSAM, you are fighting against us migrants!" But no, we just want to reduce the percentage of irregular migrants.'

In Oujda, I overheard discussions between my informants and other participants, who were baffled by the idea of '*réduire le pourcentage*' (reducing the percentage) of clandestine immigration. Most AMSAM members had very limited experience of engaging with civil society organisations and did not share the same vocabulary. A Cameroonian migrant, and member of AMSAM, argued that '[t]he good cause is not only fighting against migration; we also need to insist on the fight for the rights of the clandestine migrants.' Until then, my informants had vaguely talked about 'getting their rights' in AMSAM meetings, but they had not discussed how, as irregular migrants, they were entitled to forms of protection enshrined in national and international legislations.

After the forum, they were unsure about how they had been articulating the objectives of their association. They were keen to appropriate and deploy ideas and tools encountered in the discussions with established activists and practitioners. Fabien, echoing one of the main themes of the debates, asserted that '[w]e cannot stop migration. Morocco is not a country of transit but of residency.' Others wanted the association's name to include the words '*droits des migrants*' (migrants' rights) and recalled that Moroccan activists living in France encouraged them to include the term '*sans-papiers*' (without papers). Everyone agreed that changes were needed in the name and scope of the organisation, except Blaise, AMSAM's President, a man from the Central African Republic. He protested that all these issues were already covered by AMSAM's remit since its inception, articulated somewhat nebulously as having '*trois volets*' (three dimensions): providing support to migrants who sought to stay in Morocco, return home, or continue their journeys towards Europe, or elsewhere.

For a minute, we remained quiet, each one of us mulling over how best to describe the association. A Cameroonian man broke the silence, shouting: 'We are the Association against Migrants' Rights!' There were a few enthusiastic cheers but also looks of disapproval amongst other members. In my capacity as advisor to the organisation, I asked whether he meant 'for' rather than 'against' migrants' rights. Discussions continued, but the decision over changing the name and remit of the organisation was postponed until the next Sunday meeting.

AMSAM was a creative (and at times confusing) initiative by young migrants in Douar Hajja, who strove to organise themselves collectively in the face of hostile politics of migration. Despite precarious living conditions, migrants have been politically active in Morocco, setting up migrants' associations since at least the mid-2000s and forging fragile alliances with other civil society actors (Üstübici, 2016). In this chapter, I explore how migrants shift 'what it means to be political' (Squire, 2011: 5), by examining adventurers' articulation of multiple, and sometimes seemingly contradictory, political claims. I outline how the political participation of migrants from AMSAM responded to crucial concerns for adventurers over their mobility and capacity to reach the objective.

The political mobilisation of (irregular) migrants points to a radical but ambivalent potential to shift the boundaries of citizenship from below (McNevin, 2006; Castañeda, 2013; Ataç et al., 2017; Topak, 2017; Dadusc et al., 2021; Rees, 2024). Migrants have the capacity to compromise 'political moments' (Scheel, 2013: 579) and stage an intervention in the polity as political actors, regardless of their administrative status. Such a focus challenges the perception that irregular migrants are not capable of articulating political claims and reframes citizenship as constituted by acts (Isin and Nielsen, 2008). Through various disruptive practices that refuse abjection and subjugation (Tyler, 2013), migrants demonstrate their 'capacity for staging scenes of dissensus' (Rancière, 2010: 69), drawing attention to how, regardless of status, migrants are able to establish themselves as citizens with the right to have rights (Arendt, 1951; Isin and Nielsen, 2008).

AMSAM members' call for 'reducing the percentage' seems at odds with spectacular examples of (irregular) migrants' ability to disrupt and transform the political (e.g. hunger strikes to fight deportations, protests for regularisation, strikes for employment rights). However, in focusing on the birth and the first year of AMSAM, this chapter draws attention to the ambiguous and complex ways in which (irregular) migrants seek to overcome the violence and uncertainty that permeates their lives. The exploration of migrants' political subjectivity requires that we account for its heterogeneity, through a focus on migrants' multiple, uncertain, and sometimes seemingly contradictory claims and demands, as illustrated by the confusion over AMSAM's overall aim.

The imperative to 'fight irregular migration' amongst AMSAM members demonstrates how discourses and practices are entangled in complex 'workings of power' (Abu-Lughold, 1990: 42), whose analysis requires more than a romanticised account of resistance. Creative and transformative potentials to intervene in the political realm are better grasped by exploring how social beings are engaged in a multitude of projects which 'feed on as well as collide with one another' (Ortner, 1995: 191). Failing to account for and examine the diversity of migrants' political claims, in favour of homogenised and abstract considerations, risks curtailing any radical potential 'for novel forms of political subjectification' (Nyers, 2010: 138) and, crucially, contributes further to migrants' marginalisation.

The foundation of AMSAM

Pierre, then president of the migrants' association *Le Collectif*, introduced me to Alex, a Cameroonian migrant from *l'ambassade*, in the summer of 2012. This was the same Alex who later acted as priest for the ceremony in honour of Roméo's sister (Chapter 6). Pierre presented Alex as 'the president of migrants in Takaddoum', a joke title that I took seriously at first. Alex invited us over to *l'ambassade*, where he shared his wish to set up a migrants' association in Douar Hajja. When I asked why he did not join one of the few existing ones, Alex retorted that they were dormant organisations, disconnected from 'migrants' realities'. Pierre did not take offence and eagerly volunteered his help, as well as mine. As Pierre and I later walked back to *château*, I confided my unease. I was not sure what advice I could provide. Pierre insisted that I could assist him in 'showing them the way' to set up their association. This was 'a righteous deed'. He added, without malice, that it would facilitate my research project and provide him with opportunities to film more documentaries on migration.

We joined the meeting set up by Alex the following Sunday afternoon in the Cameroonian ghetto. Mattresses and blankets were tucked away. We sat with our backs against the red bricks, shielded from the sun by a blue plastic tarpaulin. Besides Idrissa, invited by Pierre, and Blaise, a man from the Central African Republic, the twenty or so attendees were Cameroonian men from *l'ambassade*. Alex started the meeting: 'We are here to establish an association to fight against illegal migration.' Incredulous, I stared at Pierre, who remained expressionless. Alex talked about the many issues he hoped the association could address, especially the 'reinsertion' of returning migrants into their home countries, the overall 'reduction of clandestine migration', and the collection of migrants' testimonials about life in Morocco, to increase awareness about the dangers of the adventure in home countries. After stressing the need to set up an executive committee and communication tools (e.g. Facebook account, email address), he turned to Pierre and me: 'We will manage all this ourselves, but our brother Pierre and our brother Sébastien will guide us.' I was not yet used to his charismatic, though preachy, oratorical skills. People listened and nodded but remained mostly silent.

Later, Pierre explained that he and Alex hoped that my presence as a white, European man would prompt people to commit time and energy, stressing that the whole enterprise looked 'more credible' with my presence. But Alex kept me at arm's length, especially in the beginning. I was not there for some of the early, informal discussions that happened in the evenings at *l'ambassade* amongst inhabitants of the ghetto. After Alex and Pierre had talked at the meeting, people agreed to meet again to formalise the committee, even though there had been little discussion about what exactly the association was set to achieve. Alex encouraged people to speak to other migrants in the neighbourhood, especially migrants from other nationalities.

The committee was set up at the next Sunday meeting. People volunteered for positions, which were allocated by consensus. In practice, it was Alex and Pierre who steered the distribution of roles. There were several secretaries, including one for cultural and sport affairs, one for projects' development, and one for women and children's affairs. The latter was directly allocated to Christine, who was the only woman involved in these early meetings. There were several spokespersons, including forthright and short-tempered Fabien, who turned out to be very effective at forging relationships with activists and practitioners from the Moroccan civil society. He was francophone but also spoke fluent English, enabling him to also reach out to Nigerians in Douar Hajja. Alain was the censor, responsible for overseeing the smooth running of meetings. There were several vice presidents, as well as general secretaries, including Moussa, who was the only Ivoirian migrant involved. Most positions also entailed an '*adjoint*' (deputy). The list was long, and everybody came out with a title, but soon after, there was some confusion over the exact allocation of roles and what their remit was. Alex and others insisted that 'a white man' as vice president would be helpful, especially when dealing with Moroccan and international NGOs. I politely refused but accepted, like Pierre, the title of advisor.

Migrants' organisations drew sarcastic and condescending comments from some NGO members about ceremonial and cumbersome 'African politics'. Yet, AMSAM members discussed their organisational arrangements as a response to what they imagined NGOs expected, so that they could be seen as a 'credible organisation'. Members did not attempt to have their organisation officially registered in Morocco, a process marred by administrative hurdles, deployed by authorities to stifle dissent (Bachelet and Hagan, 2023). They would not have been able to, as all members were undocumented. Though the association was without a formal legal basis, its members, eager to be credible, were constantly preoccupied with formalities. The drafting of an internal set of rules was a pressing concern early on, but it was never completed. While clear aims were not yet succinctly articulated, migrants discussed at length the design of their logo. They were keen to look credible in front of Moroccan and international NGOs.

Providing everyone in the association with a title was a tactic to make members feel valued and motivate them to be actively involved. Pierre and Alex wished for AMSAM to overcome divisions amongst migrants from different nationalities, who often lived in different ghettoes (see Chapter 4). Alex envisaged AMSAM as an extension of the supportive work carried out in *l'ambassade*, an established ghetto where Cameroonian migrants from the neighbourhood came for help. He did not want AMSAM to be another nationality-focused association of migrants. Several already existed in cities such as Rabat, sometimes with close ties to sub-Saharan embassies. There were also informal support groups (e.g. in case of illness) organised around ethnic ties. While AMSAM was being created, some Cameroonian businessmen were competing for the position of president of a Cameroonian migrants' association with close ties to the embassy. Adventurers were cynical about such forms of politics, which they associated with corruption, self-gain, and endless quarrels, which did little to better the living conditions of (especially irregular) migrants. Alex and other adventurers in Douar Hajja wanted to bring together migrants from different nationalities and provide real support.

To avoid AMSAM being overly associated with Cameroonians, Alex did not become president. He ingeniously took on the title of 'founding president', a lifelong position. Blaise, from the Central African Republic, was appointed president, as the oldest person amongst the members. His appointment suppressed tensions amongst outspoken members competing for the role. Though he was respected because of his age, he had no relevant experience in leading an organisation. Efforts to reach out to other migrants in and around Douar Hajja were largely unsuccessful. Most members were francophone Cameroonians, including a few dual citizens. Idrissa never returned after attending the first meeting. Moussa stopped being involved shortly after the Oujda forum, to concentrate on border crossing. The number of people present in the weekly meetings was between ten and fifteen in the first few months. After *l'ambassade* was shut down, many of its inhabitants, which formed the majority of the association members, left Douar Hajja for the borderlands. Meetings were relocated to Christine's restaurant, but the number of active members decreased rapidly, although

AMSAM could still mobilise a few more people from neighbouring ghettoes for specific events like conferences.

AMSAM members often insisted that the association 'represented' migrants living around Douar Hajja, Maâdid, and Takaddoum. Some even claimed AMSAM represented all migrants in Morocco, or even across the Maghreb. Representativeness was a crucial matter for AMSAM members, who sought to be credible interlocutors with NGOs. Even though many of the NGO practitioners who regularly interacted with AMSAM assured them that they were not looking for spokespersons on behalf of all migrants, but were keen to work with active, self-organised migrants. AMSAM members' grand claims about representativeness were shared by many other migrant activists and were apparent in trivial struggles between migrant associations over which association was the most 'representative'.

AMSAM and its members rapidly became visible actors amidst the small landscape of organisations working on migration in Morocco. Some established migrants' associations (e.g. *Le Conseil, Le Collectif*) had been in place for several years and had ties to Moroccan civil society, but AMSAM and the adventurers from Douar Hajja breathed new energy into the meetings and events they attended. Most of the AMSAM members had no experience of advocacy work. Yet, other members of the Moroccan civil society were quickly impressed by their tenacity and candour. Some AMSAM members developed strong personal relationships with Moroccan NGO members, especially Fabien with people from the *Groupe antiraciste d'accompagnement et de défense des étrangers et migrants* (GADEM) (Antiracist Group of Defence and Accompaniment of Foreigners and Migrants). AMSAM rapidly came to be valued for its work and input within debates about migration in Morocco. The association emerged at a time of strong focus on integration and regularisation in Morocco. Its members were, as an NGO practitioner put it to me, 'a reminder that not all migrants want to stay in Morocco'.

The emergence of AMSAM also occurred at a peculiar time of increased violence against migrants. AMSAM members, who had mostly been in Morocco for a year or two by summer 2012, when the association was founded, had arrived in Morocco during the tail end of what other migrants and NGO members described as a period of relative reprieve in terms of repression, although there were still serious and deadly incidents. But from the second half of 2011 especially, police brutality and exactions against migrants increased exponentially, prompting people in Douar Hajja to decry their living conditions. However, renewed repression and brutality at the border with Spain and within Morocco were only one reason behind the creation of AMSAM.

'Exposing the true realities of migration'

One of the motivations behind AMSAM's creation and mission to 'fight migration', sometimes articulated as 'reducing the percentage' of irregular migration, is better understood in the light of adventurers' concerns and dilemmas over 'exposing the true realities of migration'. During the first meeting in *l'ambassade*, Alex and Pierre appealed to a prevailing sense of unease amongst many adventurers, from *l'ambassade* and beyond. Migrants' portrayal of themselves and their journeys to their loved ones contributed to a perception of the adventure as a pathway towards success and (material) wealth, which often downplayed or obscured the suffering and violence they experienced. Adventurers discussed how they preferred not to tell the truth, out of shame or concern that their relatives might worry too much. But they knew that such images could unduly encourage their loved ones to embark on the adventure (see Chapter 6).

During the first meeting, Pierre stood up to talk about how people in home countries do not believe migrants when they say they are suffering because of deceiving pictures on social media. 'It is important to make brothers at home aware that, in Morocco, we live like this,' Pierre said, waving his arm to point out the decrepit state of *l'ambassade*. He stressed that people thinking of taking the road should know that they won't find a nice, air-conditioned office in Morocco, and that '[f]or every person that will make it to Europe, ten others will die'. When my turn came to speak, I gave some words of encouragement, but I also outlined how important it was not to echo the deceiving narratives found in the information campaigns funded by European countries to deter people from migrating. Alex quickly retorted: 'We do not want to stop all migration. Migration has been going on for decades. What we want to do is to denounce the obstacles, like violence and rape. We want to highlight the risks to avoid our brothers becoming *clandestins*. They can emigrate legally.'

Joseph, a Cameroonian man from *l'ambassade*, intervened to share a story about his younger brother in Cameroon. The latter thought Joseph's cautioning against undertaking the journey was not in good faith. He was convinced that Joseph was doing very well. Fearing for his brother's life and concerned for his wider family, Joseph explained in the meeting that he disclosed the 'true realities' of his life in Morocco to his brother. He shared pictures online, showing the hardship (e.g. on construction sites) that he faced every day. His brother decided to remain in Cameroon. He bought a piece of land, found a job, and married. This story was shared multiple times by Joseph during meetings, with his brother growing more successful each time.

Joseph later explained to me that he had fled Cameroon because he feared for his life. He had been documenting and exposing the opulent lifestyle of some local politicians, who threatened his life. He often drew parallels between his advocacy work in Cameroon and the need to expose migrants' true conditions in Morocco. Several weeks after the first meeting, Joseph drafted a leaflet for AMSAM, titled 'The West – the end of misery'. The first page is a drawing showing a mass of black silhouettes on a seemingly endless road. There is a rhetorical question about whether clandestine migration could ever be stopped. The answer is 'no' since some people would always be constrained to become clandestine migrants '*pour des raisons de survie*' (for survival). After highlighting the number of deaths on such journeys and the precarious lives of migrants, the document invites the reader to ponder on their 'choice of clandestine migration'. The document addresses people who have left already, but also those who have not yet started their journeys. Those who 'dream of a better life – the west as "El Dorado on earth"' – risk death during clandestine journeys. But 'clandestine migration' could be 'reduced' through the sharing of information, visuals, and testimonials exposing migrants' precarious living conditions.

'Fighting irregular migration' was not an endorsement of the hostile and violent migration policies across the region that aimed to selectively deter, stop, monitor, and return migrants. But this expression elicited puzzled and even hostile reactions within Moroccan civil society, including from other migrant leaders. Some joked that the association was guaranteed to receive funding from the EU. However, as AMSAM members articulated more clearly what they meant, the need to inform friends and families at home about the violence and suffering inherent to these journeys came to be recognised as legitimate, despite its ambiguousness. A jurist from a Moroccan NGO stressed that it could only be done by a migrants' association, to avoid ambiguity.

This emphasis on exposing the true conditions of the adventure was crucial to members from the first meetings. It reflected migrants' wider moral dilemma over crafting an image of themselves as successful adventurers but not deceiving their loved ones into making decisions based on skewed information (see Chapter 6). However, as members exchanged with other activists and practitioners, the presentation of AMSAM as a migrants' association that was not 'fighting against migration' but seeking to 'shed light on to migration' took on new meanings, beyond addressing families, friends, and decision-makers at home.

This was the case in the 'Number 9 campaign' (N9) launched by AMSAM alongside other Moroccan organisations, such as GADEM and AMDH (Moroccan Association for Human Rights). In March 2013, Yvan, a Cameroonian member of AMSAM, travelled with an Italian journalist to the Gourougou forest, near Nador, following a border-crossing attempt (by around 120–200 people) that was violently repressed by Moroccan and

Spanish forces. The trip resulted in a powerful but distressing video, entitled 'Number 9', depicting the last moments before Clément, a Cameroonian man, died from his injuries in the forest. The name of the video bears the number on Clément's sports jersey and echoes the common football-themed metaphors about adventurers as strikers for their families. The video became the centrepiece of a campaign to denounce brutal measures against migrants at the Morocco–Europe border, which received international coverage (Bachelet, 2013).

Some AMSAM members, especially Fabien who had close ties with GADEM, argued that the video needed to be deployed to denounce hostile politics of migration by documenting the infringement of migrants' rights and their brutal treatment at the hands of both Spanish and Moroccan authorities. Others, especially Alex, insisted that the original focus on raising awareness amongst the general population in Cameroon and beyond should remain the priority. Especially as many were worried that a focus on denouncing Moroccan and Spanish practices might expose them and lead to repercussions from the authorities. Migrant leaders had been harassed and intimidated by Moroccan authorities. One AMSAM member, who had returned to Cameroon, was interviewed by a media outlet about the video.

The bridge

In early 2013, I supported AMSAM in the creation of a leaflet about the association and its work, intended for actors in Moroccan civil society, including potential funders and supportive organisations, but also for potential new members amongst migrant communities. Six months after the association was founded, its members still struggled to agree on how to clearly present what they wanted to achieve. The leaflet describes AMSAM as an association 'by and for migrants', which aims to shed light on migration. It enumerates a range of pell-mell activities, such as: signposting migrants to appropriate services offered by NGOs, informing them about their rights, collaborating with other organisations to find solutions to migrants' problems, facilitating peaceful relations between migrants and Moroccans, advocating for the respect of migrants' rights, and denouncing the ill-effects of hostile politics of migration and bad governance in sub-Saharan and Maghrebi states. These different aims were compiled during meetings, but the reference to 'rights' was mostly my input.

Adventurers in AMSAM had little, if any, experience in advocacy and political organisation. Alex had run a small record label before. He drew on his organisational and communication skills, but he had no background in civil society. Some AMSAM members confided in me that, prior to getting involved in the association, they did not know what an NGO was. Members (at least initially) struggled to produce the standard documents (e.g. reports, funding applications, receipts) that NGOs required from them in order to collaborate. Keeping the remit of AMSAM blurry allowed members to engage in a variety of activities, as long as they remained within AMSAM's vague mission. They responded to arising opportunities for collaboration with NGOs (e.g. Caritas, GADEM, AMDH, etc.) and sought to come up with their own initiatives, although they had no financial resources of their own.

In the few written documents produced by AMSAM, as well as during conversations and meetings, migrants described their association as a 'bridge' between migrants and NGOs. Adventurers often complained about international and Moroccan NGOs, stressing that they were not providing adequate care or support. AMSAM's emphasis on transparency and exposing the 'true realities' of migrants' living conditions was, especially at the beginning, geared towards 'denouncing' perceived injustices at the hands of NGOs, especially Caritas, which had a support centre located just a short walk from Douar Hajja. Cameroonian men from *l'ambassade* accused Caritas and its staff and volunteers of privileging certain nationalities, calling it an NGO for Congolese people. Adventurers complained that NGOs in general were profiteering from migrants' suffering, 'eating money' from the EU and other institutions that was intended for migrants. It is not so surprising that adventurers sought more control over their dealings with NGOs since decisions about how much support migrants would receive affected their lives greatly. Migrants' grievances could be more easily addressed to NGOs than to the Moroccan authorities and large international organisations, like UNHCR.

Exchanges were brokered through the development of close relationships between AMSAM members and NGO practitioners, notably between Fabien and members of GADEM. Fabien, myself, and my flatmate, Stéphane, who worked at GADEM, struck up a friendship and often met up to discuss migration issues. Stéphane advised Fabien on articulating his ideas and developing projects for AMSAM, often with a strong emphasis on matters pertaining to the respect of migrants' rights. Fabien and Alex also established a good working relationship with Pierre-Marie, the manager of Caritas's migrants' centre just outside Douar Hajja. There were regular meetings between AMSAM and Caritas, which occasionally took place in the migrant ghettoes of Douar Hajja.

As a 'bridge', AMSAM members dispelled rumours and passed on information to other migrants about the range of support Caritas, GADEM, and other NGOs could offer. They accompanied other migrants to receive help and support (e.g. medical assistance). Through their contacts, they shared information with NGOs about issues and events affecting migrants in Rabat and in the borderlands. This was crucial for humanitarian NGOs, such as Caritas, who needed to anticipate needs and the movement of people from the borderlands, but also for more advocacy-oriented human rights organisations, such as GADEM, who needed reliable information from the field. Such exchanges also regularly took place in a dedicated forum in Rabat, *Plateforme Nationale Protection Migrants* (national forum for the protection of migrants), where NGOs and migrants' associations such as AMSAM met to discuss wider issues and coordinate responses.

As they grew in confidence and experience, AMSAM members devised their own projects and solicited minor financial help from NGOs such as Caritas. For instance, they established an emergency accommodation, to help resourceless migrants needing temporary shelter in Douar Hajja. This was set up in Christine's restaurant, with some of the expenses covered by Caritas. AMSAM members were often discussing new ideas and seeking to foster new connections with NGOs. There were disagreements over what to pursue, as well as an element of rivalry between some members. Few of these projects came to anything, since members had little time and money. The heterogeneity of concerns and projects within one same organisation was not surprising. What was remarkable was the continued emphasis on holding meetings for the whole membership (which was loosely defined and in principle open to whoever wanted to come along) every Sunday, despite their precarious living conditions.

The heterogeneity and ambiguity of AMSAM's objectives and multiple projects recall the ambiguity of adventurers' articulation of their objective as looking for their lives (see Chapter 2). Besides the overarching emphasis on 'exposing the true realities of migration', members of AMSAM described the work of the association to others (especially migrants) as fitting within '*trois volets*' (three dimensions). The association was there to support all migrants, whether they wished to return to their home country, remain in Morocco, or continue towards Europe (or elsewhere). It was established to help all migrants face up to uncertainty, illegality, and immobility, regardless of where they wanted to go to next. Members of AMSAM had complex and ambiguous migratory projects, like most adventurers in Douar Hajja and Maâdid who were constantly reassessing their journeys and life projects, trying to look for opportunities and agonising over whether to stay, try crossing (again) into Spain, or return home. AMSAM provided a platform through which adventurers were able to scale up practices of mutual help already happening amongst migrants (see Chapter 6). They collaborated with a range of actors, notably NGOs, even though these were not equal relationships. Some members occasionally complained that they felt they were being used, that people in NGOs were just extracting information from them. In denouncing their unjust treatment, members of AMSAM progressively articulated demands by drawing on the language of rights.

'Getting our rights'

Shortly after the first AMSAM meeting in summer 2012, several migrants were stabbed in racially motivated attacks on the streets of Douar Hajja and Maâdid. Young men from Western and Central Africa mobilised and started a march. There were tens of migrants, including many Cameroonians from *l'ambassade* and some representatives of other migrants' organisations. They walked on the main avenue, towards the adjacent neighbourhood of Souissi, where the men were aiming to protest outside sub-Saharan countries' embassies. I was out of town, and Pierre later showed me pictures of people shouting and marching behind a man holding up a pair of trousers, soaked with blood and hanging from a stick.

A few days later, after I returned to Rabat, people in *l'ambassade* explained to me that they had gone to Souissi '*pour obtenir nos droits*' (to get our rights). They were angry about their treatment in Morocco and the lack of support from their diplomatic representatives. Some of the latter did come out of the embassies but only issued vague promises to help migrants lodge a complaint with the Moroccan police and to ease some of the criteria to obtain a consular registration card. Early discussions about 'rights' at AMSAM focused on receiving fair treatment from consulates and embassies, on an equal basis with students, businessmen, and other migrants from sub-Saharan countries. In the ghettoes of Douar Hajja and Maâdid, adventurers complained about the violence perpetrated by the Moroccan authorities as well as the Spanish border guards, but they had come to expect it. They were appalled by the contempt, lack of support, and outright hostility from their own diplomatic representatives. This was illustrated by the slow response to the situation tens of migrants, including Idrissa, faced when stuck at the Morocco–Mauritania border (see Chapter 2). Some of the ghettoes bore symbolic names such as *le consulat* or *l'ambassade*. These names highlight adventurers' capacity and efforts to organise themselves politically, especially in the absence of support from their diplomatic representatives.

The march increased AMSAM's visibility amongst other adventurers in Douar Hajja and Maâdid, who often broadly talked about 'injustice' in their ghettoes. They shared stories and commented on their unfair and brutal treatment at the hands of the Moroccan authorities and the general population but also, as discussed above, at the hands of NGOs and diplomatic representatives. AMSAM members wanted to denounce their position as second-class citizens, compared to students and migrant workers with valid immigration documents. The political construction of adventurers as irregular migrants involved a myriad of actors and processes (Coutin, 2000), including diplomatic representatives, who even collaborated with Moroccan authorities. Pierre-Marie in Caritas recalled how some ambassadors of sub-Saharan countries had referred to irregular migrants as 'criminals' when discussing vulnerability issues with the NGO.

The focus of migrants' discontent and the articulation of the demands they put to their diplomatic representatives were inscribed in entrenched forms of injustice, affecting adventurers and their efforts to carve out 'a life more bearable'. This sense of injustice connected events and conditions in countries of origin with the hardship of the adventure (as illustrated by Joseph's story above) but also with a wider world order in which they felt left out (Ferguson, 2002; Jackson, 2011). In complaining about the inaction (and damaging actions) of their diplomatic representatives, adventurers drew connections to the socio-economic and political issues, such as corruption in home countries, which had contributed to stifling opportunities and prompted people to take the road. In meetings and events, AMSAM members talked about the need to document and address their arduous living conditions and the treatment they received in Morocco, but also about the need to tackle the general political and socio-economic environment in their home countries. Cameroonian men in *l'ambassade* sought to *'indexer'* (denounce) the negligence of decision-makers from Western and Central African countries, who had failed them at home and then also abandoned them to violence and uncertainty in Morocco.

Such a focus recalls the emphasis on tackling the root causes of migration in the global efforts to selectively enforce bordering measures and deter the mobility of undesirable migrants. However, discussions about injustice in the ghettoes of Douar Hajja and Maâdid did not stop at the responsibility of authorities from their own countries. One late morning, as I was joining Moussa in *le consulat*, I found my informant and his roommates chatting about politics, after they had unsuccessfully looked for work. They invited me to join their discussion of corruption in the Ivory Coast and of the shadowy political and economic networks between France and its former colonies. We sat in a thick cloud of cigarette smoke, our conversation accompanied by Zouglou music, faintly oozing from a mobile phone's speaker. There was an uncanny, if unsurprising, echo between their words and the lyrics of the songs playing: *'Nos dirigeants sont dirigés'* (Our leaders are led), one Ivoirian man stated, the words ringing back to a song by Ivoirian singer, Tiken Jah Fakoly, which had played a moment before. Another man turned towards me: 'In the Ivory Coast, we are told we are foreigners. In Burkina Faso, we are told we are foreigners. In Mali too. Your grandparents did this; they put up borders. We are divided. Do you have family working in the administration?' Someone else laughed and cut him off before I could think of an answer: 'One day, we will get rid of all our leaders at once and abolish borders in Africa.'

They pressed me to listen to another track, downloaded in a cyber, a song by Burkinabé artist, Sams'K Le Jah, in which he addresses African youth, recalling a glorious past and highlighting that, if Africa is '400 years behind', it is because of the trade of enslaved people, which has enriched European capitals. Shortly after mentioning the Senegalese Tirailleurs, who died 'protecting democracy in Europe', he lists some of the assassinated leaders: Sankara, Lumumba, and the others who sought to foster change but were assassinated. Once the phone's speaker went quiet, one of Moussa's roommates broke the long silence:

> This is why we go to Europe. We go looking for our right, our grandparents' right. Africa will change. The adventurer who goes out and returns will not go to the *maquis* to down a few bottles. He will know what to do with the money in order to evolve. But catching up will be hard.

Adventurers' quest for the objective was inscribed in unequal relationships with a long (post)colonial history. Idrissa made me listen to Burkinabé leader Thomas Sankara's 1987 speech, 'Against the debt', delivered at the Organisation of African Unity, while we sat in his room. In ghettoes and informal businesses, adventurers watched telenovelas but also rolling news, discussing together international sport as much as socio-political issues. They reflected back on the historical and contemporary ties between Africa and Europe, which affected their lives, mobility, and futures. As a moral endeavour, the adventure was not just about meeting the expectations of friends and families but also about seizing the right to cross to Europe, as a legacy of such past and current links: from slavery and colonialism to the more contemporary interventions by Europe's political and economic forces in their home countries, which they described as plundered by corrupt elite and foreigners.

References to rights in discussions about politics and injustice were often vague. Adventurers had diverse education levels and usually limited experiences of engaging with civil society organisations or politics. But AMSAM quickly became involved in events and exchanges with other civil society organisations in the first year after its foundation, the year that marked a rapid escalation in violence but also in advocacy work, which contributed to the shift in Moroccan politics of migration at the end of summer 2013 (see Chapter 1). AMSAM members rapidly acquired new tools through their interactions with more established human rights organisations and through their own advocacy work. They read up on international conventions and talked about human rights.

Initially, AMSAM members had refused the adjective 'political' for their organisation. They associated politics with deceitful manoeuvring, senseless quarrels, and the pursuit of personal interests. Most AMSAM members, especially Fabien, started employing the term 'political' as their interactions with NGOs and activists increased. Yet, tensions over the meaning of 'political' as deceitful manoeuvring endured, since members worried that other migrants might, in turn, accuse them of exploiting migrants' suffering for their own gain. Like with the Number 9 campaign, AMSAM members often had debates on whether they should focus more on 'politics' or 'social work'. Yet, the vocabulary of rights, along with references to international treaties and legislations, became more prominent.

In spring 2013, in response to the arbitrary arrests and deportations of migrants, a group of Senegalese migrants organised a sit-in outside their embassy, to denounce the diplomats' silence and complicity with the Moroccan government. The Senegalese diplomatic authorities called for the intervention of the Moroccan police, who arrested some participants, including some within the grounds of the embassy itself. Almost a year after the march to Souissi, AMSAM members joined other migrant associations and NGOs for sit-ins outside the tribunal. They wrote letters to sub-Saharan embassies to complain. Rather than simply decrying injustice, the letters of protest, following advice from Moroccan human rights activists, included long quotations from the Vienna convention on consular relations, highlighting diplomats' duty of care towards all nationals.

AMSAM's advocacy work and its focus on 'exposing the true realities of migration' became articulated through a discourse of rights that went beyond mere references to 'injustice'. Fabien confided that, before getting involved with AMSAM and exchanging with NGOs, he 'did not even know that migrants had rights'. Members became acquainted with new ideas and notions, such as regularisation or the rights of *sans-papiers*, which they used to articulate a broad range of claims that were not limited to a host state. They joined networks of activists, scholars, and practitioners, sharing information and conceiving joint actions to defend the rights of migrants. Such networks extended beyond the Mediterranean Sea and the Sahara Desert, through platforms such as Migreurop or *Loujna-Tounkaranké*. AMSAM took part in sit-ins, protests, and meetings, as well as online activities, where the focus on regularisation was prominent. AMSAM also gathered evidence, along with GADEM and other associations, to compile an alternative report on Morocco's application of the International Convention on the Protection of the Rights of All Migrant Workers and Members of Their Families (GADEM *et al.*, 2013). Yet, most of AMSAM's members were still attempting to leave Douar Hajja and Morocco altogether.

A migratory association

All this work took a toll on members. The number of active members dwindled after a few months, especially after the end of *l'ambassade*. Six months after its foundation, AMSAM was made up of a small core of dedicated members: Alex, Fabien, Blaise, and a few others. They were constantly solicited by practitioners, journalists, students, researchers, and activists for information. They had to rush across the city to support migrants and liaise with civil society organisations as 'volunteers'. Fabien often accompanied migrants to their medical appointments before attending his. As Fabien put it, when another migrant from Douar Hajja insisted on getting his help, despite Fabien being ill: 'Me too. I have the same problems as you.' They received 'transport money' from NGOs who were organising events, but this was little and did not make up for the lack of wages for migrant leaders, especially when compared to employed staff members in NGOs (or researchers). This was something that AMSAM members regularly pointed out. They had to dispel rumours circulating amongst other migrants about their involvement in advocacy and social work leading to lucrative opportunities.

As they carved out some space for themselves in the Moroccan civil society landscape, members of AMSAM and other migrants' associations forged fragile relationships with Moroccan and international NGOs, to bring about changes in Moroccan society. This was illustrated in the overall theme ('another Maghreb and a different politics of migration are possible') of the Oujda forum in October 2012. Fighting for migrants' rights has been enmeshed with efforts to consolidate freedoms and rights in Morocco. The Moroccan general secretary of an organisation explained that his commitment to advocacy work around migration issues in Morocco was also for the benefit and future of his own children. Migrants, notably representatives from *Le Conseil*, took part in some of the 'February 20 Movement' protests in 2011 and 2012, calling for political reform in Morocco during the so-called Arab Spring protests across the wider region. Although this was not without frictions, migrant leaders stressed that they were also part of Moroccan society and sought to elicit wider changes, for the benefit of citizens from Morocco and elsewhere. Although this did not work, Alex sought to build links with local youth organisations and to incorporate Moroccan inhabitants of Douar Hajja, Maâdid, and Takaddoum as members of AMSAM. Yet, while members of AMSAM called for the regularisation of migrants and for the respect of human rights in Morocco, they continued attempting to cross into Spain.

AMSAM is *'une association migratoire'* (a migratory association), Alex once said, a slip of the tongue when he meant to describe AMSAM as an association of migrants. Adventurers within AMSAM regularly travelled to the borderlands for border-crossing attempts. Invoking the 'three dimensions', Alex often stressed that all migrants should get involved with the association, that their 'personal journeys' would not be an issue, whether they wished to stay in Morocco, return home, or attempt crossing into Europe. AMSAM members could be holding banners asking for regularisation during protests outside the tribunal or the parliament, and the next day be leaving for the forests near Nador. When I expressed my puzzlement, Fabien gave me his typically laconic answer: 'Why not?' Fabien and other adventurers stressed that 'fighting' for migrants' rights and articulating political claims in Morocco was not in contradiction with border-crossing attempts. Both activities were about carving out a better life in the face of adversity. AMSAM members often transformed their failed border-crossing attempts into 'field missions'. Fabien and others would return to Douar Hajja after a failed attempt near Tangier or Nador and type up 'mission reports' in a cyber. They reported on the current situation in the borderlands and gave examples of police brutality, sharing this information with NGOs and other migrants' associations.

The continued mobility of the people involved in the association allowed its members to keep a close tab on what was happening across Morocco. It was useful to their collaboration with Rabat-based organisations. When Alain settled in the marginal neighbourhood of Boukhalef near Tangier, he was described as an AMSAM member acting as the local antenna in Tangier and working to provide crucial updates. This was during a period marked by increased police brutality across northern Morocco, in the first half of 2013. One Cameroonian man from *l'ambassade*, who mostly lived in the north and only returned to Douar Hajja occasionally, was the leader of a group of migrants who went on hunger strikes and refused to board a flight deporting them to Senegal in 2014. It was through him that NGOs received the information they needed to intervene.

However, the mobility of AMSAM members was disruptive. It prevented continuity and stifled the development of projects, as people disappeared with little notice. Alex stressed that people never ceased to be AMSAM members, sometimes portraying it as a lifelong membership. He dreamed that the association would one day have offices in other Moroccan cities, as well as in members' home countries. When two inhabitants of *l'ambassade* returned to their home countries, by undertaking the journey back through the Sahara, there were talks of them founding 'sister organisations' for AMSAM in Cameroon and Nigeria. However, nothing seems to have happened. Like other adventurers, after leaving Morocco, they cut off contact with many of the people they knew.

Some members shared with me their plan to use what they had learned with AMSAM in whatever context they would find themselves next, to expose injustice and seek out better living conditions. Many expected that the fight for a better life would continue, even if they made it to Europe. They also talked about being active in socio-political initiatives in their countries of origin. Discussing what he had experienced and learned with AMSAM, Hervé explained that he was hoping to make it to Europe and later return to Cameroon to set up an organisation for children who lived on the streets, a position he had once been in. Moussa often said that he was 'a revolutionary fighting injustice everywhere'. In his involvement with AMSAM, he emphasised that he had learned much and was hoping to study law and human rights in Europe. Through AMSAM, adventurers were also broadening the scope of their own 'objective', by learning new skills, gaining valuable experiences, and exploring new paths for 'finding their lives'.

Conclusion

To better account for their political subjectivity, it is necessary to examine closely how (irregular) migrants articulate multiple, ambiguous, and sometimes seemingly contradictory political claims. They shift understandings of what it means to be political by underscoring how citizenship is not a prerequisite of political involvement. Despite being constructed as irregular migrants, adventurers retain their 'faculty of action' (Arendt, 1969: 179). This has radical implications. In discussing the violently repressed protest (hunger strike and occupation) by Sans-Papiers at the Saint-Bernard church in France in 1996, Etienne Balibar (2004: 42) argues that 'we', the political community, 'owe' them. He claims that the protest by those irregular migrants has 'recreated citizenship among us, insofar as it is not an institution, nor a status, but a collective practice' (2004: 42). We must, however, be careful not to homogenise the political participation of migrants when looking for its disruptive potential.

The engagement of adventurers from Central and Western Africa seeking to 'expose the true realities of migration' provides nuance to conceptions of the political that privilege radical disruption over participation in an established order, and often focus on migrants seeking recognition from a (Western) host state. AMSAM members pursued overlapping and sometimes conflicting claims, as illustrated by the 'Number 9' campaign. For migrants, being political does not equate with a uniform set of demands. We must recognise that a 'movement's stated goals are not always as coherent or undisputed as researchers assume' (Coutin, 1993: 170). Ambiguities and contradictions are inherent to social movements, as they are to migration (Rubin, 1998).

AMSAM members interpellated not only Moroccan and European authorities, but also NGOs and their own diplomatic representatives. The heterogeneous set of objectives within AMSAM (i.e. the 'three dimensions') mirrored how members were constantly gauging opportunities to reach the lives they imagined for themselves. They often simultaneously considered staying, continuing, and returning. AMSAM members argued for their regularisation and, at the same time, kept preparing attacks in the borderlands. This showcases how irregular migrants can navigate the political realm, with a newly acquired vocabulary of migrants' rights, to 'find their lives' in an uncertain political context, marked by violence. Their active but fragile involvement in Moroccan civil society demonstrates how the rights of migrants were also entangled with wider social and political issues in Morocco. AMSAM members contributed to wider debates and advocacy work. Like other migrants in Douar Hajja and Maâdid, AMSAM members were prepared to make a life for themselves in Morocco, if conditions were right, and to fight for it. Most remained disillusioned by the continuous infringement of their rights, precarious living conditions, and the persistence of racism and violence. One year after its birth, as Moroccan authorities made promising announcements about a shift in politics of migration, the majority of the members of this organisation had returned to their home countries, crossed into Europe, or travelled elsewhere.

Note

1. This is a pseudonym. The real name of the association was once altered to reflect changes in how members presented it (as explored in this chapter), but I retain AMSAM for ease of reading.

Adventure: a radical movement towards life

This book has sought to provide an ethnographic account that probes, nuances, and humanises experiences of entrapment amongst young men from Central and Western Africa stuck in Morocco and facing the violence and uncertainty of hostile bordering regimes. To examine the moral, gendered, affective, social, and political dimensions of migrants' fraught experiences of mobility, the book was articulated around migrants' emic notion of 'the adventure' as an epic quest to carve out a better life and future for themselves (and their loved ones). Denied safe and legal ways of migrating, adventurers set out to carve out and seize opportunities matching their own (and their loved ones') ambitions. For the young men living in the ghettoes of Douar Hajja and Maâdid, the adventure was about '*chercher sa vie*' (looking for one's life) and '*se chercher*' (looking for one's self). It was a transformative, initiatory journey, through which they could assert themselves as agents of their own destinies, despite uncertain, illegalising processes. Ready to 'shock' and 'eat the border', they portrayed themselves as constantly braced to face up to violence and suffering with courage and strength. A focus on the notion of adventure deconstructs the pervasive narratives of a 'migration crisis' and a 'sub-Saharan problem', sheds light on the violent consequences of hostile migration policies and practices, and accounts for how migrants themselves made sense of their entrapped mobility.

In contributing to contemporary, interdisciplinary scholarship that has taken seriously the emic notion of the adventure, I theorise the latter as an existential yearning for a better life and future for people brutally immobilised by bordering processes. The adventure is an individual quest for emancipation amongst a collective endeavour of people who challenge global inequities in the distribution of the ability to circulate to and settle in a place one has not been assigned to within the 'national order of things' (Malkki, 1995a). In the book, I examine how the adventure entails a mode of being in (and moving through) the world for migrants facing violent, racialised migration regimes. I argue that the adventure requires the cultivation of fragile skills (e.g. resourcefulness), dispositions (e.g. keeping the right mentality), and relationships (e.g. travelling companions) to continue their journey and, hopefully, achieve victory ('*boza*'). Away from ready-made labels and categories of migration, I argue that a closer look at the adventure provides analytical tools to apprehend with both depth and nuance migrants' efforts to overcome their forced immobility. Such a focus brings insights that resonate with the conditions facing other illegalised and racialised migrants (e.g. USA–Mexico border) across a world marked not just by faster means of travel but the multiplication of crude and sophisticated fortifications and filtering processes by state and non-state actors which do not fully succeed in eradicating people's aspirations – though they often succeed in fostering harm and destruction.

The adventure is a powerful and evocative idiom for the articulation of imaginaries and aspirations about a life 'more bearable' that can only be reached by taking the road. It provides a moral template for migrants who are denied the comfort of safer routes but who nevertheless project themselves to a place and time where they hope to reach 'the objective' and carve out meaningful and dignified living conditions. Adventurers are astute and resourceful fighters against a bordered world where certain racialised categories of people are depicted as undesirable, even if some are filtered in to accommodate the needs of the privileged within global and exploitative economic processes. The adventure is not a crisis but a radical movement towards life, in which migrants defy enduring precarity and the tangible risk of death to pursue transformative projects. It calls for the recognition of political subjectivities that are often obfuscated in dominant discourses, but which articulate complex demands on a wide range of state and non-state actors.

The construction of migration and migrants as both favoured analytical objects of funded research and scarecrows of an enduring moral panic raises epistemological and ontological challenges. As argued by Abdelmalek Sayad, the figure of the migrant and the phenomenon of migration are both the object of discourses which are 'imposed' (2006: 53), and often articulated in reference to a problem. Public discourse peddles widespread and destructive narratives that reduce migrants to threatening invaders, dangerous criminals, or voiceless victims. Debates have often centred around crisis, a powerful and evocative notion that persists in capturing the imagination of many decision-makers and members of the wider public, calling for the continuous deployment of restrictive measures to selectively deter, control, manage, and deport people. These often only succeed in making journeys longer and more dangerous, as illustrated by the rising number of deaths amongst migrants in the Mediterranean region and beyond. Scholarship has provided important tools to debunk deceiving narratives and to examine the entanglements of multiple actors in the power-laden processes that (re)produce, transform, and contest borders. While the notion of crisis carries less sway in scholarly depictions, studies of migration in anthropology and beyond continue to grapple with the challenge of studying migratory phenomena without reifying the pervasive categories and labels that often obfuscate analysis (e.g. transit). Research practices around migration are also embedded in lucrative and unequal processes that constitute migration and migrants as objects of knowledge and power.

In steering away from aesthetics of despair and fearmongering narratives, the book provided insights into interdisciplinary debates (e.g. illegality, uncertainty, immobility, violence, suffering, transit, etc.) without sensationalising the violence and suffering migrants were subjected to, or their own capacity to act. I have focused on tracing the radical potential of adventurers' own understandings of the frictions between hopeful quests and bordering regimes. This is essential to draw out the complexity and existential depth of young men's lives, journeys, and stories. The notion of 'the adventure' provides migrants with the tools to make sense of, navigate, and challenge the violence and uncertainty of bordering regimes. It contributes to a more layered analysis of migration policies and practices in the wider region. In the Moroccan context, the focus on adventurers in marginal neighbourhoods highlights the fragile and ambiguous emplacement of migrants, as bordering measures impede their life and migratory projects by enforcing brutal patterns of stasis and movement.

In 2024, as I write this conclusion just over ten years after the end of fieldwork in these neighbourhoods, migration and the 'sub-Saharan problem' still dominate public debate in Morocco and beyond. Adventurers continue to attack the border with Spain amidst inadequate provision and a shift in politics of migration that has largely failed to deliver its promises. However, most of my informants are gone. In finishing this book, I have been drawn back to the question of endings. As argued by Bredeloup (2013), the adventure has a beginning and an end, which are both marked by the imperative to succeed, though the end might well be death. The adventurers I met in Douar Hajja and Maâdid have continued to grapple with their transformative projects. Many have stopped calling themselves adventurers, stressing that they were no longer in the same situation (i.e. always ready to pack up and get on a boat or scale the razor-wire-topped fences). Yet, their struggle to navigate and confront the wider forces impeding their imaginaries, aspirations, and hopes has mostly continued.

I have kept in touch with several of my close informants, through social media and regular, extensive stays in Morocco for other projects on migration. With each visit, the number of migrants I knew who still lived in Douar Hajja and Maâdid decreased a little more. New adventurers kept arriving, albeit in fewer numbers. The people I had met had gone back to their home countries, crossed into Europe, travelled onwards (e.g. Libya), or moved elsewhere in Morocco (Tangier) or to a different neighbourhood in Rabat. Some just disappeared. When COVID-19 travel restrictions were lifted in 2022, I was able to return to Morocco, after an absence of two years. There seemed to be no one I knew in the shops, ghettoes, and streets of Douar Hajja and Maâdid.

In October 2023, I sat with Blaise under a tall rubber tree overlooking the terrace of a café in Youssoufia, a neighbourhood close to Douar Hajja and Maâdid, where he had moved to feel safer. This was one of the places where, ten years before, migrant leaders, including Blaise, Alex, and Fabien, regularly met to discuss the establishment of a hub for migrants' associations, to coordinate advocacy and support work. The foundation of this hub marked a further step in the development of migrants' political subjectivity. It has continued to exist but has been marred by difficulties (e.g. internal rivalries, lack of sustainable funds, fraught relationships with other NGOs, etc.).

Sharing his disillusion with politics of migration in Morocco, Blaise highlighted the continued violence and infringement of migrants' rights by Moroccan authorities. But he also highlighted some improvements since 2013. The regularisation processes had enabled some migrants to obtain documents and find some level of security and comfort. They could send money home, thanks to new regulations, and they could even visit their family. Blaise was able to travel back to the Central African Republic after a very long absence. But this was not enough. Blaise complained that, in many ways, things were 'the same as before' for migrants.

Our meeting took place during one of my trips to interview members of Moroccan civil society for a project on the repression of solidarity actors. Blaise and many others stressed that there had been a progressive '*durcissement*' (hardening) of Morocco's approach to migration, particularly since the organisation of large operations of forced dispersal, from the borderlands towards southern Moroccan regions, in 2015 and especially 2018. Long-standing activists in migrants' associations shared a bitter sense of disenchantment. Many had obtained papers to regularise their immigration status but struggled to renew them. There were few opportunities for migrants to make a decent living. They continued to experience forms of everyday and institutional racism from the authorities and the media but also ordinary citizens in Morocco, as well as a particularly aggressive ultranationalist movement peddling far-right tropes such as 'grand replacement' (Hagan and Bachelet, 2024). Even in Rabat, there were daily arrests and forced dispersals targeting racialised Black migrants. As one Guinean leader from the hub of migrants' associations, a man who has been in Morocco for over twenty years, put it to me:

Migration in Morocco is *flou* [vague]. It has not been pursued with sincerity. We believed in this project. But people do not see a way out. People are discouraged. You meet with people and realise that they even find it difficult to just respond to your greetings. You need to be *coriace* [tough, resilient].

A few weeks after my conversation with this Guinean leader, dozens of migrants were killed at the Morocco–Spain border, near Nador (Association Marocaine des Droits Humains, 2022). In the aftermath, many of my interlocutors shared that they felt a physical as well as a moral '*épuisement*' (exhaustion).

Weary of discussing politics of migration and unfulfilled expectations, Blaise and I moved on to jollier things, sharing news about people we knew from ghettoes in Douar Hajja and Maâdid, especially former members of AMSAM. Few were still in Morocco. Alex and Christine made it to Spain in 2016. This departure was a big blow to the association, which was already short of active members. Fabien had to work even harder on consolidating AMSAM's work and ties to other organisations, and on looking for funds to support projects and studies. He also had a regular job in a call centre. His boss objected to his 'political activities', preventing him from taking time off to attend events. He managed to travel the following year, eventually obtaining refugee status in the UK. Moussa, who had stopped being involved in AMSAM already, left Morocco around that time too. He had obtained refugee status and was resettled in North America. Most AMSAM members have either returned back to their countries of origin (e.g. Cameroon) or, after several years trying, managed to cross the border into Spain, usually irregularly. Many have settled in German, French, Belgian, and Spanish cities.

Blaise had stayed on and remained committed to the association. AMSAM has continued to be an important part of the wider landscape of civil society organisations working on migration. Over more than a decade of existence, they have produced reports on migratory issues, including in the south of the country, which has remained a blind spot for many civil society organisations and researchers. Several migrants' associations have been recognised by Moroccan authorities, reflecting a wider tactic of co-optation in the handling of dissent by Moroccan authorities (Hagan and Bachelet, 2023). But AMSAM has not, seemingly because of their vocal advocacy work and close ties to Moroccan organisations that have been overtly critical of Morocco's record on politics of migration and human rights. This has prevented them from receiving and managing funds themselves, and greatly hampered the development of AMSAM and its activities. A few other migrants have joined, but in late 2023, Blaise was mostly alone.

Recruiting more active members has been a concern shared by many migrants' associations. Blaise and other migrant leaders from the hub blamed the dire conditions for migrants in general but also the specific difficulties faced by active members of migrants' associations. The relationships between migrants and the wider civil society have remained fraught, complex, and often unequal. It has also been difficult for migrant activists to maintain a balance between committing to the demands and struggles of advocacy work and pursuing one's life and migratory goals. Blaise reflected:

> In 2012 and 2013, we were many [in AMSAM]. Many people came to Morocco to cross the border. They are gone. Migrants think that *les militants* [activists] have a lot of money. Then they discover that this is not the case. So, they leave. That's the issue. The situation is difficult. There is no work. No opportunities. It is discouraging. If, unlike us, the person does not know what activism entails, then they will give up. *Militer* [to be an activist] is a sacrifice.

Feeling nostalgic after reminiscing about both joyful and gruesome moments, we got up and walked over to Douar Hajja. 'The Douar Hajja you knew is gone,' Blaise told me, listing places such as restaurants and ghettoes, where adventurers used to hang out. All of them were shut. People were gone. Several were dead or had vanished. Only *le consulat* was still going. Jamal had found a group of Sudanese migrants to rent to recently, marking changes in the make-up of adventurers and the migratory routes through Morocco and the rest of the African continent. We walked past the alleyway leading to *l'ambassade*, but neither of us was inclined to walk down and stare at the door of the Cameroonian ghetto, which had been sealed by the police in 2012.

Blaise drew my attention to how few Black migrants there were compared to 2013. We only saw a handful of men working by the wholesaler, carrying bags of flour, and a few more near *château* looking for work. Blaise repeated that the neighbourhood had changed. The number of migrants decreased throughout the second half of the 2010s, because of increasing waves of arrests and deportations once the regularisation processes were completed. More left during the COVID-19 pandemic, as there was no support from state authorities for migrants. The concentration of migrants around Rabat had shifted, mostly to Salé, Blaise said. Douar Hajja, like Maâdid, was not as central to migratory routes as before. In 2023, new plans from local and national authorities for the urban development of Rabat have singled out five '*insalubre*' (substandard) neighbourhoods, including Douar Hajja and Maâdid, as priority zones for either rehabilitation work or complete destruction.

While walking back, I asked Blaise if he still considered himself an adventurer. He chuckled and said that, for him, and for other migrant leaders who had been in Morocco for so many years, 'the adventure is over. We have no intention to cross the border by the sea.' I knew that this was only partially true. Several leaders of migrants' associations found opportunities to travel to Europe, thanks to their work and invitations from NGOs. Some never returned. Such (limited) opportunities for mobility were sometimes part of the motivation for people to join migrants' associations. Migrant leaders who stressed that the adventure was over often simply meant that they were not willing to risk their lives crossing the sea. They had not entirely given up on leaving Morocco and reaching Europe. Blaise, then in his fifties, no longer considered burning the border to be a viable option. He was not sure how much longer he would stay in Morocco. Like other migrants, he had renewed his immigration papers by registering himself under the status of auto-entrepreneur (sole trader). But he struggled to make ends meet and hoped to travel to France, where his daughter studied for a masters. He was looking for a way.

After each large crossing of young men from Western and Central Africa into the Spanish enclaves of Ceuta and Melilla, videos from journalists or from migrants themselves often circulate online. The men are seen running in urban areas, taking their tops off and celebrating by shouting '*boza*', a term widely used amongst adventurers to mean crossing into Europe. It is also a rallying cry for victory. They point their fingers upwards to thank God and address the cameras, saying that their time in Morocco is over, often calling out and waving to their mothers through the lens.

Many of my informants have shared in such celebrations after several years of trying. I have followed some of their journeys into Europe through Facebook posts and occasional phone calls, although contact has eroded over the years. Alain managed to cross into Spain with Roméo after mending their relationship. They lived near Madrid for a while. Alain posted happy pictures of himself in beautiful surroundings on social media. But when I spoke to him, he emphasised how difficult everyday life was: 'It is like we have never *mbeng* [crossed into Europe].' Adventurers often continued to struggle and used the epic and pugilistic language of the adventure (e.g. fighting) when describing their lives in Europe. There, other forms of violence, abuse, and exploitation await racialised Black men constructed as illegal. Those who made it to Europe often continued to travel and look for opportunities. They navigated complex bureaucracies for immigration papers. They often found themselves again in the informal sector, with meagre earnings and challenging conditions (e.g. night shifts as security guards). Still, they slowly built lives, and even founded families. Alain moved to Germany and had a child. In 2018, I travelled to Brussels with my family to attend Pierre's wedding as his best man. We were greeted outside Brussels-Midi station by a Cameroonian man from *l'ambassade* who reminisced over hardship in Morocco but stressed that things were not easy in Belgium.

Idrissa and I speak on the phone a few times a year. He has been working in Saudi Arabia since his chaotic journey home. He often starts the conversation by asking for advice, sharing that he still thinks about returning to Morocco. The company he has worked at for many years faced bankruptcy recently. Socio-political issues in Burkina Faso and the Ivory Coast have led some of his relatives to flee and have made returning difficult for him. He does not want to find himself in an irregular situation again, he told me, but his options are limited. Like many others, he has continued to carefully think about the best ways to find and reach the life and future he aspires to, despite the limited opportunities for travel and settlement afforded to him by unequal bordering regimes.

Adventurers in Douar Hajja and Maâdid suffered the dehumanising effects of a global governance of migration rooted in the inequities of (post)colonial relationships across the European and African continents. Denied accessible routes to the (material) success, comfort, and security that they projected on to '*le dehors*' (the outside), adventurers undertook dangerous, lengthy, but hopeful journeys to seize a better future for themselves and their families. Transnational bordering regimes that organise the selective deterrence, control, arrest, and deportation of migrants partake in the construction of certain racialised subjects as undesirable, dangerous, and undeserving. Such processes have continued to affect adventurers' capacity to live and move beyond the Mediterranean Sea. Often, they had already anticipated this in Douar Hajja and Maâdid. In a poem he wrote in *l'ambassade*, titled *Espoir* (Hope), Ismael imagined himself after crossing into Europe: 'The struggle continues.' He said something similar on the phone when I caught up with him after he had arrived in Spain and found out that opportunities to make a living were narrow and arduous still.

The exploration of hostile politics of migration and their consequences calls for the analysis of the discourses, policies, and other practices targeting these contemporary 'wretched of the earth' (Fanon, 1963), but also for a closer examination of their lives and stories. This is essential to avoid further marginalising migrants. This book contributes to such debates by examining how young men from Central and Western Africa deployed the notion of the adventure and other terms (e.g. objective, chance, mentality, etc.) to make sense of their impeded mobilities, precarious lives, and uncertain futures. Such a focus is essential to provide a nuanced account of migrants' efforts to navigate a volatile terrain where migration is constructed by powerful actors as a problem to solve, a challenge to overcome, and a crisis to stifle (Chapter 1). Exploring the emic notion through which adventurers imagined, discussed, and acted on their curbed mobility decentres the fears and putative needs of nation-states. Migrants sought to reach 'the objective', understood as a better life where they could develop themselves and their talents. Their journeys were not a straight line towards Europe (Chapter 2). They strove to be actors and not simply spectators or recipients of their own destinies through the display of courage and strength, while acknowledging that chance and more powerful forces were at play (Chapter 3). In the shadow of a Moroccan state that neglected or brutalised them, migrants organised themselves. They set up their own living arrangements and opened businesses (Chapters 4 and 5). As a loose collective, adventurers negotiated complex relationships and moral dilemmas and pursued individual journeys while relying on necessary help and support from travelling companions (Chapter 6). A focus on the adventure foregrounds the creative forms of political subjectivity and agency amongst those constructed as racialised, illegal migrants (Chapters 7 and 8).

The figure of the adventurer is a far cry from dominant portrayals of migrants as unwelcome threats, victims, or criminals. This book does not claim the emic notion of the adventure as a universal analytical tool. In places where it is used by migrants themselves, it provides insights into their efforts to sustain the capacity to be actors of their lives and journeys amidst wider forces, and sheds light on to their precarious anchoring in places like Douar Hajja and Maâdid, where migrants (often reluctantly) partook in the social, economic, and political life of these neighbourhoods, but under exploitative and violent conditions. It is crucial not to romanticise such accounts, nor to overstate migrants' ability to act in the face of hostile bordering regimes. Like the 'space of non-existence' (Coutin, 2000: 28), the adventure should not be romanticised, for it entails uncertainty, precarity, violence, and suffering. People could 'go mad' while striving to maintain 'the right mentality'. As explored in this book, adventurous journeys involve limited political agency, complex moral dilemmas, and the forging of ambiguous and power-laden relationships with a wide range of actors, including other migrants. However, an analytical focus on migrants' understanding of their entrapped mobility through the emic notion of the adventure also offers a chance to depart from miserabilist accounts of suffering, which have been at the heart of public debate as well as scholarship (see Robbins, 2013).

In parallel to fearmongering accounts, migration is the focus of pitiful portrayals of suffering, calls for compassionate responses, and appeals to a common humanity, sometimes by the very decision-makers advocating for tough measures to curb migration. Hannah Arendt argues that pity and compassion have no place in the public sphere. Compassion is irrelevant because it suppresses 'the worldly space between men where political matters are located' (Arendt, 1963: 86). Pity requires the continued 'existence of the unhappy' (Arendt, 1963: 86). Rather than boundless sentiments, Arendt proposes the principle of solidarity as a basis for revolutionary politics. As she puts it, 'it is out of pity that men are attracted towards *"les hommes faibles*", but it is out of solidarity that they establish deliberately and, as it were, dispassionately a community of interest with the oppressed and exploited' (Arendt, 1963: 88; original emphasis). Solidarity can inspire and motivate people to act.

Within studies of migration, solidarity requires engaging in earnest with how people make sense of their own experiences of violence and suffering. Aharony criticises Arendt's analysis of totalitarian regimes for arguing that 'the survivors of the concentration camps were not capable of reflecting on their experience in any meaningful way' (Aharony, 2015: 6). In her critical engagement with Arendt's understanding of totalitarianism, one of Aharony's main motivations is to demonstrate that 'survivors' testimonies are much more relevant, precisely in thinking about horrors and resisting their thoughtfulness, than Arendt was willing to admit' (Aharony, 2015: 6). A commitment to exploring the diversity of human experience and a belief that what people have to say about their own lives matters are inherent to most anthropological scholarship and ethnographic practices. In the context of hostile politics of migration and their deadly consequences, a focus on how migrants make sense of and act on their entrapped mobilities is crucial, especially to carve out spaces for radical imagination and the pursuit of alter-politics (Haiven and Khasnabish, 2014; Hage, 2015). Beyond the deconstruction of state-sanctioned categories and labels, the analysis of illegal migration must be grounded in migrants' own understandings of their entrapped mobility and (limited) capacity to act. Failing to do so further partakes in enduring marginalising processes and curtails the emergence of radically different stories to counter hegemonic narratives of crisis. As Ismael wrote in his poem, written on the rooftop of *l'ambassade* in between shifts on construction sites:

> Tomorrow, why not believe,
> Tomorrow, why ever doubt,
> Tomorrow, there might be glory.
> Tomorrow, there might be love.[1]

Note

1. See Bachelet (2014b) for a translation of the whole poem.

References

Abu-Lughod, Lila (1990) 'The romance of resistance: tracing transformations of power through Bedouin women', *American Anthropologist*, 17:1, 41–55.

Agamben, Giorgio. (1998) *Homo sacer: sovereign power and bare life*. Stanford, CA: Stanford University Press.

Agier, Michel (2011) *Managing the undesirables: refugee camps and humanitarian government*. Cambridge: Polity Press.

Agier, Michel (2022) *La peur des autres: Essai sur l'indésirabilité*. Paris: Éditions Payot & Rivages.

Aharony, Michal (2015) *Hannah Arendt and the limits of total domination: the holocaust, plurality, and resistance*. London: Routledge.

Ahmed, Sara, Castada, Claudia, Fortier, Anne-Marie, et al. (eds) (2003) *Uprootings/regroundings*. London: Routledge.

Alain-El Mansouri, Béatrice (2004) *Profil de la Ville de Rabat*. UN-Habitat and NEPAD Cities: Programme des Nations Unies pour les Établissements Humains.

Alami, Aida (2018) 'Morocco unleashes a harsh crackdown on sub-Saharan migrants', *New York Times*, 22 October.

Alami M'Chichi, Houria (2008) 'Les migrations des subsahariens au Maroc à travers la presse: une relation à l'autre difficile', in Lahlou, Mehdi (ed.), *Migration, droits de l'Homme et développement*. Rabat: Friedrich Ebert Stitfung.

Alexander, Isabella (2019) 'Trapped on the island: the politics of race and belonging in Jazīrat al-Maghrib', *The Journal of North African Studies*, 24:5, 786–806. DOI: 10.1080/13629387.2018.1483880.

Alexander-Nathani, Isabella (2021) *Burning at Europe's borders: an ethnography on the African migrant experience in Morocco*. New York: Oxford University Press.

Alioua, Mehdi (2005) 'La migration transnationale des Africains subsahariens au Maghreb: l'exemple de l'étape marocaine', *Maghreb-Machrek*, 185, 37–58.

Alioua, Mehdi (2007) 'Nouveaux et anciens espaces de circulation internationale au Maroc: les grandes villes marocaines, relais migratoires émergents de la migration transnationale des Africains subsahariens au Maghreb', *Revue des mondes musulmans et de la Méditerranée*, 119–20, 35–58.

Alioua, Mehdi (2009) 'Le "passage au politique" des transmigrants subsahariens au Maroc: imaginaire migratoire, réorganisation collective et mobilisation politique en situation de migration transnationale', in Bensaâd, Ali (ed.), *Le Maghreb à l'épreuve des migration subsahariennes: immigration sur émigration*, 279–303. Paris: Karthala.

Alioua, Mehdi (2011) 'L'étape marocaine des transmigrants subsahariens en route vers l'Europe: l'épreuve de la construction des réseaux et de leurs territoires', PhD thesis: Université de Toulouse.

Alioua, Mehdi (2015) 'L'irresponsabilité des responsables de la politique migratoire', Tel Quel, 14 February. Available at: http://telquel.ma/2015/02/14/lirresponsabilite-responsables-politique-migratoire_1434329 (accessed: 19 February 2024).

Alioua, Mehdi, and Ferrié, Jean-Noël (eds) (2017) *La nouvelle politique migratoire marocaine*. Rabat: Konrad-Adenauer-Stiftung.

Alpes, Maybritt Jill (2014) 'Imagining a future in "bush": migration aspirations at times of crisis in Anglophone Cameroon', *Identities: Global Studies in Culture and Power*, 21:3, 259–74.

Alpes, Maybritt Jill, Lo Coco, Daniela, Calderó Delgado, Clara, *et al.* (2021) *Return mania: mapping policies and practices in the EuroMed region*. Brussels: EuroMed Rights' Migration & Asylum Programme.

Amnesty International (2014) *The human cost of Fortress Europe: human rights violations against migrants and refugees at Europe's borders*. London: Amnesty International. Available at: www.amnesty.org/en/documents/EUR05/001/2014/en/ (accessed: 19 February 2024).

Anderson, Benedict (1983) *Imagined communities: reflections on the origin and spread of nationalism*. London: Verso.

Andersson, Ruben (2014) *Illegality, Inc.: clandestine migration and the business of bordering Europe*. Oakland, CA: University of California Press.

Andersson, Ruben (2016) 'Europe's failed "fight" against irregular migration: ethnographic notes on a counterproductive industry', *Journal of Ethnic and Migration Studies*, 42:7, 1055–75.

Anzaldúa, Gloria (1987) *Borderlands/La frontera: the new mestiza*. San Francisco, CA: Aunt Lute Books.

Arab, Chadia (2018) *Dames de fraises, doigts de fée: les invisibles de la migration saisonnière marocaine en Espagne*. Casablanca: En Toutes Lettres.

Arab, Chadia, and Sempere Souvannavong, Juan David (2009) 'Les jeunes *harragas* maghrébins se dirigeant vers l'Espagne: des rêveurs aux "brûleurs de frontières"', *Migrations Société*, 125, 191–206. DOI: 10.3917/migra.125.0191.

Arendt, Hannah (1951) *On the origins of totalitarianism*. New York: Harcourt, Brace and Company.

Arendt, Hannah (1963) *On revolution*. New York: Viking Press.

Arendt, Hannah (1969) *On violence*. New York: Harcourt, Brace, Jovanovich.

Aris Escarcena, Juan Pablo (2022) 'Ceuta: the humanitarian and the Fortress Europe', *Antipode*, 54, 64–85. DOI: 10.1111/anti.12758.

Asociación por Derechos Humanos de Andalucía (2014) *Droits de l'Homme à la Frontière Sud 2014*. Sevilla: APDHA. Available at: www.apdha.org/media/frontiere_sud%202014.pdf (accessed: 19 February 2024).

Association Marocaine des Droits Humains (2022) *The tragedy at the Barrio Chino border crossing*. Nador: AMDH.

Association Marocaine d'Études et de Recherches en Migration (2008) *Enquête sur l'immigration subsaharienne au Maroc: rapport préliminaire*. Rabat: AMERM.

Ataç, Ilker, Rygiel, Kim, and Stierl, Maurice (eds) (2017) *The contentious politics of refugee and migrant protest and solidarity movements: remaking citizenship from the margins*. London: Routledge.

Babo, Alfred (2017) '*Ivoirité* and citizenship in Ivory Coast: the controversial policy of Ivorian authenticité', in Lawrance, Benjamin N., and Stevens, Jacqueline

(eds), *Citizenship in question: evidentiary birthright and statelessness*, 200–16. Durham, NC: Duke University Press.
Bachelet, Sébastien (2013) 'Migrants in Morocco: "go home or face death"', *Jadaliyya*, 9 August. Available at: www.jadaliyya.com/Details/29268 (accessed: 19 February 2024).
Bachelet, Sébastien (2014a) 'Morocco trials a "radically new" politics of migration for sub-Saharan Africans', *African Argument*, 15 January. Available at: http://africanarguments.org/2014/01/15/morocco-trials-a-radically-new-politics-of-migration-for-sub-saharan-africans-by-sebastien-bachelet/ (accessed: 19 February 2024).
Bachelet, Sébastien (2014b) 'Sub-Saharan migrants' quest for hope and other dangerous pursuits', *Jadaliyya*, 16 June. Available at: http://tiny.cc/13iywz (accessed: 19 February 2024).
Bachelet, Sébastien (2019) '"Looking for one's life": trapped mobilities and adventure in Morocco', *Migration and Society*, 2:1, 40–54. DOI: 10.3167/arms.2019.020105.
Bachelet, Sébastien, and Hagan, Maria (2023) 'Migration, race, and gender: the policing of subversive solidarity actors in Morocco', *L'Année du Maghreb*, 30, 1–16. DOI: 10.4000/anneemaghreb.12574.
Bachelet, Sébastien, and Palladino, Mariangela (2024) '"Être vraiment vrai": truth, in/visibility and migration in Morocco', *Identities: Global Studies in Culture and Power*, 31:3, 313–32. DOI: 10.1080/1070289X.2023.2233857.
Badiou, Alain (2008) 'The communist hypothesis', *New Left Review*, 49, 29–42.
Badran, Sammy Zeyad (2022) *Killing contention: demobilization in Morocco during the Arab Spring*. Syracuse, NY: Syracuse University Press.
Bajalia, A. George (2021) 'Dima Africa, daily darija: im/migrant sociality, settlement, and state policy in Tangier, Morocco', *The Journal of North African Studies*, 26:5, 973–92.
Bal, Ellen, and Willems, Roos (2014) 'Introduction: aspiring migrants, local crises and the imagination of futures "away from home"', *Identities: Global Studies in Culture and Power*, 21:3, 249–58.
Baldwin-Edwards, Martin (2006) '"Between a rock and a hard place": North Africa as a region of emigration, immigration and transit migration', *Review of African Political Economy*, 33:108, 311–24.
Balibar, Étienne (2004) *We, the people of Europe? Reflections on transnational citizenship*. Princeton, NJ: Princeton University Press.
Barros, Lucile, Lahlou, Mehdi, Escoffier, Claire, *et al.* (2002) *L'immigration irrégulière subsaharienne à travers et vers le Maroc*. Geneva: Bureau International du Travail.
Bartels, Inken (2017) '"We must do it gently": the contested implementation of the IOM's migration management in Morocco', *Migration Studies*, 5:3, 315–36.
Becker, Cynthia (2002) '"We are real slaves, real Ismkhan": memories of the trans-Saharan slave trade in the Tafilalet of South-Eastern Morocco', *The Journal of North African Studies*, 7:4, 97–121.
Belfquih, M'Hammed, and Fadloullah, Abdellatif (1986) *Mécanismes et formes de croissance urbaine au Maroc: cas de l'agglomération de Rabat-Salé*. Rabat: Librairie El Maârif.
Belguendouz, Abdelkrim (2003) *Le Maroc non-Africain gendarme de l'Europe?: alerte au projet de loi 02–03 relative à l'entrée et au séjour des étrangers au Maroc, à l'émigration et l'immigration irrégulières*. Rabat: Imprimerie Beni Snassen.

Belguendouz, Abdelkrim (2005) 'Expansion et sous-traitance des logiques d'enfermement de l'Union européenne: l'exemple du Maroc', *Cultures & Conflits*, 57, 155–219.
Belloni, Milena (2016) '"My uncle cannot say 'no' if I reach Libya": Unpacking the social dynamics of border-crossing among Eritreans heading to Europe', *Human Geography*, 9:2, 47–56.
Belloni, Milena (2019) *The big gamble: the migration of Eritreans to Europe*. Oakland, CA: University of California Press.
Benjelloun, Sara (2021) 'Morocco's new migration policy: between geostrategic interests and incomplete implementation', *The Journal of North African Studies*, 26:5, 875–92. DOI: 10.1080/13629387.2020.1800207.
Bensaâd, Ali (2005) 'Le Maghreb pris entre deux feux', *Le Monde*, 28 October.
Bensaâd, Ali (ed.) (2009) *Le Maghreb à l'épreuve des migration subsahariennes: immigration sur émigration*. Paris: Karthala.
Bernardot, Marc (2008) *Camps d'etrangers*. Paris: Terra.
Berriane, Johara (2015) 'Sub-Saharan students in Morocco: determinants, everyday life, and future plans of a high-skilled migrant group', *The Journal of North African Studies*, 20:4, 573–89. DOI: 10.1080/13629387.2015.1065042.
Berriane, Mohamed, de Haas, Hein, and Natter, Katharina (2015) 'Introduction: revisiting Moroccan migrations', *The Journal of North African Studies*, 20:4, 503–21. DOI: 10.1080/13629387.2015.1065036.
Berzock, Kathleen Bickford (2019) *Caravans of gold, fragments in time: art, culture, and exchange across medieval Saharan Africa*. Princeton, NJ: Princeton University Press.
Besteman, Catherine (2019) *Militarized global apartheid*. Durham, NC: Duke University Press.
Bigo, Didier (2002) 'Security and immigration: toward a critique of the governmentality of unease', *Alternatives*, 27:1, 63–92.
Bloch, Ernst (1959) *The principle of hope*. Vol. 1. Cambridge: MIT Press.
Blunt, Alison, and Dowling, Robyn (2006) *Home*. London: Routledge.
Boccagni, Paolo (2017) *Migration and the search for home: mapping domestic space in migrants' everyday lives*. New York: Palgrave Macmillan.
Boccagni, Paolo, Murcia, Pérez, Eduardo, Louis, et al. (2020) *Thinking home on the move: a conversation across disciplines*. Bingley: Emerald Publishing Ltd.
Boccagni, Paolo, and Miranda-Nieto, Alejandro (2022) 'Home in question: uncovering meanings, desires and dilemmas of non-home', *European Journal of Cultural Studies*, 25:2, 515–32.
Boehm, Deborah A. (2008) '"Now I am a man and a woman!": gendered moves and migrations in a transnational Mexican community', *Latin American Perspectives*, 35:1, 16–30. DOI: 10.1177/0094582X07310843.
Boswell, Christina (2003) 'The "external dimension" of EU immigration and asylum policy', *International Affairs*, 79:3, 619–38.
Bourgeois, Philippe (2008) *In search of respect: selling crack in El Barrio*. Cambridge: Cambridge University Press.
Bourhaba, Othmane, and Hamimida, Mama (2021) 'Does informal economy reduce poverty? Evidence from Morocco', *International Journal of Economics and Management Research*, 1:4, 90–106.
Brambilla, Chiara, and Pötzcsh, Holger (2017) 'In/visibility', in Schimanski, Johan, and Wolfe, Stephen F. (eds), *Border aesthetics: concepts and intersections*, 68–89. New York: Berghahn Books.

Braudel, Fernand (2000) *The Mediterranean and the Mediterranean world in the age of Philip II*. London: The Folio Society.
Bredeloup, Sylvie (2008) 'L'Aventurier: une Figure de la Migration Africaine', *Cahiers Internationaux de Sociologie*, 2:125, 281–306.
Bredeloup, Sylvie (2013) 'The figure of the adventurer as an African migrant', *Journal of African Cultural Studies*, 25:2, 170–82.
Bredeloup, Sylvie (2014) *Migrations d'aventure: terrains Africains*. Paris: Éditions du Comité des Travaux Historiques et Scientifiques.
Bredeloup, Sylvie (2016) 'The migratory adventure as a moral experience', in Kleist, Nauja, and Thorsen, Dorte (eds), *Hope and uncertainty in contemporary African migration*, 134–53. London: Routledge.
Bredeloup, Sylvie, and Pliez, Olivier (2005) 'Introduction: migrations entre les deux rives du Sahara', *Autrepart*, 36, 3–20.
Buehler, Matt (2015) 'Continuity through co-optation: rural politics and regime resilience in Morocco and Mauritania', *Mediterranean Politics*, 20:3, 364–85. DOI: 10.1080/13629395.2015.1071453.
Bureau, Jeanne (2020) 'Camerounais à Oran (Algérie): Parcours migratoires, insertions urbaines et lieux de sociabilité', PhD thesis: Université de Paris.
Butler, Judith (2016) *Frames of war: when is life grievable?* London: Verso.
Cabot, Heath (2019) 'The business of anthropology and the European refugee regime', *American Ethnologist*, 46:3, 261–75.
Cabot, Heath, and Ramsay, Georgina (2021) 'Deexceptionalizing displacement: an introduction', *Humanity: An International Journal of Human Rights, Humanitarianism, and Development*, 12:3, 286–99.
Çağlar, Ayşe, and Schiller, Nina Glick (2016) *Migrants & city-making: dispossession, displacement, and urban regeneration*. Durham, NC: Duke University Press.
Cancellieri, Adriano (2017) 'Towards a progressive home-making: the ambivalence of migrants' experience in a multicultural condominium', *Journal of Housing and the Built Environment*, 32:1, 49–61.
Candea, Matei (2007) 'Arbitrary locations: in defence of the bounded field-site', *The Journal of the Royal Anthropology Institute*, 13:1, 167–84.
Carling, Jørgen (2007) 'Migration control and migration fatalities at the Spanish–African borders', *International Migration Review*, 41:2, 316–43.
Casas-Cortes, Maribel, Cobarrubias, Sebastian, and Pickles, John (2015) 'Riding routes and itinerant borders: autonomy of migration and border externalization', *Antipode*, 47, 894–914. DOI: 10.1111/anti.12148.
Castañeda, Heide (2013) 'Medical aid as protest: acts of citizenship for unauthorized im/migrants and refugees', *Citizenship Studies*, 17:2, 227–40.
Chambers, Iain (2008) *Mediterranean crossings: the politics of an interrupted modernity*. Durham, NC: Duke University Press.
Chappatte, André (2014) 'Night life in southern urban Mali: being a Muslim *maquisard* in Bougouni', *The Journal of the Royal Anthropological Institute*, 20:3, 526–44.
Cheikh, Mériam, and Péraldi, Michel (2009) *Des femmes sur les routes: voyages au féminin entre Afrique et Méditerranée: expériences et compétences*. Casablanca: Le Fennec.
Chekkat, Rafik (2020) 'Négrophobie: les damnés du Maghreb', *Orient XXI*, 11 August. Available at: https://orientxxi.info/magazine/negrophobie-les-damnes-du-maghreb,4046 (accessed: 19 February 2024).

Cherti, Myriam, and Collyer, Michael (2015) 'Immigration and pensée d'etat: Moroccan migration policy changes as transformation of "geopolitical culture"', *The Journal of North African Studies*, 20:4, 590–604.

Cherti, Myriam, and Grant, Peter (2013) *The myth of transit: sub-Saharan migration in Morocco*. London: Institute for Public Policy Research.

Collyer, Michael (2006) 'Undocumented sub-Saharan African migrants in Morocco', in Sørensen, Ninna (ed.), *Mediterranean transit migration*, 129–46. Copenhagen: Danish Institute for International Studies.

Collyer, Michael (2007) 'In-between places: trans-Saharan transit migrants in Morocco and the fragmented journey to Europe', *Antipode*, 39:4, 668–90.

Collyer, Michael (2010) 'Stranded migrants and the fragmented journey', *Journal of Refugee Studies*, 23:3, 273–93.

Collyer, Michael, and de Haas, Hein (2012) 'Developing dynamic categorisations of transit migration', *Population, Space and Place*, 18:4, 468–81.

Collyer, Michael, Cherti, Myriam, Lacroix, Thomas, et al. (2009) 'Migration and development: the Euro-Moroccan experience', *Journal of Ethnic and Migration Studies*, 35:10, 1555–70.

Colson, Elizabeth (2003) 'Forced migration and the anthropological response', *Journal of Refugee Studies*, 16:1, 1–18.

Conseil national des droits de l'Homme (2013) *Étrangers et droits de l'homme au Maroc: pour une politique d'asile et d'immigration radicalement nouvelle*. Rabat: CNDH. Available at: www.cndh.org.ma/fr/rapports-thematiques/conclusions-et-recommandations-du-rapport-etrangers-et-droits-de-lhomme-au (accessed: 19 February 2024).

Cooper, Elizabeth, and Pratten, David (eds) (2015) *Ethnographies of uncertainty in Africa*. London: Palgrave Macmillan.

Corsín Jiménez, Alberto (2011) 'Trust in anthropology', *Anthropological Theory*, 11:2, 177–96.

Coutin, Susan Bibler (1993) *The culture of protest: religious activism and the US sanctuary movement*. Boulder, CO: Westview Press.

Coutin, Susan Bibler (2000) *Legalizing moves: Salvadoran immigrants' struggle for US residency*. Ann Arbor, MI: University of Michigan Press.

Coutin, Susan Bibler, and Vogel, Erica (2016) 'Migrant narratives and ethnographic tropes: navigating tragedy, creating possibilities', *Journal of Contemporary Ethnography*, 45:6, 631–44.

Craig, Sienna R. (2020) *The ends of kinship: connecting Himalayan lives between Nepal and New York*. Seattle, WA: University of Washington Press.

Crapanzano, Vincent (2004) *Imaginative horizons: an essay in literary-philosophical anthropology*. Chicago, IL: University of Chicago Press.

Crawley, Heaven, and Skleparis, Dimitris (2018) 'Refugees, migrants, neither, both: categorical fetishism and the politics of bounding in Europe's "migration crisis"', *Journal of Ethnic and Migration Studies*, 44:1, 48–64. DOI: 10.1080/1369183X.2017.1348224.

Crawley, Heaven, McMahon, Simon, and Jones, Katharine (2016) *Victims and villains: migrant voices in the British media*. Coventry: Centre for Trust, Peace and Social Relations.

Cross, Hannah M. (2009) 'The EU migration regime and West African clandestine migrants', *Journal of Contemporary European Research*, 5:2, 171–87.

Cuttitta, Paola (2020) 'Non-governmental/civil society organizations and the European Union-externalisation of migration management in Tunisia and Egypt', *Population, Space and Place*, 26:7, 1–13.

Daadaoui, Mohamed (2010) 'Rituals of power and political parties in Morocco: limited elections as positional strategies', *Middle Eastern Studies*, 46:2, 195–219.
Dadusc, Deanna, Grazioli, Margherita, and Martinez, Miguel A. (eds) (2021) *Resisting citizenship: migrant housing squats against state enclosures*. London: Routledge.
De Coninck, David (2020) 'Migrant categorizations and European public opinion: diverging attitudes towards immigrants and refugees', *Journal of Ethnic and Migration Studies*, 46:9, 1667–86.
De Genova, Nicholas (2002) 'Migrant "illegality" and deportability in everyday life', *Annual Review of Anthropology*, 31, 419–47.
De Genova, Nicholas (2005) *Working the boundaries: race, space and 'illegality' in Mexican Chicago*. Durham, NC: Duke University Press.
De Genova, Nicholas (2018) 'The "migrant crisis" as racial crisis: do *Black Lives Matter* in Europe?', *Ethnic and Racial Studies*, 41:10, 1765–82.
De Genova, Nicholas, and Peutz, Nathalie (eds) (2010) *The deportation regime: sovereignty, space, and the freedom of movement*. Durham, NC: Duke University Press.
De Genova, Nicholas, and Tazzioli, Martina (eds) (2016) 'Europe/crisis: new keywords of "the crisis" in and of "Europe"', Near Futures Online, 1. Available at: https://nearfuturesonline.org/wp-content/uploads/2016/01/New-Keywords-Collective_12.pdf (accessed: 23 February 2024).
De Haas, Hein (2007) 'Morocco's migration experience: a transnational perspective', *International Migration*, 45:4, 39–70.
De Haas, Hein (2023) *How migration really works: a factual guide to the most divisive issue in politics*. London: Penguin.
De León, Jason (2015) *The land of open graves: living and dying on the migrant trail*. Oakland, CA: University of California Press.
De Smet, Brecht, and El Kahlaoui, Soraya (2021) 'Putting the margins at the centre: at the edges of protest in Morocco and Egypt', *Partecipazione e Conflitto*, 14:2, 621–43. DOI: 10.1285/i20356609v14i2p621.
Di Nunzio, Marco (2015) 'Embracing uncertainty: young people on the move in Addis Ababa's inner city', in Cooper, Elizabeth, and Pratten, David (eds), *Ethnographies of uncertainty in Africa*, 149–72. London: Palgrave Macmillan.
Di Nunzio, Marco (2019) *The act of living: street life, marginality, and development in urban Ethiopia*. Ithaca, NY: Cornell University Press.
Directorate-General for Neighbourhood and Enlargement Negotiations (2023) 'EU migration support in Morocco'. Available at: https://neighbourhood-enlargement.ec.europa.eu/system/files/2023-03/EU_support_migration_morocco.pdf (accessed: 19 February 2024).
Düvell, Franck (2012) 'Transit migration: a blurred and politicised concept', *Population, Space and Place*, 18:4, 415–27.
Dzenovska, Dace (2014). 'Bordering encounters, sociality and distribution of the ability to live a "normal life"', *Social Anthropology*, 22:3, 271–87.
Edogué Ntang, Jean-Louis, and Péraldi, Michel (2011) 'Un ancrage discret: l'établissement des migrations subsahariennes dans la capitale marocaine', in Péraldi, Michel (ed.), *D'une Afrique à l'autre: migrations subsahariennes au Maroc*, 37–54. Paris: Karthala.
El-Enany, Nadine (2020) *(B)ordering Britain: law, race and empire*. Manchester: Manchester University Press.
El Guabli, Brahim (2023) *Moroccan other-archives: history and citizenship after state violence*. New York: Fordham University Press.

El Hamel, Chouki (2002) '"Race", slavery and Islam in Maghribi Mediterranean thought: the question of the Haratin in Morocco', *Journal of North African Studies*, 7:3, 29–52.
El Hamel, Chouki (2013) *Black Morocco: a history of slavery, race, and Islam*. New York: Cambridge University Press.
Elliot, Alice (2015) 'Paused subjects: waiting for migration in North Africa', *Time & Society*, 25:1, 102–16. DOI: 10.1177/0961463X15588090.
Elliot, Alice (2016) 'The makeup of destiny: predestination and the labor of hope in a Moroccan emigrant town', *American Ethnologist*, 43:3, 488–99.
Elliot, Alice (2021) *The outside: migration as life in Morocco*. Bloomington, IN: Indiana University Press.
Elmadmad, Khadija (2009) *Le Maroc et la convention sur la protection des droits de tous les travailleurs migrants et des membres de leur famille*. San Domenico di Fiesole: Institut Universitaire Européen.
El Qadim, Nora (2015) *Le gouvernement asymétrique des migrations: Maroc/Union Européenne*. Paris: Dalloz.
El Qadim, Nora, Isleyen, Beste, Ansems De Vries, Leonie, *et al.* (2021) '(Im)moral borders in practice', *Geopolitics*, 26:5, 1608–38.
Erdal, Marta Bivand, and Oeppen, Ceri (2018) 'Forced to leave? The discursive and analytical significance of describing migration as forced and voluntary', *Journal of Ethnic and Migration Studies*, 44:6, 981–98.
Errazzouki, Samia (2013) 'Complicity and indifference: racism in Morocco', *Jadaliyya*, 1 August. Available at: www.jadaliyya.com/pages/index/13324/complicity-and-indifference_racism-in-morocco (accessed: 19 February 2024).
Escoffier, Claire (2008) *Transmigrant-e-s africain-e-s au Maghreb: une question de vie ou de mort*. Paris: L'Harmattan.
Essahel, Habiba (2011) 'Politiques de réhabilitation des quartiers non réglementaires au Maroc et mobilisation(s) des habitants: etudes de cas dans l'agglomération de Rabat (Rabat, Témara, Skhirat)', PhD thesis: Université François-Rabelais.
European Commission (2023) 'EU launches new cooperation programmes with Morocco worth €624 million green transition, migration and reforms', *European Commission*, 2 March. Available at: https://ec.europa.eu/commission/presscorner/detail/en/ip_23_423 (accessed: 19 February 2024).
European Court of Auditors (2019) *EU support to Morocco: limited results so far*. Brussels: European Union. Available at: www.eca.europa.eu/lists/ecadocuments/sr19_09/sr_morocco_en.pdf (accessed: 19 February 2024).
Faleh, Ali, Bokbot, Mohamed, and Alaoui, Mokhlis Derkaoui (2009) 'Les Subsahariens entre transit au Maroc et immigration clandestine en Espagne', *Papeles de Geografía*, 49–50, 27–40.
Fanon, Franz (1963) *The wretched of the earth*. New York: Grove Press.
Farmer, Paul (1996) 'On suffering and structural violence: a view from below', *Daedalus*, 125:1, 261–83.
Fassin, Didier (2005) 'Compassion and repression: the moral economy of immigration policies in France', *Cultural Anthropology*, 20:3, 362–87.
Fassin, Didier (2011) 'Policing borders, producing boundaries: the governmentality of immigration in dark times', *Annual Review of Anthropology*, 40, 213–26.
Fassin, Didier, and D'Halluin, Estelle (2005) 'The truth from the body: medical certificates as ultimate evidence for asylum seekers', *American Anthropologist*, 107:4, 597–608.

Feldman, Gregory (2012) *The migration apparatus: security, labor, and policymaking in the European Union*. Stanford, CA: Stanford University Press.

Ferguson, James (1999) *Expectations of modernity: myths and meanings of urban life on the Zambian copperbelt*. Berkeley, CA: University of California Press.

Ferguson, James (2002) 'Of mimicry and membership: Africans and the "New World Society"', *Cultural Anthropology*, 17:4, 551–69.

Friedman, Jane, Sahraoui, Nina, and Tastsoglou, Envangelina (eds) (2022) *Gender-based violence in migration: interdisciplinary, feminist and intersectional approaches*. Cham: Palgrave Macmillan.

Friedman, Sara L. (2010) 'Determining "truth" at the border: immigration interviews, Chinese marital migrants, and Taiwan's sovereignty dilemmas', *Citizenship Studies*, 14:2, 167–83.

Frontex (2023) *Risk analysis for 2023–2024*. Warsaw: Frontex. Available at: www.frontex.europa.eu/media-centre/news/news-release/frontex-risk-analysis-2023-2024-discusses-challenges-at-eu-external-borders-J6yq05 (accessed: 19 February 2024).

Gaibazzi, Paolo (2015a) 'The quest for luck: fate, fortune, work and the unexpected among Gambian Soninke hustlers', *Critical African Studies*, 7:3, 227–42.

Gaibazzi, Paolo (2015b) *Bush bound: young men and rural permanence in migrant West Africa*. New York: Berghan Books.

Gaibazzi, Paolo, Bellagamba, Alice, and Dünnwald, Stephan (eds) (2017) *EurAfrican borders and migration management: political cultures, contested spaces, and ordinary lives*. New York: Palgrave Macmillan.

Gambetta, Diego (1988) 'Can we trust trust?', in Gambetta, Diego (ed.), *Trust: making and breaking cooperative relations*, 213–37. New York: Blackwell.

Gandoulou, Justin-Daniel (1989) *Au cœur de la sape: mœurs et aventures d'un Congolais à Paris*. Paris: L'Harmattan

Gazzotti, Lorena (2021a) *Immigration nation: aid, control, and border politics in Morocco*. Cambridge: Cambridge University Press.

Gazzotti, Lorena (2021b) '(Un)making illegality: border control, racialized bodies and differential regimes of illegality in Morocco', *The Sociological Review*, 69:2, 277–95.

Gazzotti, Lorena, and Hagan, Maria (2021) 'Dispersal and dispossession as bordering: exploring migration governance through mobility in post-2013 Morocco', *The Journal of North African Studies*, 26:5, 912–31.

Geschiere, Peter (2013) *Witchcraft, intimacy and trust: Africa in comparison*. Chicago, IL: University of Chicago Press.

Gidley, Ben (2013) 'Landscapes of belonging, portraits of life: researching everyday multiculture in an inner-city estate', *Identities: Global Studies in Culture and Power*, 20:4, 361–76.

Gillespie, Richard (2002) 'Spain's pursuit of security in the western Mediterranean', *European Security*, 11:2, 48–74.

Gilroy, Paul (2006) *After empire: multicultural or postcolonial melancholia*. London: Routledge.

Goldschmidt, Élie (2002) 'Migrants congolais en route vers l'Europe', *Les Temps Modernes*, 620:1, 208–39.

Goldschmidt, Élie (2006) 'Storming the fences: Morocco and Europe's anti-migration policy', *Middle East Report*, 239. Available at: https://merip.org/2006/06/storming-the-fences/ (accessed: 23 February 2024).

Good, Anthony (2007) *Anthropology and expertise in the asylum courts*. London: Routledge.
Gouyon, Marien (2022) 'Sheep in a pen: how the externalisation of EU borders impacts the lives of gay refugees in Morocco', in Camminga, B., and Marnell, John (eds), *Queer and trans African mobilities: migration, asylum, and diaspora*, 97–115. London: Zed Books.
Greatrick, Aydan, and Fiddian-Qasmiyeh, Elena (2017) 'The roles of performance and creative writing workshops in refugee-related research', *Refugee Hosts*, 1 March. Available at: https://refugeehosts.org/2017/03/01/the-roles-of-performance-and-creative-writing-workshops-in-refugee-related-research/ (accessed: 19 February 2024).
Gross-Wyrtzen, Leslie (2020) 'Contained and abandoned in the "humane" border: Black migrants' immobility and survival in Moroccan urban space', *Environment and Planning D: Society and Space*, 38:5, 887–904.
Gross-Wyrtzen, Leslie (2023) '"There is no race here": on Blackness, slavery, and disavowal in North Africa and North African studies', *The Journal of North African Studies*, 28:3, 635–65.
Gross-Wyrtzen, Leslie, and Gazzotti, Lorena (2021) 'Telling histories of the present: postcolonial perspectives on Morocco's "radically new" migration policy', *The Journal of North African Studies*, 26:5, 827–43. DOI: 10.1080/13629387.2020.1800204.
Gross-Wyrtzen, Leslie, and El Yacoubi, Zineb Rachdi (2022) Externalizing otherness: the racialization of belonging in the Morocco–EU border. *Geoforum*, 155, 103673. DOI: 10.1016/j.geoforum.2022.103673.
Groupe antiraciste d'accompagnement et de défense des étrangers et migrants (2006) *La chasse aux migrants aux frontières Sud de l'Europe: conséquences des politiques migratoires européennes. Les refoulements de décembre 2006 au Maroc*. Rabat: GADEM.
Groupe antiraciste d'accompagnement et de défense des étrangers et migrants (2013) *Rapport relatif à l'application par le Maroc de la Convention internationale sur la protection des droits de tous les travailleurs migrants et des membres de leur famille*. Rabat: GADEM.
Groupe antiraciste d'accompagnement et de défense des étrangers et migrants (2018a) *Coûts et blessures: Rapport sur les opérations des forces de l'ordre menées dans le nord du Maroc entre juillet et septembre 2018*. Rabat: GADEM.
Groupe antiraciste d'accompagnement et de défense des étrangers et migrants (2018b) *Expulsions gratuites: note d'analyse sur les mesures d'éloignement mises en œuvre hors tout cadre légal entre septembre et octobre 2018*. Rabat: GADEM.
Groupe antiraciste d'accompagnement et de défense des étrangers et migrants and Fédération Internationale pour les Droits Humains (2015) *Maroc: entre rafles et régularisations – Bilan d'une politique migratoire indécise*. Rabat, Paris: GADEM, FIDH. Available at: www.gadem-asso.org/rapport-fidh-et-gadem-maroc-entre-rafles-et-regularisations-bilan-dune-politique-migratoire-indecise/ (accessed: 19 February 2024).
Groupe antiraciste d'accompagnement et de défense des étrangers et migrants et al. (2015) *Ceuta & Melilla, centre de tri à ciel ouvert aux portes de l'Afrique*. Available at: www.gadem-asso.org/ceuta-et-melilla-centres-de-tri-a-ciel-ouvert-aux-portes-de-lafrique-2/ (accessed: 19 February 2024).
Hagan, Maria, and Bachelet, Sébastien (2023) '*We know who you are*': hostile migration politics and the criminalisation of solidarity actors in France and Morocco.

Tangier: Litograf. Available at: https://sebastienbachelet.com/crimes-of-solidarity (accessed: 19 February 2024).
Hagan, Maria, and Bachelet, Sébastien (2024) ' "Traitors to Morocco": a campaign of harassment and racist abuse targets a human rights association', *Border Criminologies Blog*, 12 February. Available at: https://blogs.law.ox.ac.uk/border-criminologies-blog/blog-post/2024/02/traitors-morocco-campaign-harassment-and-racist-abuse (accessed: 19 February 2024).
Hage, Ghassan (2003) *Against paranoid nationalism: searching for hope in a shrinking society*. Sydney: Pluto Press.
Hage, Ghassan (2005) 'A not so multi-sited ethnography of a not so imagined community', *Anthropological Theory*, 5:4, 463–75.
Hage, Ghassan (ed.) (2009) *Waiting*. Melbourne: Melbourne University Press.
Hage, Ghassan (2015) *Alter-politics: critical anthropology and the radical imagination*. Melbourne: Melbourne University Press.
Hage, Ghassan (2016) '*État de siège*: a dying domesticating colonialism?', *American Ethnologist*, 43:1, 38–49.
Haiven, Max, and Khasnabish, Alex (2014) *The radical imagination: social movement research in the age of austerity*. London: Zed Books.
Hamlin, Rebecca (2021) *Crossings: how we label and react to people on the move*. Stanford, CA: Stanford University Press.
Han, Clara (2012) *Life in debt: times of care and violence in neoliberal Chile*. Berkeley, CA: University of California Press.
Hannoum, Abdelmajid (2020) *Living Tangier: migration, race, and illegality in a Moroccan city*. Philadelphia, PA: University of Pennsylvania Press.
Hannoum, Abdelmajid (2021) *The invention of the Maghreb: between Africa and the Middle East*. Cambridge: Cambridge University Press.
Hart, Keith (1970) 'Small-scale entrepreneurs in Ghana and development planning', *The Journal of Development Studies*, 6:4, 104–20.
Haut Commissariat au Plan (2020) *La migration internationale au Maroc*. Available at: www.hcp.ma/downloads/Enquete-Nationale-sur-la-Migration_t22402.html (accessed: 30 August 2024).
Haut Commissariat au Plan (2021) *La migration forcée au Maroc, résultats de l'enquête nationale de 2021, rapport détaillé*. Available at: www.hcp.ma/Note-sur-les-resultats-de-l-enquete-nationale-sur-la-migration-forcee-de-2021_a2715.html (accessed: 19 February 2024).
Holmes, Seth M., and Castañeda, Heide (2016) 'Representing the "European refugee crisis" in Germany and beyond: deservingness and difference, life and death', *American Ethnologist*, 43:1, 12–24.
Honwana, Alcinda (2012) *The time of youth: work, social change, and politics in Africa*. Boulder, CO: Kumarian Press.
Human Rights Watch (2022) *'They'll get you no matter what': Morocco's playbook to crush dissent*. New York: HRW. Available at: www.hrw.org/report/2022/07/28/theyll-get-you-no-matter-what/moroccos-playbook-crush-dissent (accessed: 19 February 2024).
Huysmans, Jef (2008) 'The jargon of exception: on Schmitt, Agamben and the absence of political society', *International Political Sociology*, 2:2, 165–83.
Infantino, Federica (2011) 'Barbès à Casa? Lieux cosmopolites d'Afrique dans la métropole marocaine', in Péraldi, Michel (ed.), *D'une Afrique à l'autre: migrations subsahariennes au Maroc*, 73–100. Paris: Karthala.
Institut National d'Aménagement Urbain (1984) *Évaluation du premier projet de développement urbain: Douar Hajja–Mâadid*. Rabat: INAU.

Isin, Engin F., and Rygiel, Kim (2007) 'Abject spaces: frontiers, zones, camps', in Dauphinee, Elizabeth, and Masters, Cristina (eds), *The logics of biopower and the war on terror: living, dying, surviving*, 181–203. New York: Palgrave Macmillan.

Isin, Engin F., and Nielsen, Greg M. (eds) (2008) *Acts of citizenship*. London: Zed Books.

Jackson, Michael (2002) *The politics of storytelling: violence, transgression and intersubjectivity*. Copenhagen: Museum Tusculanum Press.

Jackson, Michael (2005) *Existential anthropology: events, exigencies and effects*. Oxford: Berghahn Books.

Jackson, Michael (2011) *Life within limits: well-being in a world of want*. Durham, NC: Duke University Press.

Jackson, Michael (2013) *The politics of storytelling: variations on a theme by Hannah Arendt* (second edition). Copenhagen: Museum Tusculanum Press.

Jackson, Michael, and Piette, Albert (eds) (2015) *What is existential anthropology?* Oxford: Berghahn Books.

Jansen, Stef (2014) 'On not moving well enough: temporal reasoning in Sarajevo yearnings for "normal lives"', *Current Anthropology*, 55:S9, S74–S84.

Jansen, Stef (2016) 'For a relational, historical ethnography of hope: indeterminacy and determination in the Bosnian and Herzegovinian meantime', *History and Anthropology*, 27:4, 447–64. DOI: 10.1080/02757206.2016.1201481.

Jansen, Stef, and Löfving, Staffan (eds) (2008) *Struggles for home: violence, hope and the movement of people*. Oxford: Berghahn Books.

Jiménez-Alvarez, Mercedes G., Espiñeira, Keina, and Gazzotti, Lorena (2021) 'Migration policy and international human rights frameworks in Morocco: tensions and contradictions', *The Journal of North African Studies*, 26:5, 893–911. DOI: 10.1080/13629387.2020.1800208.

Jones, Hannah, Gunaratnam, Yasmin, Bhattacharyya, Gargi, et al. (2017) *Go home? The politics of immigration controversies*. Manchester: Manchester University Press.

Jones, Reece (2016) *Violent borders: refugees and the right to move*. London: Verso.

Kausch, Kristina (2009) 'The European Union and political reform in Morocco', *Mediterranean Politics*, 14:2, 165–79.

Kettani, Meryem, and Péraldi, Michel (2011) 'Les mondes du travail: segmentations et informalités', in Péraldi, Michel (ed.), *D'une Afrique à l'autre migrations subsahariennes au Maroc*, 55–72. Paris: Karthala.

Khosravi, Shahram (2010) *'Illegal' traveller: an auto-ethnography of borders*. London: Palgrave Macmillan.

Khrouz, Nadia (2019) *L'étranger au Maroc: droit et pratiques*. Paris: L'Harmattan.

Khrouz, Nadia, and Lanza, Nazarena (eds) (2015) *Migrants au Maroc: cosmopolitisme, présence d'étrangers et transformations sociales*. Rabat: Konrad-Adenauer-Stiftung.

Khrouz, Nadia, Ouardi, Adila, and Rachidi, Hicham (2009) *Maroc: le cadre juridique relatif à la condition des étrangers au regard de l'application du pouvoir exécutif et de l'interprétation du juge*. Rabat: GADEM.

Kleinman, Julie (2019) *Adventure capital: migration and the making of an African hub in Paris*. Oakland, CA: University of California Press.

Kleist, Nauja (2016) 'Introduction: studying hope and uncertainty in African migration', in Kleist, Nauja, and Thorsen, Dorte (eds), *Hope and uncertainty in contemporary African migration*, 1–20. London: Routledge.

Kleist, Nauja, and Jansen, Stef (2016) 'Introduction: hope over time – crisis, immobility and future-making', *History and Anthropology*, 27:4, 373–92.

Kleist, Nauja, and Thorsen, Dorte (2016) *Hope and uncertainty in contemporary African migration*. London: Routledge.
Laacher, Smaïn (2007) *Le peuple des clandestins*. Paris: Calmann-Lévy.
Lanza, Nazarena (2011) 'Les domestiques sénégalaises au Maroc: un travail servile entre tradition et modernité', in Péraldi, Michel (ed.), *D'une Afrique à l'autre migrations subsahariennes au Maroc*, 121–45. Paris: Karthala.
Law, Ian (2014) *Mediterranean racisms: connections and complexities in the racialization of the Mediterranean region*. London: Palgrave Macmillan.
Le Cour Grandmaison, Olivier, Gilles, Lhuilier, and Valluy, Jérôme (2007) *Le retour des camps? Sangatte, Lampedusa, Guantanamo...*. Paris: Autrement.
Lemaizi, Salaheddine (2022) *Politique migratoire au Maroc: entre pressions européennes et chantage marocain*. Bruxelles: Racines.
Lems, Annika (2016) 'Placing displacement: place-making in a world of movement', *Ethnos: Journal of Anthropology*, 81:2, 315–37.
Lems, Annika (2018) *Being-here: placemaking in a world of movement*. Oxford: Berghan Books.
Linn, Rachel (2011) '"Change within continuity": the equity and reconciliation commission and political reform in Morocco', *The Journal of North African Studies*, 16:1, 1–17.
López-Sala, Ana (2015) 'Exploring dissuasion as a (geo)political instrument in irregular migration control at the southern Spanish maritime border', *Geopolitics*, 20:3, 513–34.
Lucht, Hans (2011) *Darkness before daybreak: African migrants living on the margins in southern Italy today*. Oakland, CA: University of California Press.
Lutterbeck, Derek (2006) 'Policing migration in the Mediterranean', *Mediterranean Politics*, 11:1, 59–82.
Maâ, Anissa (2023) 'Autonomy of migration in the light of deportation: ethnographic and theoretical accounts of entangled appropriations of voluntary returns from Morocco', *Environment and Planning D: Society and Space*, 41:1, 92–109.
MacGaffey, Janet, and Bazenguissa-Ganga, Rémy (2000) *Congo–Paris: transnational traders on the margins of the law*. Oxford: James Currey.
Maghraoui, Driss (2009) 'Introduction: interpreting reform in Morocco', *Mediterranean Politics*, 14:2, 143–49.
Mains, Daniel (2017) 'Too much time: changing conceptions of boredom, progress, and the future among young men in urban Ethiopia, 2003–2015', *Focaal: Journal of Global and Historical Anthropology*, 78, 38–51. DOI: 10.3167/fcl.2017.780104.
Malkki, Liisa H. (1995a) 'Refugees and exile: from "refugee studies" to the national order of things', *Annual Review of Anthropology*, 24:1, 493–523.
Malkki, Liisa H. (1995b) *Purity and exile: violence, memory, and national cosmology among Hutu refugees in Tanzania*. Chicago, IL: University of Chicago Press.
Malkki, Liisa H. (1996) 'Speechless emissaries: refugees, humanitarianism, and dehistoricization', *Cultural Anthropology*, 11:3, 377–404.
Mallett, Shelley (2004) 'Understanding home: a critical review of the literature', *The Sociological Review*, 52:1, 62–89.
Marcus, George E. (1995) 'Ethnography in/of the world system: the emergence of multi-sited ethnography', *Annual Review of Anthropology*, 24:1, 95–117.
Marshall-Fratani, Ruth (2006) 'The war of "who is who": autochtony, nationalism, and citizenship in the Ivoirian crisis', *African Studies Review*, 49:2, 9–43.
Masquelier, Adeline (2019) *Fada: boredom and belonging in Niger*. Chicago, IL: University of Chicago Press.

Mayblin, Lucy, and Turner, Joe (2020) *Migration studies and colonialism*. Cambridge: Polity Press.
Mbembe, Achille (2003) 'Necropolitics', *Public Culture*, 15:1, 11–40. DOI: 10.1215/08992363-15-1-11.
McConnachie, Kirsten (2014) *Governing refugees: justice, order and legal pluralism*. New York: Routledge.
M'charek, Amade (2020) '*Harraga*: burning borders, navigating colonialism', *Sociological Review Monographs*, 68:2, 418–39.
McMurray, David A. (2001) *In and out of Morocco: smuggling and migration in a frontier boomtown*. Minneapolis, MN: University of Minnesota Press.
McNevin, Anne (2006) 'Political belonging in a neoliberal era: the struggle of the sans-papiers', *Citizenship Studies*, 10:2, 135–51.
Médecins Sans Frontières (2013) *Violence, vulnerability and migration: trapped at the gates of Europe*. Geneva: MSF. Available at: www.msf.org/violence-vulnerability-and-migration-trapped-gates-europe (accessed: 19 February 2024).
Melly, Caroline M. (2011) 'Titanic tales of missing men: reconfigurations of national identity and gendered presence in Dakar, Senegal', *American Ethnologist*, 38:2, 361–76.
Ménard, Anaïs, and Bedert, Maarten (2021) 'Introduction: the role of social imagination in strategies of im/mobility in Sierra Leone and Liberia', *African Diaspora*, 13:1–2, 1–18.
Menin, Laura (2016) '"Anti-Black racism": debating racial prejudices and the legacies of slavery in Morocco', *SWAB-WPS*, 2, 2016.
Menin, Laura (2020) '"Dans la peau d'un noir": Senegalese students and young professionals in Rabat, Morocco', *Anthropologia*, 7:1, 165–88.
Menjívar, Cecelia (2014) 'Immigration law beyond borders: externalizing and internalizing border controls in an era of securitization', *Annual Review of Law and Social Science*, 10:1, 353–69.
Mezzadra, Sandro, and Nielson, Brett (2013) *Border as method, or, the multiplication of labor*. Durham, NC: Duke University Press.
Migreurop (2007) *Guerre aux migrants: le livre noir de Ceuta et Melilla*. Paris: Sylepse.
Misra, Sasi, and Kumar, E. Sendil (2000) 'Resourcefulness: a proximal conceptualisation of entrepreneurial behaviour', *The Journal of Entrepreneurship*, 9:2, 135–54.
Möllering, Guido (2001) 'The nature of trust: from Georg Simmel to a theory of expectation, interpretation and suspension', *Sociology*, 35:2, 403–20.
Mortensen, Emilie Lund (2021) 'Becoming responsible in exile: reimagining manhood among Syrian men in Amman', *Contemporary Islam*, 15:2, 201–13.
Mourji, Fouzi, Alioua, Mehdi, and Radi, Saadia (2016) *Les migrants subsahariens au Maroc: enjeux d'une migration de résidence*. Rabat: Konrad Adenauer Stiftung.
Naguib, Rabia (2020) 'Legitimacy and "transitional continuity" in a monarchical regime: case of Morocco', *International Journal of Public Administration*, 43:5, 404–24. DOI: 10.1080/01900692.2019.1672733.
Narotzky, Susana, and Besnier, Niko (2014) 'Crisis, value, and hope: rethinking the economy: an introduction to supplement 9', *Current Anthropology*, 55:S9, S4–S16. DOI: 10.1086/676327.
Natter, Katharina (2014) 'The formation of Morocco's policy towards irregular migration (2000–2007): political Rationale and Policy Processes', *International Migration*, 52:5, 15–28. DOI: 10.1111/imig.12114

Natter, Katharina (2021) 'Crafting a "liberal monarchy": regime consolidation and immigration policy reform in Morocco', *The Journal of North African Studies*, 26:5, 850–74.
Natter, Katharina (2022) *The politics of immigration beyond liberal states: Morocco and Tunisia in comparative perspective*. Cambridge: Cambridge University Press.
Navez-Bouchanine, Françoise (ed.) (2002) *Effets sociaux des politiques urbaines: l'entre-deux des politiques institutionnelles et des dynamiques sociales*. Paris: Karthala.
Navez-Bouchanine, Françoise (2003) 'The case of Rabat – Salé, Morocco', in Wakely, Patrick (ed.), *Understanding slums: case studies for the global report on human settlements 2003*, 224–25. Nairobi: UN-Habitat. Available at: www.ucl.ac.uk/dpu-projects/Global_Report/pdfs/Rabat.pdf (accessed: 19 February 2024).
Norman, Kelsey P. (2016) 'Between Europe and Africa: Morocco as a country of immigration', *The Journal of the Middle East and Africa*, 7:4, 421–39.
Norman, Kelsey P. (2020) 'Migration diplomacy and policy liberalization in Morocco and Turkey', *International Migration Review*, 54:4, 1158–83.
Nyers, Peter (2010) 'No one is illegal between city and nation', *Studies in Social Justice*, 4:2, 127–43.
Obeid, Michelle (2023) 'Sovereignty at what price? Existential displacement at the Lebanese/Syrian border', *The Journal of Royal Anthropological Institute*, 29:4, 783–801.
Ojo, Sanya, Nwankwo, Sonny, and Gbadamosi, Ayantunji (2013) 'African diaspora entrepreneurs: navigating entrepreneurial spaces in "home" and "host" countries', *The International Journal of Entrepreneurship and Innovation*, 14:4, 289–99.
Olwig, Karen Fog (2018) 'Migration as adventure: narrative self-representation among Caribbean migrants in Denmark', *Ethnos: Journal of Anthropology*, 83:1, 156–71.
Oosterom, Marjoke (2021) 'Are rural young people stuck in waithood?', in Sumberg, James (ed.), *Youth and the rural economy in Africa: hard work and hazard*, 141–54. Boston, MA: CABI.
Ortner, Sherry B. (1995) 'Resistance and the problem of ethnographic refusal', *Comparative Studies in Society and History*, 37:1, 173–93.
Ortner, Sherry B. (2016) 'Dark anthropology and its others: theory since the eighties', *HAU: Journal of Ethnographic Theory*, 6:1, 47–73.
Osella, Filippo, and Osella, Caroline (2000) 'Migration, money and masculinity in Kerala', *The Journal of the Royal Anthropological Institute*, 6:1, 117–33.
Pallister-Wilkins, Polly (2022) *Humanitarian borders: unequal mobility and saving lives*. London: Verso.
Pandolfo, Stefania (2007) '"The burning": finitude and the politico-theological imagination of illegal migration', *Anthropological Theory*, 7:3, 329–63.
Panebianco, Stefania (2022) 'The EU and migration in the Mediterranean: EU borders' control by proxy', *Journal of Ethnic and Migration Studies*, 48:6, 1398–416. DOI: 10.1080/1369183X.2020.1851468.
Péraldi, Michel (ed.) (2011) *D'une Afrique à l'autre: migrations subsahariennes au Maroc*. Paris: Karthala.
Perl, Gerhild (2020) 'The production of illicit lives: racial governmentality and colonial legacies across the Strait of Gibraltar', *Zeitschrift für Ethnologie*, 145:2, 255–74.

Pian, Anaïk (2009) *Aux nouvelles frontières de l'Europe: l'aventure incertaine des Sénégalais au Maroc*. Paris: La Dispute.
Pickerill, Emily (2011) 'Informal and entrepreneurial strategies among sub-Saharan migrants in Morocco', *The Journal of North African Studies*, 16:3, 395–413.
Pine, Frances (2014) 'Migration as hope: space, time, and imagining the future', *Current Anthropology*, 55:S9, S95–S104.
Pouessel, Stéphanie (2012) *Noirs au Maghreb: enjeux identitaires*. Tunis: Karthala.
Rachidi, Ilhem (2022) 'Morocco and Algeria: a long rivalry', *Carnegie Endowment for International Peace*, 3 May. Available at: https://carnegieendowment.org/sada/87055 (accessed: 19 February 2024).
Rajaram, Prem Kumar, and Grundy-Warr, Carl (2004) 'The irregular migrant as homo sacer: migration and detention in Australia, Malaysia, and Thailand', *International Migration*, 42:1, 33–63.
Ramsay, Georgina (2020) 'Time and the other in crisis: how anthropology makes its displaced object', *Anthropological Theory*, 20:4, 385–413.
Rancière, Jacques (2010) *Dissensus: on politics and aesthetics*, trans. Corcoran, Steven. London: Continuum.
Redfield, Peter (2005) 'Doctors, borders, and life in crisis', *Cultural Anthropology*, 20:3, 328–61.
Rees, Peter (2024) 'The nomos of citizenship: migrant rights, law and the possibility of justice', *Contemporary Political Theory*, 23:4, 529–48 [Preprint]. DOI: 10.1057/s41296-023-00672-y.
Reeves, Madeleine (2012) 'Black work, green money: remittances, ritual, and domestic economies in southern Kyrgyzstan', *Slavic Review*, 71:1, 108–34.
Rehn, Alf, and Taalas, Saara (2004) 'Crime and assumptions in entrepreneurship', in Hjorth, Daniel, and Steyaert, Chris (eds), *Narrative and discursive approaches in entrepreneurship*, 144–59. Cheltenham: Edward Elgar.
Rhani, Zakaria, Nabalssi, Khalid, and Benalioua, Mariam (2022) '"The Rif again!" Popular uprisings and resurgent violence in post-transitional Morocco', *The Journal of North African Studies*, 27:2, 326–61. DOI: 10.1080/13629387.2020.1780921.
Richmond, Anthony H. (1994) *Global apartheid: refugees, racism and the new world order*. Oxford: Oxford University Press.
Richter, Line (2022) 'Moral borderwork: policies, policing, and practices of migrant smuggling at the EU–Morocco border', *Geopolitics*, 27:5, 1430–49.
Robbins, Joel (2013) 'Beyond the suffering subject: towards an anthropology of the good', *The Journal of the Royal Anthropology Institute*, 19:3, 447–62.
Rodier, Claire (2012) *Xénophobie business: à quoi servent les contrôles migratoires?* Paris: La Découverte.
Roitman, Janet (2013) *Anti-crisis*. Durham, NC: Duke University Press.
Römhild, Regina (2017) 'Beyond the bound of the ethnic: for postmigrant cultural and social research', *Journal of Aesthetics and Culture*, 9:2, 69–75.
Rotter, Rebecca (2016) 'Waiting in the asylum determination process: just an empty interlude?', *Time & Society*, 25:1, 80–101.
Rouch, Jean (1956) *Migrations au Ghana: Gold Coast. Enquêtes 1953–1955*. Paris: Société des Africaniste.
Royaume du Maroc: Ministère de la Jeunesse, de la Culture et de la Communication (2013) 'Migration: royal instructions bring a new vision for a national and humanist migration policy', *Maroc Portail National*, 12 September. Available at: www.

maroc.ma/en/news/migration-royal-instructions-bring-new-vision-national-and-humanist-migration-policy-release (accessed: 19 February 2024).
Rubin, Jeffrey (1998) 'Ambiguity and contradiction in a radical popular movement', in Alvarez, Sonia E., Dagnino, Evelina, and Escobar, Arturo (eds), *Cultures of politics/politics of cultures: re-visioning Latin American social movements*, 141–64. New York: Routledge.
Sadai, Célia (2021) 'Racisme anti-Noirs au Maghreb: dévoilement(s) d'un tabou', *Hérodote*, 180:1, 131–48.
Sahraoui, Nina (2020) 'Gendering the care/control nexus of the humanitarian border: women's bodies and gendered control of mobility in a European borderland', *Environment and Planning D: Society and Space*, 38:5, 905–22. DOI: 10.1177/026377582092548.
Salazar, Noel B. (2011) 'The power of imagination in transnational mobilities', *Identities: Global Studies in Culture and Power*, 18:6, 576–98.
Salazar, Noel B., and Smart, Alan (2011) 'Anthropological takes on (im)mobility', *Identities: Global Studies in Culture and Power*, 18:6, i–ix.
Salter, Mark B. (2006) 'The global visa regime and the political technologies of the international self: borders, bodies, biopolitics', *Alternatives: Global, Local, Political*, 31:2, 167–89.
Samers, Michael (2004) 'An emerging geopolitics of "illegal" immigration in the European Union', *European Journal of Migration and Law*, 6:1, 27–45.
Sassen, Saskia (2000) 'Women's burden: counter-geographies of globalization and the feminization of survival', *Journal of International Affairs*, 53:2, 503–24.
Sayad, Abdelmalek (2006) *L'immigration ou les paradoxes de l'altérité*. Paris: Raisons d'Agir.
Schapendonk, Joris (2015) 'What if networks move? Dynamic social networking in the context of African migration to Europe', *Population, Space and Place*, 21:8, 809–19.
Scheel, Stephan (2013) 'Autonomy of migration despite its securitisation? Facing the terms and conditions of biometric rebordering', *Millennium: Journal of International Studies*, 41:3, 575–600.
Scheele, Judith (2012) *Smugglers and saints of the Sahara: regional connectivity in the twentieth century*. Cambridge: Cambridge University Press.
Scheper-Hughes, Nancy (1995) 'The primacy of the ethical: propositions for a militant anthropology', *Ethnography*, 36:3, 409–40.
Scheper-Hughes, Nancy (2000) 'Ire in Ireland', *Current Anthropology*, 1:1, 117–40.
Schielke, Samuli (2008) 'Boredom and despair in rural Egypt', *Contemporary Islam*, 2:3, 251–70.
Schielke, Samuli (2020) *Migrant dreams: Egyptian workers in the Gulf states*. Cairo: American University in Cairo Press.
Schmoll, Camille (2020) *Les damnées de la mer: femmes et frontières en Méditerranée*. Paris: La Découverte.
Schmoll, Camille, and Semi, Giovanni (2013) 'Shadow circuits: urban spaces and mobilities across the Mediterranean', *Identities: Global Studies in Culture and Power*, 20:4, 377–92.
Schuster, Liza (2005) 'The realities of a new asylum paradigm', *COMPAS Working Paper*, 20.
Souiah, Farida (2012) 'Les *harraga* algériens', *Migrations Société*, 143:5, 105–20.

Squire, Vicki (2011) *The contested politics of mobility: borderzones and irregularity*. Abingdon: Routledge.
Stasik, Michael, Hänsch, Valerie, and Mains, Daniel (2020) 'Temporalities of waiting in Africa', *Critical African Studies*, 12:1, 1–9. DOI: 10.1080/21681392.2020.1717361.
Stock, Inka (2012) 'Transit to nowhere: how sub-Saharan African migrants in Morocco confront life in forced immobility', PhD thesis: University of Nottingham.
Stock, Inka (2016) 'Transnational social fields in forced immobility: relations of young sub-Saharan African migrants in Morocco with their families and friends', *Identities: Global Studies in Culture and Power*, 23:4, 407–21.
Stock, Inka (2019) *Time, migration and forced immobility: sub-Saharan African migrants in Morocco*. Bristol: Bristol University Press.
Stock, Inka, Üstübici, Ayşen, and Schultz, Susanne U. (2019) 'Externalization at work: responses to migration policies from the Global South', *Comparative Migration Studies*, 7:1, 1–9.
Szörényi, Anna (2006) 'The images speak for themselves? Reading refugee coffee-table books', *Visual Studies*, 21:1, 24–41.
Tarrius, Alain (2002) *La mondialisation par le bas: les nouveaux nomades des économies souterraines*. Paris: Balland.
Ticktin, Miriam (2006) 'Where ethics and politics meet: the violence of humanitarianism in France', *American Ethnologist*, 33:1, 33–49.
Timera, Mahamet (2009) 'Aventuriers ou orphelins de la migration internationale: nouveaux et ancien migrants "subsahariens" au Maroc', *Politique Africaine*, 115:3, 175–95.
Topak, Özgün E. (2017) 'Migrant protest in times of crisis: politics, ethics and the sacred from below', *Citizenship Studies*, 21:1, 1–21.
Tošić, Jelena, and Lems, Annika (2019) 'Introduction. African-European trajectories of (im)mobility: exploring entanglements of experiences, legacies and regimes of contemporary migration', *Migration and Society*, 2:1, 1–11.
Traoré, Mahmoud, and Le Dantec, Bruno (2012) *Partir et Raconter: Une odyssée clandestine*. Paris: Lignes.
Tyler, Imogen (2013) *Revolting subjects: social abjection and resistance in neoliberal Britain*. London: Zed Books.
Tyszler, Elsa (2015) *Ceuta and Melilla: centres de tri à ciel ouvert aux portes de l'Afrique. Joint report: Migreurop, GADEM, Cimade, APDHA*. Available at: www.lacimade.org/publication/ceuta-et-melilla-centres-de-tri-a-ciel-ouvert-aux-portes-de-lafrique/ (accessed: 23 February 2024).
Tyszler, Elsa (2018) '"Boza!" disent aussi les femmes', *Vacarme*, 83:2, 82–91.
Tyszler, Elsa (2019) 'From controlling mobilities to control over women's bodies: gendered effects of EU border externalization in Morocco', *Comparative Migration Studies*, 7:1, 1–20. DOI: 10.1186/s40878-019-0128-4.
United Nations (2018) *Global compact for safe, orderly, and regular migration: intergovernmentally negotiated and agreed outcome*. Available at: https://refugeesmigrants.un.org/sites/default/files/180713_agreed_outcome_global_compact_for_migration.pdf (accessed: 19 February 2024).
United Nations Department of Economic and Social Affairs (2020) *International Migration Stock*. Available at: www.un.org/en/desa/international-migration-2020-highlights#:~:text=The%20report,%20International%20Migration%202

020%20Highlights,%20by%20the%20Population%20Division (accessed: 25 June 2024).
Üstübici, Ayşen (2016) 'Political activism between journey and settlement: irregular migrant mobilisation in Morocco', *Geopolitics*, 21:2, 303–24.
Valenzuela, Abel (2001) 'Day labourers as entrepreneurs?', *Journal of Ethnic and Migration Studies*, 27:2, 335–52.
Van Houtum, Henk, and Pijpers, Roos (2007) 'The European Union as a gated community: the two-faced border and immigration regime of the EU', *Antipode*, 39:2, 291–309.
Vigh, Henrik (2006) 'The colour of destruction: on racialization, geno-globality and the social imaginary in Bissau', *Anthropological Theory*, 6:4, 481–500.
Vigh, Henrik (2008) 'Crisis and chronicity: anthropological perspectives on continuous conflict and decline', *Ethnos: Journal of Anthropology*, 73:1, 5–24.
Vigh, Henrik (2009a) 'Motion squared: a second look at the concept of social navigation', *Anthropological Theory*, 9:4, 419–38.
Vigh, Henrik (2009b) 'Wayward migration: on imagined futures and technological voids', *Ethnos: Journal of Anthropology*, 74:1, 91–109.
Viruell-Fuentes, Edna A. (2006) '"My heart is always there": the transnational practices of first-generation Mexican immigrant and second-generation Mexican American women', *Identities: Global Studies in Culture and Power*, 13:3, 335–62. DOI: 10.1080/10702890600838076.
Waterbury, John (1970) *The commander of the faithful: the Moroccan political elite; a study in segmented politics*. London: Trinity Press.
Wender, Anne Sophie, Laflamme-Marsan, Marie-José, and Rachidi, Hicham (2004) *La situation alarmante des migrants subsahariens en transit au Maroc et les conséquences des politiques de l'Union Européenne*. Paris: Cimade. Available at: www.lacimade.org/wp-content/uploads/2009/03/rapportMarocCimade.pdf (accessed: 19 February 2024).
Wilkins, Annabelle (2019) *Migration, work and home-making in the city: dwelling and belonging among Vietnamese communities in London*. London: Routledge.
Willen, Sarah (2005) 'Birthing "invisible" children: state power, NGO activism, and reproductive health among "illegal migrant" workers in Tel Aviv, Israel', *Journal of Middle East Women's Studies*, 1:2, 55–88.
Willen, Sarah (2019) *Fighting for dignity: migrant lives at Israel's margins*. Philadelphia, PA: University of Pennsylvania Press.
Williams, Jill M. (2015) 'From humanitarian exceptionalism to contingent care: care and enforcement at the humanitarian border', *Political Geography*, 47, 11–20.
Wilmott, Annabelle Cathryn (2017) 'The politics of photography: visual depictions of Syrian refugees in U.K. online media', *Visual Communication Quarterly*, 24:2, 67–82.
Wolff, Sarah (2008) 'Border management in the Mediterranean: internal, external and ethical challenges', *Cambridge Review of International Affairs*, 21:2, 253–71.
Woolley, Agnes (2014) *Contemporary asylum narratives: representing refugees in the twenty-first century*. London: Palgrave Macmillan.
Wright, John (2002) 'Morocco: the last great slave market?', *The Journal of North African Studies*, 7:3, 53–66.
Yene, Fabien Didier (2010) *Migrant au Pied du Mur*. Paris: Séguier.
Zapata-Barrero, Ricard, and De Witte, Nynke (2007) 'The Spanish governance of EU borders: normative questions', *Mediterranean Politics*, 12:1, 85–90.

Zetter, Roger (2007) 'More labels, fewer refugees: remaking the refugee label in an era of globalization', *Journal of Refugee Studies*, 20:2, 172–92.

Zhang, Sheldon X., Sanchez, Gabriella E., and Achilli, Luigi (2018) 'Crimes of solidarity in mobility: alternative views on migrant smuggling', *The ANNALS of the American Academy of Political and Social Science*, 676:1, 6–15.

Zigon, Jarrett (2009) 'Hope dies last: two aspects of hope in contemporary Moscow', *Anthropological Theory*, 9:3, 253–71.

Zournazi, Mary, and Hage, Ghassan (2002) ' "On the side of life": joy and the capacity of being', in Zournazi, Mary (ed.), *Hope: new philosophies for change*, 150–71. New York: Routledge.

Zournazi, Mary, and Lingis, Alphonso (2002) 'Murmurs of life', in Zournazi, Mary (ed.), *Hope: new philosophies for change*, 22–41. New York: Routledge.

Index

Notes: Page numbers in *italic* refer to photographs; 'n.' after a page reference indicates the number of a note on that page.

Action Plan for Morocco (1999) 30
activists 14, 17, 65, 180
adventure, the (*l'aventure*) 9, 11, 14, 16, 57–58, 66, 88, 190–91
    as existential yearning 2–4, 7, 8, 19, 185
    the objective and 49, 59, 186
    as quest 1, 8, 10, 71, 185
    with suffering 12–13
adventurers (*aventuriers*) 1–2, 7, 9–11, 66, 84n.6, 139
    choices for 15, 16, 50, 56, 76
    doing research with 14–19
    in Douar Hajja and Maâdid 8, 13, 17, 89
    families of 57, 73, 84n.5, 129, 191
    in forest camps 70, 77, 136, 149
    hope of 12, 76, 187, 192
    man as 69–73
    the objective and 8, 18, 24, 49–51, 60, 64, 75
agency (*la chance*) 24, 25, 59–60, 68, 69, 76, 193
Agier Michel 7
AIDS 41, 151
alcohol 82, 97, 121
Algeria 15, 42, 72, 112, 116, 125n.4, 133
    border xiii, xvi, 32, 35, 39, 45n.6, 46n.8, 51–52, 56, 70, 87, 140–41, 165
    migration to 33, 53, 54, 58

Alioua, Mehdi 42
ambassade, l' (the embassy), Douar Hajja 15, 17–18, 21, 87, *104*, 168, 190
    as AMSAM headquarters 165, 166
    attack on 85–86
    with informal restaurants 115–16
    life in 88, 89–95, 101, 111, 113–15
    migrants in 52–54, 56, 59, 108, 142–44, 153
AMDH *see* Association Marocaine des Droits Humains
AMSAM *see* Association Migration sub-Saharienne au Maroc
Anderson, Benedict 134
anthropology 2, 12, 18, 111, 130–31
anti-Black racism 148, 149–53
Antiracist Group of Defence and Accompaniment of Foreigners and Migrants *see* Groupe antiraciste d'accompagnement et de défense des étrangers et migrants
Arendt, Hannah 193–94
'*association de migrants*' *see* migrants' organisation
*Association Marocaine des Droits Humain*s (AMDH, Moroccan Association of Human Rights) 27, 173

Association Migration sub-Saharienne au Maroc (AMSAM, Sub-Saharan Migration Association in Morocco) 184n.1, 185
   with 'exposing the true realities of migration,' 172–76
   membership 165–71, 173–84, 188–90
   migrant rights and 177–80, 181
asylum xiii, 26n.3, 30, 35–40, 144, 153
aventure, l' see adventure, the
aventuriers see adventurers

Balibar, Etienne 183
Barros, Lucile 46n.10
Bayane, Al (newspaper) 21
becoming mad see *devenir fou*
begging ('*fissabila*,' '*taper salām*') 80, 108–9, 117, 124, 135
Black Hawk Down (film) 89, 102n.1
Black migrants 27, 133, 137, 190
   labour and exploitation of 110, 124
   as targets xiii, 3, 5, 25, 28, 34, 39, 41–44, 149–52, 162, 188
Blackness 42–43, 149
'*bonne mentalité, la*' see right mentality
borders xvi, 29, 32, 39, 44n.2, 45n.4, 45n.6, 46n.8, 165, 189
   attacks xiii, 2, 8, 57, 61, 70, 71, 83, 95, 129, 137, 184, 187
   crossing attempts xiii, 12, 25, 61, 64, 68, 74, 88, 102, 112, 115, 124, 139–41, 161, 182, 191
   crossing failures 2, 9, 18, 56–58, 66, 80, 81, 90, 131, 142, 173–74
   guards xiv, 28, 34, 51, 52, 53, 61, 70, 77, 79–81, 101, 177
   violence and 27, 28, 35, 50, 173–74
boredom 24, 62, 68, 74, 83, 101, 109
bosses 108, 112, 115–21, 136
boza (to cross into Europe) xiv, 8, 68, 84n.1, 186, 191
Braudel, Fernand 44n.1
Bredeloup, Sylvie 13–14, 187
Burkina Faso 1, 15, 48, 51, 133, 178, 192
businesses 24–25, 101, 110, 124, 154
   bosses 108, 112, 115–21, 136

informal restaurants 57–58, 61–62, 74, 84n.5, 90, 99–100, *107*, 108–9, 115–23, 125n.6, 136, 179

Cabot, Heath 6
Cameroonians xiv, xvi, 57, 61, 93, *106–7*
   ghettoes xiii, 15, 17–18, 21, *105*, 165, 168, 190
   migrants 109, 141, 172–73
Caritas 26n.4, 76, 78, 91, 134, 175–76, 178
   with housing 97–98
   mental health issues and 82
CCSM see *Collectif des Communautés sub-Sahariennes au Maroc*
Central Africa, migrants from Western and 27–28, 31–34, 48, 56, 60, 65, 75–76
Ceuta, Spain 5, 27–28, 30–32, 35, 44n.3, 191
chance 1, 9, 12, 83
   the adventure and 59, 66
   courage, strength and 24, 69, 73–80, 84n.7, 129, 131
chance, la see agency
Chappatte, André 125n.6
chercher sa vie see search for 'one's life'
children 5, 16, 18–19, 21, 35, 57, 156
Christians 78, 131, 151
clandestins (illegal people) xii, 71, 101, 172
clochards (tramps) 55, 67, 85, 94, 150
CMSM see *Conseil des Migrants Sub-Sahariens au Maroc*
CNDH see *Conseil national des droits de l'Homme*
Collectif des Communautés sub-Sahariennes au Maroc (CCSM, *Le Collectif*, The Collective of Sub-Saharan Communities in Morocco) 17, 165, 168
Collyer, Michael 130
colonialism 3, 33, 41–44, 64, 111, 179, 192
Colson, Elizabeth 137
Committee of the International Convention on the Protection of the Rights of All Migrant

Workers and Members of Their Families 36
Congolese people 78, 109, 117, 175
Conseil des Migrants Sub-Sahariens au Maroc (CMSM, *Le Conseil*, Sub-Saharan Migrants Council in Morocco) 165, 181
Conseil national des droits de l'Homme (CNDH, National Human Rights Council) 36
consulat, le (the consulate), Douar Hajja
  life in 87–88, 93–95, 99, 101, 116–17
  migrants in xiii, xvi, 15, 60, 62, 65, 69, 74, 81, 93, *104*, *105*, 109, 133, 143, 146–47, 190
conviviality 149, 154, 155, 163
corruption 59, 64, 74, 125n.3, 157, 170, 178–79
Corsín Jiménez, Alberto 136
courage
  strength, chance and 24, 69, 73–80, 84n.7, 129, 131
  strength and xvii, 1, 9, 66, 68, 76, 77, 79, 83, 84n.7, 131, 137–38, 144, 185, 193
COVID-19 pandemic 40, 188, 190
crisis 12, 65, 67–68, 86, 136, 186–87, 192
  migration 43, 185
  narratives 4–7, 194
  trope of 1, 5
  to cross into Europe *see boza*
cybers 57, 74, 109, 121–22, 127, 147, 157, 182

deaths 127, 153, 179
  labour and 111
  migrants 5, 27, 28, 35, 42, 44n.2, 70, 86, 140–41, 142, 148, 173–74, 189
'*débrouillardise*' (resourcefulness) 8, 55, 88, 110, 132, 133
dehors, le (the outside) 20, 49, 155, 192
Democratic Republic of Congo 31, 118
devenir fou (becoming mad) 9, 12, 24, 68–69, 80–83, 143

Douar Hajja, Rabat 1, 18, 26nn.4–6, 88, *103–7*, 108, 177
  adventurers in 8, 13, 17, 89
  jobs in 113–15
  migrants in xiii–xiv, 48, 50, 59–61, 67–68, 81, 187–88, 193
  neighborhood xii–xiii, 13, 15, 19–23, 157, 190
  stuckedness in 3, 9, 11, 24, 50, 56, 60–61, 64, 68, 69, 83
  see also ambassade, l'; *consulat, le*
drugs 41, 82, 150, 157, 164

Economic Community of West African States (ECOWAS) 38
economy, informal 24, 51, 111, 120, 124, 125n.3, 154
ECOWAS *see* Economic Community of West African States
Edogué Ntang, Jean-Louis 25n.2, 125n.4
El Hamel, Chouki 43
Elliot, Alice 60, 158
El Yazami, Driss 36
embassy, the *see ambassade, l'*
enslaved people 47n.15, 47n.17, 64, 95, 147, 152
  slavery and 111, 148, 163, 179
  trading of 41, 43, 44, 47n.16
entrepreneurs 110–11, 115–20, 122, 191
Essahel, Habiba 22
EU *see* European Union
EU Emergency Trust Fund (EUTF) 46n.11, 47n.12
Europe xiv, 8, 40, 68, 84n.1, 186, 191
  see also mbeng
European Agency for the Management of Operational Cooperation at the External Border 29
European Border and Coast Guard Agency *see* Frontex
European Court of Auditors 46n.11
European Economic Community 30
European Union (EU) 5, 44, 47n.12, 50, 173, 175
  imagined futures in 63–64
  with migration 28–29
  Morocco and 30–31, 34, 35, 46n.11
EUTF *see* EU Emergency Trust Fund

Fakoly, Tiken Jah 178
families 57, 73, 84n.5, 129, 141–44, 172, 191
Faye, Ismaila 42
'February 20 Movement' 181
'*fissabila*' *see* begging
forest camps 77, 117, 136, 149
   informal 18, 26n.4, 32, 69, 93
   living conditions 25n.2, 70, 81, 87, 91, 108, 141
Forum Social Maghrébin (FSM) 165
foyer 93–96, 98–99, 102, 102n.3, 148, 150
France 54, 62–65, 131, 166, 178, 183, 191
Frontex (European Border and Coast Guard Agency) 29, 45n.4
FSM *see Forum Social Maghrébin*

GADEM *see Groupe antiraciste d'accompagnement et de défense des étrangers et migrants*
Gaibazzi, Paolo 77–78
gender 11–12, 62, 71, 185
Germany 54, 65, 191
Ghana 8, 11, 54, 111
ghettoes 15, 17–18, 21, *104–6*, 165, 168, 190
   foyer and 93–96, 98–99, 102, 102n.3, 148, 150
   living conditions 85–89
   Malian 78, *103*, *106*
   overcrowding in xiii, xiv, 24, 87–88, 91, 94–95, 97, 137
   see also ambassade, l'; *consulat, le*
Gilroy, Paul 155
Global Forum on Migration and Development (2018) 38
globalisation 64, 84n.5, 122
God 23, 77, 79, 83, 131, 139, 160
Golden Sands (*les Sables d'Or*) xiv–xvi, 15, 52
Groupe antiraciste d'accompagnement et de défense des étrangers et migrants (GADEM, Antiracist Group of Defence and Accompaniment of Foreigners and Migrants) 36, 39, 171, 173, 175–76

Guardia Civil, Spain 70, 141
Guinea 15, 31, 47n.16, 73, 115

Hage, Ghassan 5, 11
Han, Clara 129
Hart, Keith 111
Haut-Commissariat au Plan (HCP) 39
health 12, 36, 82–83, 91, 149
High-Level Working Group (HLWG) on Migration and Asylum 30
home 56–58, 62–63, 66–67, 82, 85, 88–89, 99
home-making practices 13, 24, 89, 102
Honwana, Alcinda 74
hope 1, 24, 69, 79
   of adventurers 12, 76, 187, 192
   migrants with 2, 48–50, 192
housing 20–22, 24, 87–89, 93–102, 128, 150
human rights 20, 27, 34, 36, 86, 173, 180

illegality 4, 16, 29, 32, 41, 43–45
   Blackness and 149
   'space of non-existence' and 7
   uncertainty, immobility and 8, 176
illegal people *see clandestins*
imagination xv, 76, 134, 158, 186, 194
   migrants and 62–64
   the outside and 58–65
immobility 2, 4, 11, 13–14, 50, 64, 71, 186–87
   entrapped mobility 1, 3, 6–7, 15, 185, 193, 194
   uncertainty, illegality and 8, 176
   see also stuckedness
Institut National d'Aménagement et d'Urbanisme (INAU) 26n.5
Integrated External Surveillance System (SIVE), Spain 30
Intergovernmental Conference to Adopt the Global Compact on Safe, Orderly and Regular Migration (2018) 38, 39
International Convention on the Protection of the Rights of All Migrant Workers and Members of Their Families 34, 36, 180

International Journal of Middle East Studies xviin.1
International Organisation for Migration (IOM) voluntary return programme 56, 58, 82, 85
Ireland 155, 159, 162
Ivoirian migrants xiii, 65, 69, 93–95, 104, *105*, 169

Jackson, Michael 11, 63
jobs, in Douar Hajja and Maâdid 113–15
see also labour
journeys, fragmented 52–56

labels 6–7, 25n.1, 29, 49, 71, 110, 186–87, 194
labour xiii, 31, 54, 119, 125n.4, 157
  forced 111–13, 114, 116, 121, 124, 130
  informal economy and 24, 51, 111, 120, 124, 125n.3, 154
  jobs in Douar Hajja and Maâdid 113–15
  wages 112, 115, 117, 134, 150, 181
  working conditions 110, 111–13, 123–24
landlords 15, 96, 100, 102, 116, 118, 160
  at *le consulat* 93
  exploitation by 24, 85–86, 92, 94, 97–98, 101, 120, 150, 163
laws, Morocco 34, 37
'*l-brrā*' (the outside) 20, 155, 158–59
Le Jah, Sams'K 179
Lemaizi, Salaheddine 47n.14
Libya 29, 58
life
  in *l'ambassade* 88, 89–95, 101, 111, 113–15
  boredom of everyday 24, 62, 68, 83, 101, 109
  in *le consulat* 87–88, 93–95, 99, 101, 116–17
  search for one's 1, 8, 60, 185
  suffering as school of 130–32
life more bearable, a (*une vie plus supportable*) 3, 10, 19, 24, 59, 77, 178

Lingis, Alphonso 69
living conditions 31, 54, 82, 115, 132, 144, 157, 162
  forest camps 25n.2, 70, 81, 87, 91, 108, 141
  ghettoes 85–89
Loujna-Tounkaranké 180
Lucht, Hans 11

Maâdid, Rabat 1, 18, 26n.4, 26n.6, 88, *103*, 108, 177
  adventurers in 8, 13, 17, 89
  jobs in 113–15
  migrants in xiii–xiv, 48, 50, 59–61, 67–68, 81, 187–88, 193
  name and origins of 26n.5
  neighborhood 15, 19–23, 157
  stuckedness in 3, 9, 11, 24, 50, 56, 60–61, 68, 69
madness 9, 12, 24, 68–69, 80–83, 143
Mali 15, 31, 32, 47n.16, 52, 54, 114–15, 178
Malian ghetto 78, *104*, 106
Malian migrants 147–48, 153
man, as adventurer 69–73
maquis (informal restaurants) 115, 125n.6, 179
Maroc Hebdo (magazine) 41
Mauritania 15, 51–53, 177
Mawlay Isma'il (Sultan) (1672–1727) 47n.15
mbeng (thinking about entering Europe) 122, 129, 132, 191
  defined 126n.8, 145n.1
  wasting and spoiling 135–41, 142, 144
Médecins Sans Frontières (MSF, Doctors without Borders) 35, 83
Melilla, Spain 5, 44n.3, 76, 81, 84n.3, 101, 191
  with border violence 27, 28, 35
  forest camps near 32, 69, 77
  fortification of 30, 31
mental health 12, 82–83
mentalité (mentality) 25, 128, 137
  see also right mentality
migrants *see specific topics*
migrants' organisation ('*association de migrants*') 18, 169, 177

migration
  illegal 4, 29, 46n.10, 46n.11, 48, 168, 194
  reasons for 51, 53, 54, 57, 59, 72–73, 159, 172–73
  true realities of 16, 172–76, 180, 183
  see also specific topics
migration politics 3, 14, 17, 28, 34, 184, 187, 189
  hostile 4, 7, 30, 63–66, 68, 167, 173, 174, 185, 192, 194
  transnational 4, 6, 23, 27, 44
  2013 and new 35–40, 42, 140, 179, 188
migration regimes 2, 3, 5, 7, 18, 19, 185
migratory projects 25, 32–33, 60, 98, 142, 176, 187
migratory routes 29, 31–32, 45n.4, 87, 91, 125n.6, 190
Migreurop 180
military 26n.3, 29–30, 69–70
Ministry of Foreign Affairs, African Cooperation and Moroccan Expatriates 40
Ministry of Moroccans Residing Abroad and Migration Affairs 36, 40
mobility 11, 24, 33
  entrapped 1, 3, 6–7, 15, 185, 193, 194
  migrant businesses and 121–24
  see also immobility
Mobility Partnership Agreement (2013) 46n.11
Mohamed VI (King of Morocco) 36, 37, 38, 67
money 2, 57–58, 60, 63, 72, 139, 165
  begging for 80, 108–9, 117, 124, 135
  integration 92, 94
  transport xvi, 181
Moroccan Association of Human Rights see Association Marocaine des Droits Humains
Morocco 18, 37, 67, 80, 157, 180
  EU and 30–31, 34, 35, 46n.11
  Mauritania and 51–53, 177
  stuckedness in 1, 7, 8, 11, 14, 33, 58, 82, 83, 185
MSF see Médecins Sans Frontières
Muslims 16, 30, 78, 131, 151
'myth of return,' 62, 99

N9 campaign see Number 9 campaign
names, changing 16, 151
national forum for the protection of migrants see Plateforme Nationale Protection Migrants
National Human Rights Council see Conseil national des droits de l'Homme
nationalities, of migrants 45nn.4–5
National Strategy on Immigration and Asylum see Stratégie Nationale d'Immigration et d'Asile
Natter, Katharina 37
NDICI – Global Europe see Neighbourhood, Development and International Cooperation Instrument – Global Europe
Ndour, Charles 42
Neighbourhood, Development and International Cooperation Instrument – Global Europe (NDICI – Global Europe) 40
ngandas (informal restaurants) 115, 125n.6
NGOs (nongovernmental organisations) 18, 26n.3, 36, 74, 169, 173, 178
  migrants and 174–77
  practitioners 4, 65, 129, 171, 175
  workers 26n.4, 48, 51, 111
  see also Caritas
Niger 32, 91
Nigeria 31, 46n.8, 47n.16, 54, 182
Nigerians 91, 119, 134, 151, 169
nongovernmental organisations see NGOs
'Number 9' (video) 174
Number 9 (N9) campaign 173, 180, 183
'Number 9,' migrants as 142

objective, the
  adventurers and 8, 18, 24, 49–51, 60, 64, 75
  the adventure and 49, 59, 186

Index

objects, of success 63
'original people,' 20, 163
outside, the 158–59
   le dehors 20, 49, 155, 192
   imagining 58–65

passports 15, 26n.3, 51, 63, 85, 112, 133
Péraldi, Michel 25n.2, 125n.4
phones 63, 136, 141, 145n.2, 148, 178
Piette, Albert 11
Plateforme Nationale Protection Migrants (national forum for the protection of migrants) 176
poetry 69, 72, 192, 194
police xv, 86, 149, 161, 163, 182, 190
   encounters 26n.3, 51, 53
   Guardia Civil 70, 141
   Moroccan 80, 177, 180
   raids xiii, 15, 22, 24, 39, 42, 82–83, 87, 97–99, 112, 115, 120, 155
poverty 12, 22–23, 59, 74, 125n.3, 130, 144, 160
profiteering 5, 110, 125, 175
protests 167, 177, 180, 181, 182

queer community 10
quest, the adventure as 1, 8, 10, 71, 185
question subsaharienne, La see sub-Saharan issue, the
Qur'an 125n.1, 151

race 23, 32, 44, 64, 163
   hierarchies 15, 151, 152
   migration and 41–43
   migration regimes and 2, 7, 19, 185
racism 73, 115, 130, 145
   anti-Black 148, 149–53
   violence and xv, 42–44, 148, 153–54, 163, 177
rape 53, 172
Refugee Convention (1951) 26n.3
refugees
   camps 7, 88
   UNHCR 15–16, 52, 54, 82, 94, 153, 175
relationships 1, 9, 17, 145, 179
   migrants and locals 153–63

   romantic xv–xvi, 11, 67, 73, 75, 138
   social 125, 128–30, 133, 135, 144
   with trust between migrants 128, 129–30, 136–41
research, with adventurers 14–19
Réseau marocain des journalistes des migrations (RMJM) 47n.14
resourcefulness *see 'débrouillardise'*
restaurants, informal 57–58, 61–62, 74, 84n.5, 90, 99–100, *106*, 108–9, 115–23, 125n.6, 136, 179
right mentality (*la 'bonne mentalité'*), 23, 80–81, 101, 109, 141, 160, 193
   with courage and strength 9, 77, 83, 84n.7, 131, 137–38, 144
   suffering and 113, 131, 137
   trust with sharing of 129, 135, 138, 140, 144
RMJM *see* Réseau marocain des journalistes des migrations
Robbins, Joel 131
rubber dinghies (zodiacs) xv, 12, 32, 62, 115, 124, 140–41, 161

Sables d'Or, les see Golden Sands
Sankara, Thomas 179
Sayad, Abdelmalek 183
Schengen Agreement (1985) 28
Schengen Area 62
Scheper-Hughes, Nancy 17, 18
Schmoll, Camille 122
search for 'one's life' (*chercher sa vie*) 1, 8, 60, 185
search for 'one's self' (*se chercher*) 1, 8, 65, 185
secrets 16–17, 66, 75, 139
Semi, Giovanni 122
Senegal 31, 47n.16, 52, 182
sexual violence 46n.7, 53, 172
Shamal, al- (newspaper) 41
shame 9, 17, 38, 50, 56–58, 66, 74
Single European Act (1986) 28
SIVE *see* Integrated External Surveillance System
slave *see* enslaved people
smugglers 29, 32, 40–41, 46n.11, 46nn.7–8

SNIA *see* Stratégie Nationale
    d'Immigration et d'Asile
social media 17, 27, 42, 63, 143, 172,
    187, 191
Spain 5, 27–28, 32, 44n.3, 191
    Guardia Civil 70, 141
    Morocco and 30–31, 35, 67
    see also Melilla
stereotypes 150–51, 153
Stratégie Nationale d'Immigration et
    d'Asile (SNIA, National Strategy
    on Immigration and Asylum)
    36, 38, 40
strength
    chance, courage and 24, 69, 73–80,
        84n.7, 129, 131
    courage and xvii, 1, 9, 66, 68, 76,
        77, 79, 83, 84n.7, 131, 137–38,
        144, 185, 193
stuckedness 1, 7, 8, 14, 33, 58, 82, 185
    in Douar Hajja 3, 9, 11, 24, 50, 56,
        60–61, 64, 68, 69, 83
    in Maâdid 3, 9, 11, 24, 50, 56,
        60–61, 68, 69
    at Morocco–Mauritania border
        51–53, 177
sub-Saharan issue, the (*La question
    subsaharienne*) 4, 23, 30, 44
    migrants from Western and Central
        Africa 27–28, 31–34
    migration as security problem 28–29
    race and migration 41–43
    2013 and new migration politics
        35–40
Sub-Saharan Migrants Council in
    Morocco *see Conseil des Migrants
    Sub-Sahariens au Maroc*
Sub-Saharan Migration Association
    in Morocco *see Association
    Migration sub-Saharienne
    au Maroc*
suffering 13, 113, 130–31
    shared 25, 132–37
    violence and 2–3, 7, 12, 24, 49,
        83, 129, 137, 172–73, 185,
        187, 193–94

Takaddoum 148, 156, 161, 181
    migrants in 82, 101, 123, 168, 171
    neighborhood 21

'*taper salām*,' 108, 125n.2
    see also begging
theft xiii, 35, 46n.7, 136, 140, 153
thinking about entering Europe
    see mbeng
tramps *see clochards*
transit migration 17, 24, 44, 50, 64
trauma 12, 83, 119, 131, 142
trickster stories 20, 53, 64
true realities ('*les vraies réalités*') of
    migration 16, 172–76, 180, 183
trust 46n.11, 47n.12
    between migrants 128,
        129–30, 136–41
    with sharing of right mentality 129,
        135, 138, 140, 144
truth, families and telling 141–44, 172
Tunisia 29, 40, 42, 73

UDP *see* Urban Development Plant
uncertainty 12, 24, 35, 44, 59, 89,
    91, 120
    chance and 83
    illegality, immobility and 8, 176
    with lives of migrants 74–75, 99,
        124, 137, 167
    as social resource 68
    trust and 139
    violence and 1, 7, 13, 76, 129, 167,
        178, 185, 187, 193
UN-DESA *see* United Nations
    Department of Economic and
    Social Affairs
unemployment xii–xiii, 23, 53, 67, 150,
    156, 157
UNHCR *see* United Nations High
    Commissioner for Refugees
United Nations 34, 38
United Nations Department of
    Economic and Social Affairs (UN-
    DESA) 41
United Nations High Commissioner for
    Refugees (UNHCR) 15–16, 52,
    54, 82, 94, 153, 175
Universal Declaration of Human
    Rights 34
unpredictability, violence and
    147, 161–62
Urban Development Plant (UDP)
    26n.5

Várhelyi, Olivér 40
vie plus supportable, une see life more bearable, a
violence xiii, 4, 25, 40, 53, 141, 182–83
  attacks 85–86, 99, 115, 130, 147–50, 152–54, 177
  borders and 27, 28, 35, 50, 173–74
  boredom and 95, 101, 109
  against migrants 39, 46n.7, 67–68, 70–71, 82–83, 86
  racism and xv, 42–44, 148, 153–54, 163, 177
  suffering and 2–3, 7, 12, 24, 49, 83, 129, 137, 172–73, 185, 187, 193–94
  uncertainty and 1, 7, 13, 76, 129, 167, 178, 185, 187, 193
  unpredictability and 147, 161–62
visibility 43, 111, 152, 177
'*voix d'ici et d'ailleurs, les*' (voices from here and elsewhere) workshop 156

'*vraies réalités*' of migration, *les see* true realities of migration

wages 112, 115, 117, 134, 150, 181
Western Africa 27–28, 31–34, 38, 48, 56, 60, 65, 75–76
Western Union 58, 73
whiteness 42
witchcraft 100, 134, 152
women 10, 35, 39, 52, 97, 100, 117, 146
  in Douar Hajja and Maâdid 26n.4, 108
  informal restaurant owners 108, 118–20, 121, 136
  labour and 112
  migrants 46n.9, 73, 84n.5
World Social Forum (2013) 165

Zigon, Jarrett 79
zodiacs *see* rubber dinghies

EU authorised representative for GPSR:
Easy Access System Europe, Mustamäe tee 50,
10621 Tallinn, Estonia
gpsr.requests@easproject.com

www.ingramcontent.com/pod-product-compliance
Lightning Source LLC
LaVergne TN
LVHW072154070825
818147LV00002B/8